Teaching as a
Professional Discipline

Teaching as a Professional Discipline

Geoffrey Squires

FALMER PRESS

Taylor & Francis Group

UK	Falmer Press, 1 Gunpowder Square, London, EC4A 3DE
USA	Falmer Press, 325 Chestnut Street, 8th Floor, Philadelphia, PA 19106

First published in 1999

A catalogue record for this book is available from the British Library

ISBN 0 7507 0923 5 cased

Library of Congress Cataloging-in-Publication Data are available on request

Jacket design by Caroline Archer

Typeset in 10/12pt Times by
Graphicraft Limited, Hong Kong

Printed in Great Britain by Biddles Ltd., Guildford and King's Lynn on paper which has a specified pH value on final paper manufacture of not less than 7.5 and is therefore 'acid free'.

Every effort has been made to contact copyright holders for their permission to reprint material in this book. The publishers would be grateful to hear from any copyright holder who is not here acknowledged and will undertake to rectify any errors or omissions in future editions of this book.

Contents

List of Figures and Tables

Figures

Tables

Preface

Since about 1980, my work has consisted mainly of training lecturers and tutors in further, higher and adult education, and training trainers in both the public and private sectors. I have also been involved, through research and workshops, in education for a number of professions.

What I have to say in this book is largely the outcome of these activities. My first tentative steps in this direction were recorded in an occasional paper published in 1982, but it was not until 1988 that I really began to conceptualize teaching in terms of a multi-dimensional model. Brief accounts of the emerging model appeared in my book on the undergraduate curriculum in 1990 and in various conference papers in the following years. Then, in 1994, I brought out a comprehensive training package for use in my own and others' workshops. This has proved to be invaluable as a way of testing out and developing the model with a wide range of practitioners. There have also been a number of subsequent publications dealing with various applications of the model.

In terms of schools, I thus write as an outsider and must express a due measure of caution. However much one knows about them at second hand, people who have not actually worked in schools are unlikely to have the feel for them that day-to-day practitioners have. And there are, I think, key differences between schools and post-school education, which stem not only from the age of the learners, but the existence in the former of a national curriculum and (more complex to unravel) the role and place of the teacher. Nevertheless, I hope that what I have to say will offer a different perspective on teaching, and in particular one that places it firmly in the context of other professions.

The long gestation of this work means that it is impossible for me to thank everyone who has contributed to it. However, I would like in particular to mention David McNamara, who has been the best kind of colleague, constructively critical, and Tony Becher, for his support over the years. I am grateful to Michael Eraut for his helpful comments on certain portions of the text. I would also like to acknowledge the generous assistance of David Walker with the section on Aristotle. In all cases, the responsibility for what I have said remains of course my own. I am also grateful to my colleagues on the Educational Development Team at the University of Hull, and to my family who have had to live with this and without me at times.

However, as this Preface will have made clear, my main debt is to the large number of practitioners — lecturers, teachers, tutors, trainers and managers — with whom I have worked over the years. The models that are set out here have emerged slowly, uncertainly and sometimes painstakingly through my work with them, and many of their contributions have ultimately been built into them. While my debts to the literature will be obvious, it has above all been those at the 'chalk-face' who have kept me going and moved me on, and I owe them a great deal. Theirs the trial, mine the error.

Geoffrey Squires
1st October 1998

Chapter 1

The Paradigm Problem

There can be few subjects, if any, that experience as great a degree of internal dissension as education. All disciplines, of course, have their tensions, to do with their scope, theoretical persuasion, methodology, application or other aspects of their practice. Academic life is a disputatious affair, and the historical longevity of the university as an institution may be due partly to the fact that it has found ways of managing conflicts that would leave a church in schism, fragment a political party, or drive a commercial company to the wall.

The tensions within education, however, reflect the very existence of the discipline and nature of the activity. They lead some people to doubt whether education is a proper discipline at all, as distinct from a collection of elements borrowed from other disciplines. And these tensions have practical as well as academic consequences. They place a question mark against the idea of teaching as a profession and undermine its credibility as a policy voice. They make the field peculiarly vulnerable to external pressures. And they lead to the sudden lurches and longer-term pendulum swings that typify educational practice, making it a prey to passing fads and fashions.

Many of these tensions concern what is taught and what ought to be taught — the curriculum. This is hardly surprising. The curriculum involves assumptions about the purpose of education, the nature of knowledge, the social context and the development of the learner, all contentious areas. It is also subject to more immediate political pressures to 'do something about' current problems of a moral, social or economic kind. There is a very substantial body of curriculum theory that helps us to analyse these various perspectives, claims and tensions, but the curriculum in practice seems destined always to remain an arena of conflict, reflecting as it does the unresolved issues of the society in which it exists.

However, there are also major disagreements about the process of teaching, the how rather than the what of education, and it is with these that this book is concerned. Such tensions often take the form of arguments about methods: whether the class should be taught as a whole or in small groups, whether lectures are preferable to seminars, or what the proper role of practical work is. In recent years, the development of educational and communications technology has added an extra dimension to such debates.

I shall argue in this book that such arguments are not only unproductive, but a poor way of thinking about teaching. After all, no other profession conceives of its work in terms of methods in the way that education does. Methods are involved in the practice of medicine, engineering and the law, but doctors, engineers and solicitors would not dream of reducing their work simply to this. Methods are means: they are ways of doing something, but they are not that something. One needs to look beyond methods and media to understand teaching.

This book will set out a multi-dimensional view of teaching in which methods and procedures constitute one, but only one dimension of the activity. The basis for this approach will be spelled out in Chapter 2, on The Nature of Professional Disciplines. I shall argue that all professional activities have certain basic characteristics, which suggest three basic questions: what do professionals do? what affects what they do? and how do they do it? The implications of this approach for teaching will be worked out first at the level of the course as a whole, in Chapter 3, and then at the more detailed level of the single class or teaching session, in Chapter 4. The two remaining chapters will explore the consequences of this approach for our ideas about professional expertise in general, and the training of teachers and evaluation of teaching in particular.

These ideas do not, of course, simply take vacant possession of an empty dwelling. The literature on teaching is rich in theories and models of teaching, and in addition practitioners bring with them their own personal and often implicit 'theories', which shape their practice (Marland, 1995). It is important to examine these first, not only to situate this approach in terms of current writing in the field, but to engage with what people already think and do.

One final point before we embark. I have referred only to 'teaching' rather than the 'teaching and learning' that seems to be *de rigueur* these days. Clearly, ideas about teaching must relate to ideas about learning, because the purpose of the former is in some way to enhance the latter, and there will be references to research on learning in various parts of the book. However, it is important to remember that learning goes on all the time, whether people are being taught or not. There is now widespread evidence from studies of adult learning (Brockett and Hiemstra, 1991; Candy, 1991; Gear, McIntosh and Squires, 1994; Tough, 1971) that the learning that goes on within the confines of formal education and training is only the visible tip of a much larger iceberg of ubiquitous, informal, self-directed learning. Learning happens anyway; it is teaching that is the special case, and it is for that reason that I shall focus on it, although as we shall see, the wheel will eventually come full circle.

Paradigms of Teaching

Despite the fact that Masterman (1972) identified 21 different senses in which Kuhn (1962) used the word 'paradigm', it has entered academic currency as a useful term for describing not only the way in which something is conceptualized or viewed, but the whole package of beliefs, values, attitudes and practices that goes along with that view (Burns, 1995). It will be used in that general sense here, to explore a number of different views of teaching, and the practical consequences of those views. Indeed the term is particularly apt in an educational context, because it accommodates some of the complexities of the relationship between abstract formulation, practical activity and cultural context that characterize the field.

For Kuhn, the task was to describe how one scientific paradigm came to displace another one, a process for which the Copernican revolution provided an exemplary case study. However, the problem in teaching is closer to what Masterman describes as 'multiple-paradigm science' (1972, p. 74). Here, as in some other social science fields, the problem is to explain not how one paradigm displaces another, but how a number of conflicting or competing paradigms somehow coexist. As Masterman notes, 'far from there being no paradigm, there are on the contrary too many' (*ibid.*). Thus I shall explore seven different paradigms of teaching that, while they may rise or fall in terms of relative influence, lay permanent claim to being good ways of thinking about teaching. They are: teaching as a common-sense activity, teaching as an art, teaching as a craft, teaching as an applied science, teaching as a system, teaching as reflective practice, and teaching as competence.

Each of these is an important paradigm, with a substantial literature attached, and it will be possible here only to sketch out the main features, strengths and limitations of each one. Each of them draws on sources of thinking that go well beyond education, an interesting fact in itself, but one that again will point up the limits of the analysis here. And the fact that each is treated discretely should not be taken to mean that there are no links and overlaps between them, or that one cannot draw on them eclectically, and find ways of accommodating elements of several of them. That would be to assume that teaching is an entirely homogeneous activity — that all teaching is somehow the same — and it may well be that different paradigms resonate with different teachers in relation to different aspects of their work.

Teaching as a Common-sense Activity

The idea that teaching is a common-sense activity is not one that is frequently heard in education faculties, for obvious reasons, but it is sometimes voiced by colleagues in other university departments. How else can one explain the fact that lecturers who have had no teacher training nevertheless produce their annual crop of graduates, and sometimes gain high teaching quality assessment ratings in the process? Not only that: the common-sense paradigm has a perfectly respectable theoretical pedigree, and reflects the wider attachment to common sense that is a marked feature of English culture.

The common-sense paradigm of teaching rests on two different kinds of argument. The first goes back to the experience of schooling. Few things in society are actually mandatory, as distinct from forbidden. We do not have to vote; we do not have to get married; we do not have to join the army; we do not have to work (at least not yet). But we do have to go to school (or make alternative arrangements). This massive act of social compulsion, which is without parallel in terms of scope, length and intensity, means that we all have extensive experience of being taught, and (so the argument goes) when it comes to our turn to teach others, have some ideas about how to go about this, what to do and what not to do. The parts of teaching that we have to learn are those that are usually hidden from us as pupils or students, such as the administrative arrangements and the assessment process (which is typically wrapped in mystery).

The second basis of the common-sense argument is that the things we do when we teach are, by and large, not all that different from what we do in everyday life. We organize resources, plan events, explain things to people, ask and answer questions, guide, encourage and criticize. So all we need to learn when we begin to teach are those things that we do not normally do to others, such as lecture them or assess them, and we can pick these up through a process of trial and error or by apprenticing ourselves to a more experienced teacher. The other thing we do not normally do (with the exception of giving children's parties) is to cope with a room full of young people, and so classroom management is another skill that has to be acquired. But (so the argument goes) this can be picked up as well. Thus run the common-sense arguments for a common-sense approach to teaching, and they are sometimes applied to other 'non-technical' activities, such as management or social work, as well. And if teaching really is a matter of common sense, then it follows that most people can or could do it, since most people, though not all, have common sense (it is after all common rather than universal).

However, there is a more intellectualized version of this argument, which stems from the concept of common-sense knowledge. The central endeavour of phenomenology has been to explore not only how the world appears to us and how we experience it, but what cognitive or perceptual structures we bring to these appearances and experiences. In the work of Schutz (1970) and Berger and Luckmann (1971) in particular this has led to a preoccupation with the structures and characteristics of common-sense knowledge in the everyday 'lifeworld' (*Lebenswelt*). Such knowledge is described as pre-theoretical, in that it tends to take the world for granted rather than systematically analysing, questioning or theorizing about it — although 'a-theoretical' might be a better term, since common-sense knowledge is not merely the precursor of organized knowledge, but exists in its own right. Common sense involves a certain stance *vis-à-vis* the world, which tends to accept and work with what is there. It is basically pragmatic or operational in its emphasis on actions and their consequences and places limits on the usefulness of analysis or reflection ('we don't want to get into all that'). It appeals to the shared wisdom of the tribe, although it allows for some individuality and innovation within those limits. And it is primarily concerned with know-how rather than knowledge; things are typically experienced in terms of their use (cf. Heidegger's notions of 'equipment' and 'tools') rather than as static objects of perception (Heidegger, 1962, pp. 95–9).

Another characteristic of common-sense knowledge is that despite the way it is sometimes phrased ('everyone knows that . . .') it does not aspire to strict generalization or universality; it tends to focus on the situation at hand. It is localized, specific, episodic and concrete. It addresses particular events, situations, problems. However, it is also associated with the notion of cumulative experience, and hence the idea that people can acquire it over time; young people typically lack it, and old people tend to lose it. One can thus see why it holds attractions for writers such as

Hargreaves who conceptualizes teaching in terms of 'professional common-sense knowledge' (Hargreaves, 1993, pp. 86–92). Teaching, he argues, is localized, specific, episodic and concrete, so the knowledge we need to do it is largely of that kind.

One objection to Hargreaves' notion lies in the apparent contradiction between the concepts of profession and common sense. Professions are specialized, expert, closed, sometimes almost hieratic bodies, whereas common sense is by definition common property. Professional work seems to involve a range of kinds of expertise, including formal, organized knowledge and identifiable procedures and skills. We may use our common sense or judgment to synthesize and regulate these, but there has to be something to synthesize and regulate in the first place. Professional work may involve common sense, but it is hardly reducible to it.

A different kind of objection relates to the ways in which common-sense knowledge is stored and passed on, which is often through examples, cases and stories. The term 'anecdotal' used to be a term of mere abuse in the social sciences, but more recently the importance of anecdotes as ways of sharing and storing communal knowledge and know-how has become more widely recognized. An interesting question here is how far the current emphasis on narrative research methods in teaching (see the various articles in Gudmundsdottir, 1997) should in fact be located within a common-sense paradigm. Anecdotes may play a particular role in specialized 'communities-of-practice', that is groups of people who are involved in the same kind of work, such as teaching (Brown and Duguid, 1996).

However, the problem with anecdotes is that one cannot disagree with them, as one might disagree with an argument. One cannot deny the story: one can only counter it with a different story. Thus anecdotal knowledge tends to carry a heavy normative charge, an implicit expectation about concurrence and assent. This makes it difficult for the practitioner to stand back from the practices of the group, and bring his or her analytical powers to bear. It can seem churlish to demur.

It was noted earlier that not only can the common-sense paradigm be defended in theoretical terms, but as something that reflects the wider society. The notion of common sense plays an important role in English-speaking and in particular English culture; England is, after all, the country of common land, common law, common prayer, a House of Commons. It would be interesting to explore the parallels with other countries: the French do not use *sens commun* much, and their *bon sens* appeals more to 'reason'; the German *Bauernverstand* has connotations of peasant wisdom or cunning; the Finns talk about 'countryman's sense'. In England, common sense seems to represent a permanent celebration of the demotic, a safeguard against ideological and other forms of intellectual extremism, a social bond that unites everyone from the prime minister down, perhaps a continuing inheritance from the old Anglo-Saxon culture with its moots and jury system where — at least in the historical mythology — the ordinary had its value and ordinary people had their say. And of course it serves to keep 'so-called experts' in their place.

However, it also sets limits to thought and analysis. To say that something is a matter of common sense is effectively to stop the debate, to rule out further discussion. Common sense tends to be conservative and reproductive in its instincts. It legitimizes a suspicion and ignorance of theory, abstraction, ideas, the intellect and the intellectual. It uses but debases the native English tradition of empiricism, of the appeal to experience. In what other country do people use the phrase 'purely academic' so dismissively, to mean of no real importance? In these respects, the common-sense paradigm may in the end impede our thinking about teaching and learning, as it does about much else.

Teaching as an Art

The idea that teaching is an *art* is both old-fashioned and quite recent. On the one hand, it is associated with some older books on the subject, such as Highet's *The Art of Teaching*, which first appeared in 1951 and went through many reprints (Highet, 1963). In such accounts, teaching appears as a rather subtle and ultimately mysterious activity. It is strongly associated with personal qualities and character- istics; significantly Highet begins with a long section on 'The Teacher' and has a later section on 'Great Teachers and their Pupils'. While teaching involves methods, it also involves qualities — such as liking the subject and liking the pupils — and 'abilities' such as memory, will-power and kindness. Although Highet does not argue that teachers are born, not made, and indeed talks about 'teaching' in every- day life, there is a strong sense that selection or self-selection may be as important as training. Indeed, whereas the common-sense paradigm dismisses training as unnecessary, the art paradigm in its extreme form dismisses it as impossible. Teaching is a gift.

A somewhat different perspective on the art paradigm is offered by Axelrod (1973) in his book *The University Teacher as Artist*. Here, teaching is seen as the elaboration of style; style not as decorative adjunct or superficial appearance, but as the necessary and authentic expression of a way of doing or being. If the weak- ness of the art paradigm lies in its vagueness and openness to mere posturing — teaching as 'performance' — some of its truth surely lies in the notion of style as a coherent expression of identity. The teacher-as-artist does what he or she *is*.

As Delamont (1995) makes clear in her useful overview of subsequent think- ing, the art paradigm has been marginal in most of the mainstream psychological and sociological literature on teaching. However, there are exceptions. Although Jackson does stress the importance of common sense (Jackson, 1986, pp. 10–23), his emphasis on the uncertainties of teaching and on its potential transformative role perhaps places him closer to the art paradigm than any other, although such pigeon-holing hardly does justice to his thinking. Delamont also mentions the work of Gage, which will be referred to later, but probably the most explicit formulation of the art paradigm is that of Eisner. He argues that teaching can be seen as an art in four senses: (1) that it is sometimes performed with such skill and grace that it can be described as an aesthetic experience, (2) that it involves qualitative judgements based on an unfolding course of action, (3) that it is contingent and unpredictable rather than routine, and (4) that its outcomes are often created in the process (Eisner, 1985, pp. 175–6). Tom, however, draws a distinction between the fine arts and practical arts, arguing that the latter provide a better metaphor for teaching, a point that will be picked up in the next section on craft (Tom, 1984, pp. 129–35).

However, beyond the work of these particular writers, there are reasons for thinking that the art paradigm has made something of a comeback in recent years. This is evident in subtle shifts in the discourse of research on teaching, and the increasing use of words such as 'artfulness', 'artistry', 'repertoire' and 'improvisation' in describing the process of teaching. The current interest in 'narrative', which was discussed earlier in relation to the common-sense paradigm, may also be linked to the art paradigm, although narrative is itself a problematic notion in a good deal of modern writing, and its use in educational research seems curiously old-fashioned. In one sense, these words constitute negative or residual elements: signs that rational, technical or scientific accounts have somehow failed to capture the process adequately (Dunkin, 1987b). However, they also signal a positive recognition of the indeterminacy of much teaching (Delamont, 1995) and, by extension, of the limitations of plans, scripts or procedures, the whole rational apparatus that occupies a good deal of teacher training.

The problem with the art paradigm lies as much in the art as the teaching. When teaching is said to be an art, it tends to be a rather romantic view of art that is implied, rather than the strict disciplines and rules of classicism. The emphasis is on expression and spontaneity, on creative responses to the unfolding situation, on personal authenticity and originality, rather than on more classical criteria such as good technique and sense of form. And the problem becomes more acute if one considers the contemporary arts. Whereas in the past one might identify a particular style or school of literature, painting or music as being the dominant and characteristic one in a particular period, we now seem to be in a situation that is not so much post-modernist as post-orthodox, with several different styles or traditions existing concurrently. To take just one example, there is contemporary poetry being written in relatively traditional modes, modernist poetry involving composition by field, using collage and found text, 'language' poetry that makes language itself the object of writing, performance poetry and concrete poetry, not to mention various other forms. And these are not just 'styles' in some superficial sense; they imply different views of literature, different notions of language, and different relationships with an audience, to the point where it is difficult to believe that we are talking about the same thing at all. If we cannot agree on what art is, how can we describe teaching as an art?

There may, however, be another kind of value in the art paradigm. Whatever the style or form of art, most artists would probably agree that the job is an internalized one. Learning to write, play or paint well involves a great deal of self-discipline, which may in fact be much more rigorous than any that might be imposed from the outside. In an era that places increasing emphasis on external controls — in terms of performance indicators, accountability, appraisal and the like — it is no bad thing for teachers to be reminded that the ultimate manager is oneself.

Teaching as a Craft

In contrast to the art paradigm, the craft paradigm is on the face of it much more straightforward. Whereas the arts are intuitive, personal, mysterious and typically the province of the gifted few, crafts are explicable, objective, transparent and accessible to the many, as the ubiquity of DIY attests. One can demonstrate a craft, imitate it, practise it, refine it and master it. The craft guilds are a major, if undervalued, strand in the history of European education and training. One of the tragedies of colonialism is that, with a few exceptions, the craft apprenticeship system was not exported along with the formal educational systems to the developing countries. After all, Europe developed historically on two educational legs, not one.

One can see the attractions of such a paradigm of professional work. If teaching is a craft, then one can analyse it into its elements, set up programmes to train people in it, and produce a large and skilled workforce for the schools, colleges and universities. There will be no mystery, no messing about, and it is perhaps no accident that the craft model seems strongest in that sector of the system that itself embodies such work, namely the vocational/technical Further Education colleges. The various City and Guilds teaching certificate courses are typical examples of their kind, and similarly practical courses exist for teachers and trainers in the German 'dual' system.

However, recent writing on the craft paradigm has gone well beyond the kind of straightforward practical approach adopted by Marland (1975) or, in the context of higher education, Eble (1976), although the latter also nods in the direction of the arts. In the hands of authors such as Desforges and McNamara (1979), Tom (1984), Tom and Valli (1990), Leinhardt (1990), Grimmett and MacKinnon (1992) and McNamara (1994) the concept has been extended and refined to the point where it is now a major contender for the dominant metaphor of teaching. Tom in particular adds a moral dimension to teaching as a craft, but the main thrust among all the writers is to develop a view of teaching know-how that goes beyond the general and formulaic, and attempts to capture the local, vernacular, specific reality of teaching as-it-is-done. As with the art paradigm, the craft view of teaching seems to be partly a reaction against the applied science paradigm, which views teaching in terms of the application of general principles (see Tom, 1984, pp. 135–49). But teaching (the craft writers argue) is not general, it is always particular; it is not principled, it is fashioned; not abstract, but concrete.

Logically, if craft knowledge were wholly particular and always related to the specific case or situation, it would not accumulate and develop; it would remain trapped within its own specificity, never building up into anything more than individual responses to local situations. This is indeed a problem for those who stress the particularity of knowledge about teaching, for example in action research. What we learn about one situation may enable us to deal better with the situation in question, but if it does not generalize or transfer in some way to other situations, we can hardly talk about the development of expertise. And if we can generalize it, surely we can abstract it?

One response to this (see Clandinin and Connolly, 1996) is to argue that people can use such knowledge even when it cannot be generalized in the strict sense (i.e. without qualification) because they can recognize aspects of it and make the necessary translations and adaptations to their own case; it thus has affinities with 'narrative' in literature. We cannot experience the aristocratic society of nineteenth-century Russia as portrayed in *Anna Karenina*, but we can nevertheless project ourselves into it sufficiently to understand what the characters are going through. Craft knowledge, surprisingly perhaps, therefore implies a theory of the *imagination*: of the capacity to create cognitive scenarios based on, but not restricted to, what we know or have experienced directly. It is our imagination rather than our knowledge that allows us to identify or empathize with and learn from, for example, the experience of someone who teaches a different subject in a different school — in short, to enter the world of others, however imperfectly. In this way, it is the very concreteness of craft knowledge that provides the imaginative foundations for others to build on: the best case studies are not those that are most like our own situation, but those that are most real.

The second point to be made is that although researchers commonly refer to the problems of generalizing in education and other fields, they less frequently discuss the problem of particularizing. Writing about educational narratives, case studies or action research tends to assume that one can give a description of a particular situation, but in fact such particularities are themselves shot through with generalities in the very words they use. If a situation were wholly particular or unique we would not be able to describe it at all. Even an apparently specific episode such as '*Peter came into the classroom, sat down at the back and started chatting to his friends. I told him to be quiet and get on with his work*' is riddled with generality. A 'classroom' is a general category of space; 'told' implies a kind of general authority; 'work' implies a general way of thinking about education. The point is simple, even banal: however much we may think we are concentrating on the specifics of a situation, we are always enmeshed in the inherent generality of language and the shared structures of perception and cognition. The purely particular does not exist. Craft knowledge, like other kinds of knowledge, is embedded in something more general, although not necessarily generalizable in the strict scientific sense.

This concrete, grounded strength of the craft paradigm is, however, also its limitation. However much modern writers may try to extend its scope, its historical origins and connotations lie firmly in the artisan's fashioning of materials and objects. But students are not materials and learning is not an artefact. While the process may be equally non-formulaic in relation both to objects and people, the metaphor of craft in the end restricts what is an essentially human enterprise, concerned in the case of teaching and learning with *meanings*, not artefacts. Objects do not answer back; there is no possibility of dialogue with them; if we shape them wrongly, they do not protest. The value of the craft paradigm lies in illuminating the concrete aspects of professional work. It asserts the value of doing and experience, the endlessly repeated yet never quite similar encounters with the phenomenal world. It captures some of the grittiness of teaching, the grain of a particular group, the warp and weft of the process, the almost physical resistance of problems, the palpable satisfaction of a good outcome. But it is doubtful whether it can be a sufficient paradigm of teaching.

Teaching as an Applied Science

In its strong form, the applied science paradigm assumes that professional work involves the application of scientific principles and evidence to practical tasks. Science, it is argued, investigates and discovers fundamental patterns and regularities in the natural and social world. A knowledge of these patterns allows practitioners to intervene in events with a high degree of confidence that the effects of their interventions will produce the intended results. It is not necessary for such knowledge to be complete or such predictions to be certain; as long as the results are better than would otherwise be obtained, for example by relying on trial and error, common sense or intuition, the approach is justified. Thus the shift from a law-like conception of science in the early part of the century to a more probabilistic recent one does not affect this argument. It can be noted in passing that the idea that nature exemplifies 'laws' is itself a metaphor, and a characteristically European one, whereas the conception of orderliness in traditional Chinese science involved rather a sense of organic harmony (Needham, 1956, pp. 518–83).

Whereas the art and craft paradigms have long historical roots, the applied science paradigm depends on having some science to apply, and is thus a more modern idea. (The translation of Aristotle's *poiesis* as 'applied science' (Hope, 1952, p. 233) is a retrospective and dubious imposition of a contemporary concept.) As Gage (1996) argues, applied science has played a large part in some professions such as medicine and engineering, so why not in education? Thus, for much of this century, people looked to educational psychology in particular to provide a basis for teaching and learning, in terms of fundamental laws, principles and rules.

The applied science paradigm in its weaker form includes other 'foundation' disciplines such as philosophy, history and sociology, which are believed to provide a basis for practice, a belief that underpinned much teacher training in the 1960s and 1970s but came in for increasing criticism as time went on (see Hirst, 1983; Wilkin, 1996).

Most contemporary models of teaching are in fact psychology-based models. This is true of the majority of the models contained in the various editions of Joyce and Weil's *Models of Teaching* (1996) and the relevant sections in the two editions of the *International Encyclopaedia of Teaching and Teacher Education* edited respectively by Dunkin (1987a) and Anderson (1995). Some of these models derive directly from a particular school of learning theory. Thus one can see Skinner (1954) and Bruner (1968) as expressions of behavioural and cognitive theory respectively, and Rogers (1983) and Winne (1995) as representatives of humanistic and information-processing approaches; Bandura (1986) provides the basis for a theory of social learning and teaching through modelling. More recent models, such as those advanced by Entwistle (1992) and Ramsden (1992) also derive from a particular view of learning, in this case based heavily on Marton's work on student approaches to learning within the cognitive tradition (Marton, 1977). Interactive, mastery, heuristic and competence models of teaching all stem from particular psychological theories (see Dunkin, 1987a). Even where the model of teaching is more eclectic or generic, as in the case of Dunkin and Biddle (1974), Gagné (1985) or Biggs (1993), the debt to psychology is clear.

While psychology has lit up some of the darker corners of educational work, however, it has not provided the general illumination of the whole room which was expected earlier in the century (see for example Ward, 1926). We still do not have an applied science of teaching. Attempts to summarize the general implications of learning theories for teaching (see, for example, Hilgard and Bower, 1975, pp. 606–38) hardly add up to a coherent model. There are two problems here, related respectively to the science and the application. The fact that the human or social sciences have been less successful than the natural sciences in generating high-confidence predictions is widely accepted. Two quite different explanations, however, are given for this shortfall. The first is that the human sciences are more complex in terms of the numbers and types of variables operating in human situations, and therefore require more complex methodological and statistical procedures to identify any patterns. Progress is therefore likely to be slow, and much slower than some of the pioneers in such fields originally expected, but it is being made. We are, it is argued, gradually building up a coherent understanding of human learning, for example through meta-analyses of large numbers of existing studies (Gage, 1996). Writers typically refer to such work as being in its infancy or at an early stage or having some way to go, but the assumption is that it will in fact retrace the developmental path of the natural sciences. It should be noted that this is simply a belief; despite the scientific nature of the work, there is no empirical basis for such an assumption.

The second explanation is that the existence of human consciousness introduces a qualitative difference between the non-human and human domains, because consciousness, in effect, breaks any patterns that we may identify. Even with something as basic as the hunger drive, people can choose to go on hunger strike to the point of death. Concepts such as 'reward' and 'punishment' are in fact highly subjective; some people find conventional rewards uninteresting, or conventional punishments rewarding. Culture can be defined precisely as that which is beyond nature, and there is no compelling reason to assume that it will exhibit patterns in the way that the natural world does. The problem is exemplified neatly in language, which is arguably the defining element of human culture. Language is both a patterned (syntactically) and unpredictable (semantically) phenomenon. Each language has its regularities, but each speech-act is unique. Attempts to reproduce the latter artificially run into Dreyfus's *ceteris paribus* problem: other things never are equal in the human domain (Dreyfus, 1992, pp. 57–61). The great twentieth-century project of trying to do in the human sphere, through economics, sociology and psychology, what has been done in the natural one runs apparently into the post-modernist wall: human beings are not only beyond nature, but beyond culture; consciousness, precisely because it is the capacity to think about thought, is the ultimate wild card.

This does not mean that the human sciences are useless, merely that we have to be more modest in what we expect of them. If a pattern exists 'for the most part', we can still base our decisions on it as long as we recognize that events may turn out otherwise. The human sciences can thus give us a broad steer in some aspects of professional work; but we need to realize that this is usually indicative rather than predictive. There may be rules, and even rules about rules, but in the end one is faced with a judgment as to whether to apply the rules. Thus the doctor will feed the results of, say, a 'scientific' blood test into his or her decision-making, but the final treatment decision will have to take account of a wider range of considerations, including the general condition and situation of the patient, and the time-frame and availability of medical provision and intervention.

This leads to the second problem with the applied science paradigm, which concerns the application rather than the science. Part of the problem of relating the 'foundation disciplines' of education to the practice of teaching has been precisely the lack of a conceptual framework for the latter. There has been nothing, as it were, to plug the psychology or sociology into, hence it has been difficult for teachers to relate the generalities of such disciplines to the specifics of their class-room work. This has led to a good deal of criticism of the irrelevance of such disciplines, but in fact the problem lies not with them but with education itself. The failure of 'educational theory' in the 1960s and 1970s was not in fact a failure of educational theory, but of theories in education; there was little or no educational theory *per se*. One of the arguments for the model that will be set out in Chapters 3 and 4 is that it offers a framework to which philosophical, psychological and sociological content can be related.

Even if there has been less science to apply than some writers believe, what there has been has thus been under-utilized because of the absence of a coherent model of teaching that could take account of it. I shall argue in the next chapter that the contingent nature of professional work rules out, *a priori*, the idea that teaching, or any other profession, can be seen simply as an applied science. No professional domain — whether engineering, medicine, agriculture or any other — is *merely* the application of general scientific principles. But this does not exclude drawing on scientific knowledge as one element among others in practical decisions; it merely relegates its status from a determinant to an element.

Contemporary writers in the instructional science tradition (see Gage, 1996; Stones, 1994) take a much more sophisticated view of the applicability of science to teaching and learning than their predecessors, and indeed Gage's views show an interesting shift over time. It is now widely acknowledged that whatever 'funda-mental pedagogical principles' exist must be interpreted in the light of the situation, rather than simply or directly applied. This thus admits a degree of contingency, in the form of mediating factors, into the analysis. The difference between such a view and the approach to be presented here is that for the applied scientist such contingency is a complication, a problem that intrudes upon the application pro-cess, whereas here it is regarded as a defining characteristic of professional work.

Even if all other contingencies were somehow eradicated or controlled, there would still remain the fundamental contingency of *time*. Time is important in professional fields in a way that is quite different from scientific ones; not for nothing is Heidegger's great phenomenological tract titled *Being and Time*. Time is the ever-present, inescapable consideration for the professional, whether doctor, lawyer or teacher. All that they do is done in time. Things happen in a sequence of events. The order of actions can have a crucial impact on the outcome. For the scientist, time also matters in the sense that experiments and investigations obviously occur in and over time; but their *timing* is not usually so crucial, because they do not form part of this inexorable serial flow. But it can matter greatly whether an illness is diagnosed in March or April, whether something happens at the beginning of a class or at the end, at what point a fertilizer is applied to a crop. How often the professional person says 'I wish I had done this a little earlier' or 'I wish I had waited'; how often they lament not having enough time. Thus, even if the human sciences did manage to generate strong general laws, those laws would still have to be applied in a temporal context, after something and before something else. In that sense, the 'timelessness' of science contrasts with the temporality of the professions.

Teaching as a System

The idea that professional work, such as teaching, can be seen in terms of a *system* is sometimes associated with the applied science paradigm, but actually has a quite different basis. Although some writers such as Checkland (1981) see the growth of systems theory as a response to the scientific problem of dealing with wholes rather than parts, systems thinking actually belongs to a rational rather than scientific tradition. (Schon's notion of 'technical rationality' unhelpfully conflates the two [Schon, 1983, 1987]). Systems thinking can be seen as one form of a more general rational or rationalistic paradigm, which has had a widespread influence on late twentieth-century thinking, particularly in the fields of human organization and public policy (Carley, 1980) and which has in turn generated concepts such as Herbert Simon's 'bounded rationality' (Simon, 1996). And although it would be a complex task to unravel the various historical antecedents of this, the main debt would seem to be not to Renaissance science but to the more general espousal of rationality and clarity as a means to human progress that came in later centuries, and is associated particularly with the Enlightenment. The distinction between ends and means, which is a cornerstone of rational analysis, is after all a philosophical rather than scientific one.

The modern concept of the system builds on these foundations (see Emery, 1969). The ends–means distinction remains essential, but tends to be expressed in the language of aims/goals/objectives on the one hand, and strategies/tactics/resources on the other. However, modern systems theory adds three crucial elements: (1) the idea that the means–ends nexus can be seen as a whole, that is as a system, (2) the idea that the system may itself form part of a hierarchy of supra-systems and sub-systems, and (3) that such systems may have the capacity to regulate themselves through feedback. The contribution of mathematics to modelling such systems has been important, though so far has had little impact on education. Thus what is sometimes referred to as a systems approach in education or training is based on a mixture of rational planning and systems theory. That theory developed mainly in the years following the Second World War, and as von Bertalanffy has argued, has a mechanistic strand, which developed out of the need to plan man-machine operations such as air defence, and an organismic strand, which has grown out of the study of biological systems (von Bertalanffy, 1968). Systems theory of both kinds introduced new concepts for thinking about intentional, organized human activities: notions such as synergy, dynamic interaction, equilibrium and equifinality. The work of Norbert Wiener (1948) on cybernetics contributed the crucial concept of feedback, which among other things offered a more elegant version of the behaviourists' 'knowledge of results'.

The concept of system is now pervasive in our culture, and has influenced the professions along with everything else. In education, it dovetailed neatly with the behaviourist emphasis on precise, observable and measurable objectives and out-comes, and step-by-step approaches (see Mager,1962; Skinner, 1954; Tyler, 1949) so that the 'systems approach' to teaching is in fact a composite of three things: rational analysis, systems theory and behavioural psychology. This is seen as a technology that is viable in its own right and that does not have to be grounded in basic scientific laws or principles. The arguments are purely rational ones. How can we know if we have achieved our aims if we have not specified them clearly in the first place? How can we analyse the process of teaching and learning unless we break it down clearly into all its components? How can we design or implement anything if we do not go through the rational cycle of formulating objectives, deciding strategies, selecting resources, organizing activities, implementing delivery and evaluating the results? This is not the language of science, but of a particular form of rationality.

The main contribution of systems theory to education and training has been to help people to think about teaching as a complex whole (see Patrick, 1992, pp. 109–30; Richey, 1992; Romizowski, 1988). Systems thinking highlights the extent to which the various components of a system impact upon or interact with one another; it thus reduces the dangers of treating things in isolation. It also demands a thorough analysis of the sequences and stages involved in such an activity, so that one is less likely to miss things out. The typical systems diagram thus involves not only boxes and arrows to indicate the relationships between components, but flow-charts and decision-trees to set out the sequence of events. Insofar as professional work involves the planning of complex wholes, such ration-ality has a place.

However, it is insufficient on its own, for two reasons. First, it is decon-textualized, and does not take enough account of the contingencies of teaching and learning. It may look fine on paper, but in reality all sorts of factors break in upon the neat scheme: time pressures, organizational politics, people's attitudes, and the general confusion and uncertainty that in other circumstances have been called the 'fog of war'. Systems theorists sometimes distinguish between closed and open systems, the latter having more permeable boundaries and transactions with their environments. However, once that openness gets beyond a certain point, the very concept of a system begins to break down, since it implies a certain stability of structure and function.

Even in theory, however, rational planning may not be the optimum approach, because it is essentially abstracted from the people and contexts in which it has to operate. Lindblom (1959, 1979) has argued for a form of incrementalism in the public policy domain, mainly on the grounds that policy-making is better seen as a form of negotiation between competing interests than as a rational process. This essentially political model of planning in fact applies quite well sometimes to teaching: not only may there be negotiation between the teacher and his or her peers and organization, but within the classroom between teacher and learner. The capacity to engage in continual negotiation and therefore modification is, Lindblom argues, a better guarantee of effectiveness in an unpredictable or evolving situation than a pre-ordained rational plan. As noted earlier, improvisation and spontaneity may therefore have their place in teaching along with preparation and planning.

The other basic problem with the systems approach is that it is purely a process model; it says nothing about the content of any system. It can be applied equally to firing a missile, running a small business, organizing health care or teaching primary school children. This is both its strength and its weakness. It is a powerful, generic idea, but tells us nothing about the substance of the particular activity we apply it to. It does not say anything in itself about the uniqueness of teaching and learning, and therefore cannot take account of the nature of those particular processes. It assumes that teaching and learning are clear, transparent, goal-directed, analysable, plannable and measurable activities, but it does not attempt to justify such assumptions. It has nothing to say about the functions of teaching, what teachers do. For these reasons, it is not a paradigm of teaching at all, but simply a general paradigm that happens to be applied to teaching, among other fields.

Teaching as Reflective Practice

Another example of a process paradigm is the notion of 'reflective practice'. This idea is associated in particular with the work of Schon (1983, 1987), who has related it to a number of professions (such as management and architecture) including teaching. It has also had considerable influence on other fields such as nursing and social work. Schon's work (together with that of Argyris, 1982) can be seen as part of a general reaction against 'technical rationality' and the beliefs, set out above, that professional practice could be based either on scientific principles or rational planning (although as noted earlier, their reaction tends not to distinguish between the two). The whole anti-technicist approach can be mapped neatly onto Kolb's experiential learning cycle, with its four stages of concrete experience, reflective observation, abstract conceptualization and active experimentation (Kolb, 1984). Critics of applied science or systems approaches to teaching variously place the emphasis on *experiential* learning (Boud, Cohen and Walker 1993; Weil and McGill, 1989); *reflective* practice (Calderhead and Gates, 1993; Schon, 1987); or *action* learning and research (Elliott, 1993; McGill and Beaty, 1992; Revans, 1982).

The fourth stage — abstract conceptualization — receives much less emphasis in this paradigm.

Schon argues that most professional problems are messy and inchoate, and cannot be solved purely through scientific application or rational analysis. They require a continuing process of reflection on what is happening and has happened (reflection in action, reflection on action). Such a process can improve the quality of decisions, and is contrasted with unreflective, unthinking, routine or habit-ridden behaviour. Eraut (1995) sees Schon's approach as a form of metacognition and Argyris talks about 'double loop learning', which involves questioning the frame of reference of the question (Argyris, 1994). Thus practitioners have to disengage temporarily from the immediacy of practice to think about what they are doing — and about what they are thinking about it.

There can be no objection to the idea of reflective practice in itself. As noted earlier, it is difficult to imagine any professional activity going on without an element of reflection, if it is not to become wholly routinized and habit-ridden. The need for reflection is a direct consequence of the fact that professional work is contingent; if it were simply algorithmic and rule-governed we would not need to reflect on it at all. And one can see in practical terms what Schon is talking about. The advanced driver who is told to commentate aloud on his perceptions and decisions as he is driving (reflection-in-action) and the air force pilot who is carefully debriefed after a mission (reflection-on-action) offer two examples from quite different domains, but one can see the potential use of such commentaries and debriefings in professional training.

Again, however, there are problems. If reflection is taken to be the only or main element in professional activity, it can lead to an underemphasis on substantive knowledge or relevant skills. To what extent can one reflect without an adequate knowledge-base in the field? What is one reflecting with or about? And does one have the skills needed to translate the outcomes of such reflection into action? It is all very well for a teacher to be able to produce a reflective account of a class or session, but that is not an end in itself; reflection has ultimately to feed back into action.

Moreover, the relationship between reasoning and reflection is also not clear. The latter implies something more heuristic or iterative and less logical or systematic than the former. So how do we evaluate the quality of reflection? We can apply certain criteria to reasoning (to do with the grasp of concepts, process of argument and handling of evidence) but it is not so clear how we should judge a reflective account, such as a diary, journal or logbook. When we use words like 'thoughtful', 'perceptive', 'sensitive' or 'illuminating', what kinds of judgments are we making? Presumably the adequacy of a piece of reflection has to relate not simply to the person who is doing it, and how he or she has done it, but to the situation, and this sends us back to the thorny question of what is significant. If I reflect on the colour of the ceiling in my classroom, how do we know that that is not significant (if it isn't)? On what basis do we select for reflection and analysis a relatively small number of features from the infinite detail of the class? As Albert Camus once pointed out, true naturalism in writing is an impossibility.

As noted above, reflective practice is another pure process paradigm; it tells us nothing specific about teaching or any other profession to which it relates. So what do we reflect on and with? The answer presumably is 'experience' or 'practice'; but here again one confronts the problem for the empiricist: experience and practice are not some kind of raw material mutely awaiting interpretation, they are already 'structured' and 'processed' to some degree. Cognition is already deeply implicated in perception and experience; we do not perceive or experience first and think second.

While the notion of reflective practice is undoubtedly useful as an element in professional work and training, it is thus not enough on its own. It leaves un-answered questions about the content of such reflection. It is often seen as the opposite of systems thinking, but in fact it shares with that paradigm the strength and weakness of a process paradigm, applicable to everything and nothing in par-ticular. One can also ask questions about the intellectual context of its use. The historical salience of science and technology and the related cult of the expert in American culture make it understandable that there should be periodic reactions against this, and Schon fits neatly into this pattern. He can be seen as a scion of American pragmatism; there are affinities with Dewey (on whom he did his thesis) for example, in the emphasis on experience and inquiry, a debt which he has acknowledged (Argyris and Schon, 1996, pp. 30–7). However, the impact and reception of Schon in England is another matter. This is a culture in which science and technology have long had an ambiguous status, in which experts are commonly mistrusted, in which theory and abstraction are often regarded as alien. The notion of reflection fits comfortably into a certain amateur (rather than expert) quasi-literary and anti-technological ethos, which has deep social and cultural roots. It is hardly surprising, therefore, that (as in the Gospel) the prophet has been so much honoured in this country, but also rather worrying.

Teaching as Competence

The final paradigm is that which views teaching as a matter of competence or competences (the word 'competencies' is also sometimes used, but there seems to be no consistent difference in meaning). The development of competence-based education and training in the US has been traced by Tuxworth (1982), Short (1984) and Houston (1987). The approach there developed mainly in the fields of voca-tional education and teacher education in the 1960s and 1970s, although as with most fundamental educational ideas one can find precursors, in the objectives move-ment of the 1950s (Mager, 1962; Tyler, 1949) and even the efficiency movement of the 1920s (Bobbitt, 1924; Charters, 1929). Like these two earlier examples, the competence movement focuses on what professionals can actually do rather than what they know. The bottom line is the capacity of the practitioner to perform or deliver in the real-world context, a context that may bring pressures of time, un-certainty, conflicting priorities and inadequate resources. Competence shares with behaviourism the emphasis on specific objectives and observable behaviour, but goes beyond the earlier movement in deriving those behaviours from, and relating them to, the actual work environment.

In the UK the competence movement essentially dates from the formation of the National Council for Vocational Qualifications in the mid-1980s, and the espousal by that organization of a competence-based approach (de Ville, 1986). This has led to the reformulation of most vocational and technical courses in terms of a framework of competences and levels (usually 1 to 4) although the relationship between the NCVQ (now Qualifications and Curriculum Authority) and the existing examining bodies such as the Business/Technician Education Council (BTEC) and City and Guilds was by no means always smooth. This was hardly surprising: such bodies were well established in their own right, and some of them date back to the nineteenth century. However, the NCVQ had powerful government backing, and (despite some practical criticisms) a good deal of support from employers, so the changes largely went through. These changes can best be seen not as changes in the content of the curriculum but as a re-formatting of courses in a way that emphasizes student performance and outcomes, and the assessment of these in the real work environment (where possible).

The extension of the paradigm to higher-level professional courses has been much more problematic. In some fields, such as education, nursing and social work, the competence-based approach has had considerable influence, though not usually in as detailed, specific or behavioural a form as in vocational and technical courses. Both Elliott (1991, pp. 118–34) and Barnett (1994, pp. 157–71) have argued for broader or more holistic approaches to competence in education, and in the ASSET programme for training social workers, specific competences are complemented by an analysis of the general qualities required by professionals in the field (Winter and Maisch, 1996, pp. 39–63). Such work offers an interesting though currently less influential alternative to the dominant behavioural paradigm. Other professions, such as medicine, law and engineering, have so far largely resisted such ideas, partly because they are deemed inappropriate to the field, and also probably because they are viewed as an encroachment on their autonomy by an external body.

The competence paradigm in this country is well represented by Burke (1989, 1995) and Jessup (1991), who are largely sympathetic to it. Eraut (1994) has engaged dispassionately with it, placing it in the wider context of research on expertise; the most forceful of many critics has probably been Hyland (1997). There is also now quite a large practical literature on the subject (see, for example, Fletcher, 1991). At first sight, the competence paradigm might seem very similar to the craft one, in its emphasis on practical skill. However, the notion of competence goes beyond the connotations of craft skills, since it includes everything that goes towards the delivery or performance of those skills in the real-world situation, including, for example, the appropriate matching of skill to task, and the attitudes and stamina needed to carry it through in difficult circumstances. On the other hand, 'competence' has a narrower or more definable sense than 'art', in that it implies that what people do and the way they do it can be specified in quite clear and predictable terms. Although the levels of competence (from 1 to 5) defined by the NCVQ imply increasing open-endedness and contingency in tasks and situations, the general thrust behind the competence movement is to pin down the idea of *doing*.

The potential advantages of this approach are threefold. In general terms, it places the emphasis in vocational, technical and professional fields firmly where it should be: on performance, rather than knowledge or understanding. The bottom line is what the practitioner can do, rather than what he or she can describe, analyse, reflect on or explain. In terms of the process of education and training, a competence-based approach offers clear objectives for teacher and learners alike, thus clearing away some of the curricular fog that obscures courses, and providing an explicit, shared basis for working together. Thirdly, in terms of learning and assessment, it allows one to disaggregate large blocks of learning into smaller more manageable units, and offers a way of accrediting learning that has taken place elsewhere, on other courses, in other modes or through prior experience. In many ways, therefore, it promises to free up education and training from some of its supply-side institutional and curricular rigidities, and to shift the emphasis from producer to consumer. Its advocates certainly see it as not merely a technical approach but a liberating movement.

Many of the criticisms have concerned the implementation of the approach, and the unwieldy jargon and bureaucracy that it seems to engender. Some critics argue that mere competence encourages mediocrity, and that one should be aiming at excellence, or at least allow for a range of performance, not just the criterion-referenced tick/cross. More serious charges have been laid at the unreliability of assessment, much of which has to be devolved to practitioner-assessors in work environments who may apply varying standards in their local contexts, and this has undermined the credibility of some courses. To be fair, this is a problem with any work-based assessment, and a potential weakness even in well-organized apprenticeship systems such as the German one.

However, the basic weakness of the competence paradigm lies not in the process of teaching and assessment itself, but in the prior analysis of jobs that has to be carried out in order to identify competence. Such 'functional analysis', as it is called, has some affinities with the methods of task analysis developed in the 1960s and 1970s (see Stammers and Patrick, 1975), which essentially involve a hierarchical breakdown or 'progressive desegregation' (Ellis, 1995) of the work to be performed. The terms used for this vary, but typically a whole occupation or job is divided into key elements, which are in turn subdivided into tasks, which are in turn broken down into behaviours, which in turn generate specific performance criteria. A familiar tree-like structure thus emerges, though this is not necessarily symmetrical, and the number of levels can vary. This analysis is often complemented by a specification of the knowledge and understanding that 'underpin' the competences, and a list of the range of situations or cases to which they should apply.

The problem is that although the competence approach may look logical on paper, there is no reason to believe that it is necessarily a good way of capturing what people do in their work. There are two basic issues. The first is that in all but the simplest jobs or tasks, one has to distinguish between what one does and how one does it, and the relationship between these is not simply a hierarchical one. In the model set out in Chapter 3, I shall distinguish between functions or roles on the one hand (what one does) and procedures or methods on the other (how one does it). The point may be clarified by taking an example from outside the field of education.

Let us assume that one of the functions of a doctor is to *diagnose* a medical problem, that is to come up with a plausible relationship between the symptom the patient is showing (tiredness) and the possible cause or causes of this (stress, diabetes, heart problems, and so on). We might assume that the doctor arrives at a diagnosis primarily through using verbal procedures (question and answer, talk) and physical procedures (physical examination). However, the doctor may also on occasions use biochemical procedures (blood or urine tests) and even surgical procedures (taking a sample of tissue). So the single function of diagnosis (what) may be accomplished by the use of multiple procedures (how). Conversely, each of these procedures may serve multiple functions. Surgery is usually associated with treatment rather than diagnosis, as are biochemical procedures such as putting the patient on a drip or giving him or her a blood transfusion. Physical procedures (manipulation, massage) may also be curative rather than diagnostic and doctors' talk may serve a wide range of purposes beyond the diagnostic, ranging from treatment (persuading the patient to take the whole course of pills, therapy) through counselling to education. The relationship between what doctors do (functions) and how they do it (procedures) is thus not hierarchical but orthogonal. And the same applies to other professions.

Another way of putting this is in terms of that little word 'do'. For all its apparent concreteness or obviousness, the word *do* is in fact quite problematic. 'I am preventing the spread of disease' and 'I am giving an injection' are both possible answers to the question: what are you doing? The competence approach sees this difference as one of levels (disease prevention is a general task that can be subdivided into more specific behaviours). But there are many different ways of preventing the spread of diseases (sanitation, isolation, education, and so on) and there are many different functions of injections (to inoculate, give antibiotics, supply vitamins, control diabetes, sedate, and so on). The relationship between what one does and how one does it is very complex in professional work and cannot be represented simply in terms of hierarchical levels.

The second main problem with the competence paradigm is the way it deals with contextuality and contingency. As we have seen, the competence approach tries to accommodate contextual variations through 'range statements', that is the variety of situations in which the person should be able to perform. This implies that the competence is a standard behaviour that has to be adapted or fine-tuned to the context. The problem is that contingency is not simply an adaptation of, but a basic characteristic of, professional work. The world of the professional practitioner — the doctor, engineer, social worker, teacher — is a contingent world because it is not simply or normally a rule-governed world. That is why doctors and other professionals talk so much about professional judgment, good judgment and errors of judgment. Context is a permanent aspect of what they do; it defines one dimension of their world. It is not some kind of extraneous consideration to be tacked on in the form of a range statement.

The degree of contingency is sometimes seen as the key difference between 'low-level' vocational/technical occupations and 'high-level' professional ones; hence the common argument that the competence approach is suitable for more routine, simpler tasks, but decreasingly appropriate as one moves up the occupational ladder. However, one might argue that even the simplest and most routine task is subject to some contingencies, if only those of time (normal, rushed, panic-stations), space (adequate, roomy, cramped) and resources (generous, inadequate, shoe-string). This points to the need for yet another dimension in any model of work, and it seems more logical to apply this to all occupations and tasks at all levels, recognizing that simpler jobs will produce simpler models, but still take the same basic form.

Conclusion

It would be a complex task, and one that would take us away from the main purpose of this book, to trace the influence of these seven paradigms on the various sectors of education at various times and in various places. Besides, they do not usually manifest themselves in pure or discrete form, but rather in the messy, semi-conscious and eclectic use that characterizes much of our practice. We may espouse one paradigm, and act out another in our work; or assent to one in public, while holding to another in private. We may shift from one to another over time, perhaps in the developmental sequence suggested by Pratt (1989). And, as noted at the beginning, different paradigms may reflect different aspects of our work.

The same problem arises at the level of national policies and trends. It is one thing to describe, as Wilkin (1996) does, how the 'foundations' approach to teacher education in the 1960s and 1970s has largely given way to, on the one hand, a government-backed competence approach, and on the other, an emphasis on reflect-ive practice in many university education faculties. But this is to speak only of the schools. Further education has hitherto been strongly influenced by the craft para-digm (in the various City and Guilds courses), which is not surprising in a sector that is heavily involved in teaching crafts of various kinds. In the field of training and development, the systems approach still largely rules, and again this is congru-ent with much of the language and ethos of management, with its emphasis on objectives, strategies, resources and evaluation. In higher education, the training of lecturers is a recent development, which shows various competing influences at the time of writing, and which will no doubt encounter some eloquent defenders of the common-sense and artistic paradigms.

The analysis sketched out here will, however, have served its purpose if it suggests why none of these paradigms quite fits the bill. Each one has its strengths, its truths; one cannot dismiss any of them out of hand. Indeed, a useful exercise is to ask practitioners to place the seven in order of preference. In my experience, this usually yields a wide diversity of responses and promotes lively discussion as people justify their preferences to one another. (I have yet to find two people in a group coming up with exactly the same ranking). Such an exercise helps to bring to the surface and engage the kind of tacit or hidden 'personal theories' which, as noted at the outset, teachers and intending teachers often bring to their work.

But each paradigm has its limitations. If teaching really were a matter of common sense, why do we find bad or incompetent teaching? If it is an art, why is it a (relatively) mass activity? Can an inanimate metaphor like craft really illuminate a human process? How can it be an applied science when there is not much science to apply? How can the messiness of teaching be accommodated in the notion of a system? What do we reflect with?

The next chapter will set out yet another paradigm, that of teaching as a professional activity. Again, this will prove to have its limitations, but I shall argue that it offers a more comprehensive and balanced view of teaching than any of the ones reviewed in this chapter. It will also help to relate teaching to other professions, bringing to light some interesting similarities and differences. But first we have to go back, as it were, to square one.

Chapter 2

The Nature of Professional Disciplines

Teaching, it is often asserted, is a profession. It is surprising, therefore, to find relatively little reference to other professions in most writing about teaching. True, the professional literature on management looms large in discussions of the management of educational institutions, and writing on educational counselling typically refers to counselling in general. Some parallels have been drawn with clinical decision-making and evidence-based practice in medicine. One also comes across passing references to other professions such as engineering, nursing, social work or design. But there is little sustained analysis of what it is that teachers might have in common with other professionals in terms of the nature of their work.

Insofar as there are any inter-professional references, they are usually in terms of the sociology of the professions (Hoyle, 1995). There is a well-established sociological literature on the professions and professionalization, which seemed to burgeon particularly around the 1960s (see, for example, Etzioni, 1969; Jackson, 1970; Reader, 1966). The professions seem to have reached an apogee of esteem at that point, before the growth of consumerist attacks, radical critiques and the political assault grounded in free-market economics. Such writing is concerned with the historical evolution of professions, their definition, nature and characteristics, their relations with the state and the client, and issues of access, training, status and control. All these aspects of the professions obviously have implications for teaching.

There is also a substantial literature on both initial and continuing professional education, usually in the context of higher education (Becher, 1994; Bines and Watson, 1992; Cook, 1973; Goodlad, 1984; Jarvis, 1983; Schein, 1972; Turner and Rushton, 1976). In particular, there has been a growth of interest in continuing professional development in recent years, mainly as a response to the organizational, legal, technological and social changes with which practitioners have to cope.

There is also a third strand of literature, which explores the nature of professional expertise, and how professionals do what they do. This literature addresses the relationship between theory and practice, knowledge and know-how, and the complex processes of professional problem-solving and decision-making. It is a rich vein of research and thinking, drawing on everything from detailed ethnographic analyses of professional practice to computer-based expert systems, and will be discussed in Chapter 5.

But none of these kinds of literature quite gets at the basic question that concerns us here, which is: What is the nature of professional work? What kinds of disciplines are professional disciplines? With some interesting exceptions (see, for example, Calderhead, 1987, 1995; Clark and Yinger, 1987; Kennedy, 1987) these sorts of questions are rarely asked, perhaps because they seem too abstract, too philosophical in a field that still sets great store by empirical investigation. This book is an attempt to set out a coherent view of the activity of teaching: what it is, what it involves. However, since teaching is a profession, the point of departure will be an analysis of the nature of professions and professional work in general. This will then be related specifically to teaching at the level of the course and the level of the class in Chapters 3 and 4.

I shall argue that professional work in any domain has three basic characteristics. It is *instrumental*, in the sense of aiming at some effect beyond itself; it is *contingent* in that it is dependent upon its situation or context; and it is *procedural*, in that it involves certain ways of doing things. These are not the only characteristics of professions, but they are the ones that are most relevant here, and each of them will be explored in turn.

Instrumentality

Professional work is instrumental because its purpose lies beyond itself, in trying to bring about some change or facilitate some effect. That change or effect might be a palpable artefact, such as a bridge or a building, or a change of state or condition, for example in a person's learning, health, or social situation. Although professionals may enjoy what they do, and think it is good in itself, they do not do it primarily for such intrinsic reasons; they have some external end in mind. The teacher teaches not just to teach, but to help people learn; the lawyer presents a case not just to deploy complex arguments, but to help ensure that justice is done.

In saying that the professions are instrumental, one is in no way demeaning them, or suggesting that they are somehow calculating or mean-spirited. That is what they are there for and why we need them. There are of course arguments about the degree of dependence that clients have or professionals may encourage. George Bernard Shaw notoriously regarded them as a conspiracy against the laity, and Illich (1977) criticized them as being fundamentally disabling, depriving people of the confidence and capacity to do things for themselves and one another. But that debate concerns the locus of control; it does not touch the basic purposiveness of professional activity, whoever carries it out.

Nor is the instrumentality of the professions meant to imply a broader philosophic instrumentalism. Indeed, this characteristic helps to distinguish them from some other activities. Although the work of the pure scientist or the painter has its own ends or purposes, it is not usually thought of as instrumental in the sense here of aiming to have a specific, identifiable effect on the world. And equally, the term distinguishes professional activity from a good deal of everyday life. When we say that a person is 'a bit instrumental' in his or her behaviour, it suggests too much concern with ends and not enough with relationships. But it is no criticism of the professional to call him or her instrumental; indeed the main complaint is usually that professionals are not instrumental enough, that they become so preoccupied with what they are doing that they forget the purpose and outcome of it. Thus the doctor can become fascinated with medical techniques, the barrister immersed in his own performance, the lecturer preoccupied with her own subject-matter.

One further point needs to be made about the term 'instrumental' in an educational context. In saying that teaching is an instrumental activity, I am not implying that education as a whole must be instrumental — that it has to be justified in utilitarian or vocational terms. The teacher may be instrumental in helping the learner to achieve intrinsic or liberal aims, such as self-development, rationality or wisdom. The model that I shall develop is a model of teaching, not of education; it relates to the means or process whereby educational aims or ends are achieved, not to those aims themselves. It is concerned with outcomes only insofar as they have implications for that process, and as such reverses the usual emphasis of curriculum models. Here, educational aims are treated as a variable (*rationale*) that may affect the process of teaching and learning, whereas in curriculum models they are logically the point of departure for the whole analysis.

Does this imply that the process is value-free or amoral? To some degree, yes. The model of teaching that will be set out in Chapters 3 and 4 could be used to facilitate outcomes that some people would reject as immoral. It has already been used in various kinds of training. How can this be reconciled with the moral notions that are implicit in the idea of a profession, and specifically of teaching? The answer perhaps involves another value: clarity. The fact that discussions about the process of teaching are often heavily value-laden has arguably made it more difficult for us to think clearly about *both* educational ends and educational means. Methods and techniques of teaching and assessment have come to be regarded as intrinsically good or bad, rather than as effective or ineffective in relation to a particular educational aim.

Of course teaching is not a wholly transparent activity, and cannot be regarded as a purely neutral or technical matter; the processes we use colour or inflect what we are using them for. But by focusing for once on the process of teaching and learning, and treating educational aims as a variable in that process, we may in the end get a clearer understanding of the relationship between what we aim to do and how we can do it. What distinguishes this model from many others in the field is therefore that it is actually a model of *teaching*, as distinct from education or curriculum: of teaching wherever and however it occurs, and to whatever end. In some countries and contexts (and particularly in continental Europe) it would be regarded as a pedagogical model, although if we associate pedagogy only with the teaching of children, that is too restrictive (see Knowles, 1978; Merriam and Caffarella, 1991; Tennant 1997). The model can be and has been used in relation not only to formal education, but also non-formal education and informal learning in the adult sphere (for a discussion of these distinctions, see Squires, 1993). The essential point is that the emphasis here is on the process rather than the content. One cannot entirely separate the two, and any model of education has to comprise both. But the fact that we routinely use the three different words — teaching, curriculum and education — suggests that it is legitimate to focus on one as long as we do not forget the other two, and the issue will be picked up again at the beginning of Chapter 5, after the model has been set out in detail.

Contingency

The second basic characteristic of professional work is its *contingency* — the fact that it is influenced or affected by things around it. Professional activity takes place not in a vacuum, but in a situation: it is embedded in the temporal, phenomenal world. The most obvious evidence for this is the familiar response that professionals give to some question about their practice: 'Well, it depends'. What the professional does may depend on a wide range of contextual or situational factors, which he or she has to take account of and deal with in some way. All these are rolled up in the important though complex notion of professional judgment, which involves sensing, reading or interpreting the situation and responding appropriately.

A more significant indication of the contingent nature of professional activities is the centrality of the concept of decision-making in research on professional expertise, a topic that will be explored in Chapter 5. If professional work involved only rules, there would no room for decisions; one would simply respond to the situation in the correct way (although arguably responding at all is itself a decision). But the reality for the lawyer, engineer, social worker or manager is that every day brings its load of decisions, some broad and strategic, some tactical, some highly specific, which have to be made in the light of the circumstances. And Goodnow (1982) has argued that education also should be seen in these terms.

There are of course deeper problems with the notion of contingency. Such a view of professional work challenges what was described in Chapter 1 as the applied science paradigm of professions, which sees professional practice largely as the application of general, underlying principles. By contrast, a contingency model emphasizes the particularity of professional work, the fact that each problem or case is different, if only in terms of when it occurs in the sequence of events. But if we come to know the world through its patterns, as the scientist might argue, how can we speak of knowledge where there are no patterns? If everything is contingent, situational or particular, how is it possible for the professional to build up any kind of general, cumulative expertise or wisdom? I shall come back to these issues in Chapter 5. Since professionals habitually describe what they do in contingent terms — 'it depends', 'consider it case by case', 'assess the situation', 'play it by ear', and so on — rather than in the language of general laws and rules, I shall for the moment take them at their word.

Procedurality

It is easier to describe the third basic characteristic of professions in terms of what they are not, rather than what they are. As noted in the previous chapter, one sometimes encounters the idea that professional work is really just a matter of common sense, or as the Americans sometimes put it, that professionals are really 'just plain folk'. The argument seems to be applied mainly to (a) professions that employ everyday language rather than specialized terminology, and (b) those that are accessible to common experience. Three professions in particular seem to fit the bill: teaching, social work and management. Each of these employs relatively familiar, vernacular language: indeed, when they do introduce specialized terms, they are typically accused of resorting to jargon, whereas such specialized terminology passes without comment in fields such as medicine or engineering. (The popular complaint that lawyers dress up common English in legal jargon to mystify and rip off the public also goes back a long way.) Each of these three professions also forms part of the common experience. Virtually everyone has been to school; many people have experienced social or family problems at first hand; and most people have worked in organizations. So the idea that all one needs in each case is common sense seems quite natural.

Few professionals would dismiss the importance of common sense or common knowledge in their work, but neither would they normally reduce it to this. Something else is needed. Each profession has its own way of doing what it does: a repertoire of approaches, tools, materials, techniques. These can range from pieces of equipment and software of various kinds, through identifiable methods and procedures, to the softer, subtler and less explicit ways and means, tricks of the trade, recipes, hints, tips, styles and approaches that form part of the collective professional wisdom and culture.

It is difficult to find the right term to cover all these ways and means. One possibility is the ancient Greek word *techne*, and I shall explore Aristotle's use of the term later in Chapter 5. Although the original meaning of the word is arguably broader and less cut-and-dried than the equivalent modern concept of technique, the rather mechanistic or routinized connotations of the latter inevitably colour it in ways that make it difficult to use now without giving the wrong signals.

An alternative is the modern term *procedural*. This is used by some psychologists in their distinction between declarative or propositional knowledge (knowing that) and procedural knowledge (knowing how). The original distinction is philosophical (Ryle, 1949, pp. 26–60) but this has been used more recently in psychological analyses of the nature of expertise (J.R. Anderson, 1995, pp. 236–42). Again, the connotations of the word are not quite right. The term suggests something that we not only know how to use, but are aware of using; something that has an identifable, often linear sequence of steps. Thus it does not quite capture the 'softer' aspects of professional work: it suggests Pascal's *'esprit géométrique'* rather than his *'esprit de finesse'*. Of course the same might be said of the concept of decision-making itself, which could connote a rational, explicit and conscious paradigm of expertise.

We need some way of referring to the fact that professions involve certain ways of doing things that go beyond everyday expertise or know-how. Learning to become a professional involves, among other things, learning those ways. As we get further into the concrete analysis of these, the problem of terminology may come to seem less bothersome: we may feel that we know what we are talking about with reference to the specific examples. Of the two general terms, 'procedural' seems a little freer of unwanted connotations than 'technical', so it will be preferred here. However, in saying that professions are procedural, I am not suggesting that they rely merely on explicit, cut-and-dried steps and sequences of operations. I want merely to indicate that they go beyond common sense and common experience because they involve the acquisition of certain kinds of know-how: the capacity to turn intention into effect in a particular context. (The jazz pianist Oscar Peterson once defined technique as 'the art of getting out of your own way'.) The nature of that know-how will vary from profession to profession. In some, the emphasis on technical hardware or identifiable techniques is much greater than in others, and the importance of social skills also varies. Much of what I am talking about in terms of the *procedural* is difficult to explicate and often routinized. But no picture of the professions would be complete without some reference to their means of doing what they do.

One might argue that the professions have other basic characteristics as well. For example, a good case can be made for seeing them as moral activities, an issue already touched on in the discussion of instrumentality. Or one might want to stress the fact that they are cultural constructs, which cannot really be abstracted from the network of meanings of which they form a part. They are clearly social institutions, which exercise power and influence in certain ways. The very notion of a profession is a modern Western one; and in terms of teaching we might want to question assigning that role to an individual, rather than to a group or community, and to a designated, licensed individual at that. Are we not all, as Highet suggested, at some times and in some ways, teachers? I have already referred to non-formal education and informal learning, and in the discussion of the model in the following chapters, I shall explore to what extent it can be seen as a framework not only for the teacher but for the learner: not only for teaching but for self-teaching or peer-teaching. The model should reach beyond the profession to encompass the activity of teaching wherever and however it occurs.

However, the focus in this chapter will be on the three main characteristics of professional work identified so far — instrumentality, contingency and procedurality — because they suggest three basic and powerful questions that we can ask about all professions. These questions will eventually form the three dimensions of the model, and be related to one another to provide an integrated analysis of teaching. The three questions are: *What do teachers do?* (instrumentality), *What affects what they do?* (contingency), *How do they do it?* (procedurality).

Three Basic Questions

The first question is about roles or functions rather than overt activities or behaviours. What are teachers there for? If they were not there, how would we miss them? Would we in fact miss them? And given that people have some natural capacity to learn, which they manifest in their everyday lives outside the classroom, what do teachers do for students or pupils that the latter cannot do for themselves?

The question may be clarified by referring again to medicine. What do doctors do? In one sense, we all know what doctors do: they look down our throats, tap our chests, take our blood pressure, ask us questions, and so on. But these are really answers to the third question (*How do they do it?*). To describe what doctors do in terms of roles or functions, we have to turn to a quite different kind of language. As mentioned in the previous chapter, we might say that doctors *diagnose* and *treat* medical problems. However, before they can diagnose, they need to *assess* the condition of the patient, and indeed sometimes they will assess without being able to arrive at a diagnosis, if the symptoms are nonspecific. Moreover, general practitioners sometimes do not treat us themselves, but *refer* us to someone else for treatment; and sometimes that other practitioner cannot treat us at all but can only *palliate*, by relieving the symptoms. Both treatment and palliation will usually need to be *monitored,* kept under review for some period of time, and this may involve some kind of follow-up. A *counselling* role may also be associated with the problem or its treatment, and it is arguable that if doctors want patients to manage their own health better, an element of *education* has to be involved, particularly with long-term or chronic conditions, or in a public health context. And I have omitted what might logically be thought of as the first role of the doctor, to *prevent* illness.

This kind of list — prevent, assess, diagnose, treat, palliate, refer, monitor, counsel, educate — gives us some tentative answers to the first question: what do doctors do? It also raises issues about the relative emphasis on these various functions in doctors' training and work. How important is prevention? How do doctors learn when to treat something themselves, and when to refer it to a specialist? Does the distinction between treatment and palliation underpin that between hospitals and hospices, between trying to cure a condition and enabling people to die with dignity? How confident or competent do doctors feel in their counselling role? Do they recognize that role at all? Do they in fact see themselves as health educators?

One can pose the same basic question about any other profession. What do lawyers do? What are their roles/functions? What do engineers do? Managers? Architects? Pharmacists? Nurses? Surveyors? Accountants? Social workers? The question is a deceptively simple one. In fact, the possible answers go to the heart of the nature and identity of each profession, and the arguments about the relative importance of the various roles or functions reflect fundamental disagreements about the nature and scope of that profession. It is likely, therefore, that there will never be any final or settled set of answers to the question, and we should regard all such lists as provisional. But the importance of this first of the three questions cannot be overstated. Unless we can say what it is that a profession *does* in this sense, we have literally no point of departure for analysing its practice, training its practitioners or evaluating its performance. (For a similar approach to the analysis of technical occupations, see the work on task inventories described by Patrick, 1992, pp. 189–94).

Why then do we not have ready-made and widely known lists of functions for each profession, such as the above? How on earth do professions manage to exist without such lists, if they are so important? In fact, the language for talking about roles and functions does exist already in every profession. The above tally of doctors' roles would be quite familiar to medical practitioners, although they probably wouldn't have come across them before as a systematic inventory, and might well disagree about the list. But the terms and the ideas are already part of the professional culture; all one has to do is to assemble them. This will be the case with most of what is said about teaching in this book. The concepts and ideas will usually be familiar and recognizable; it is the way of bringing them together that is likely to be new.

So what do teachers do? The answers to this question will be spelled out in detail in Chapters 3 and 4, both at the level of the course and the class. Here, I shall take just one example to illustrate what I am talking about. Teachers *explain* things (G. Brown, 1978; Cruickshank and Metcalf, 1995). But what is explaining? Clearly, it is not a teaching method in the usual sense of the phrase. One does not timetable 'explaining' from 11.15 to 12.05 in the way that one might a lecture, class or tutorial. Teachers can explain in the context of various methods. It looks as if explaining, like the doctor's diagnosis, is a generic role or function that can manifest itself in a number of different settings.

And as with diagnosis, one can see that explaining may happen in various ways. The doctor may arrive at a diagnosis through a process of systematic elim-ination, or through the checking out of an initial hunch (Elstein, Shulman and Sprafka, 1978). Likewise, there are various ways of going about explaining: breaking the task down step by step, stage by stage; back-tracking; citing relevant examples; locating the idea in a wider framework of concepts; looking for parallels, analogies or metaphors; questioning the questioner in order to help him or her explicate the mental schema that produced the question. The function procedures of explaining will in turn depend on a range of factors: the nature of the content that is being explained; the level one is working at; the characteristics of the questioner; the amount of time available; the possibility of referring to other materials; and so on. But although explaining may involve various procedures and depend on various contextual factors, it is not reducible to these. It is something that the teacher attempts to do for the learner: a role or function. It is something that the learner can turn to the teacher for.

However, it is important to state right away that it is not always the teacher who does the explaining. The learner may turn to someone else, a friend in the class, a parent or colleague, with the problem: What does this mean? How does this tie in with that? How do I go about this? One can thus talk about peer-explaining, and in some contexts, such collaborative learning is to be encouraged as valuable in itself. And although the phrase may seem odd, one can even speak of 'self-explaining'. For what else is it when a person works something out, puzzles some-thing out, figures something out, sorts something out for himself or herself? What else is 'understanding' but the capacity to explain something to oneself? When we say we do not understand something, we mean that we cannot give a satisfactory account of it to ourselves. When we can, we say we understand; although this private process of self-explaining usually needs to be checked out publicly (Have I got the hang of this properly? Have I got the right end of the stick?)

The essential, general point that comes out of this particular example is that the functions are functions of *teaching*, but not necessarily of the *teacher*. Indeed, one of the longer-term aims of education is usually to help learners to internalize, take over and own some of the functions of the teacher, so that they literally become self-teachers. That idea lies at the heart of the concept of the autonomous, lifelong learner. Gradually, we learn to do for ourselves what hitherto others have done for us.

The second basic question about professionals is: *What affects what they do?* Professionals do not do what they do in a vacuum. They operate in a context, a situation, a particular set of circumstances, a time-frame, a physical and social location. Professional work is embedded work, not abstracted or detached from the world, but very much in and of it. It has to take account of, and respond to things around it. It sometimes seems more like a juggling act, or a continuing negotiation with things around us, than anything else. Professional decisions are more often trade-offs than solutions.

To return to the medical example: the doctor will perform his or her functions in the light of three main kinds of variable: the nature of the medical *problem*; the condition and situation of the *patient*; and the context of medical *provision.* A great deal of medical education is devoted to equipping the doctor to understand the first, and even then it is widely recognized that individual doctors may be better at diagnosing and treating some kinds of problem (e.g. ear, nose and throat) than others (e.g. skin) which may be less familiar. But whatever the problem, it needs to be seen in the light of the general condition and situation of the patient. The latter may involve everything from basic characteristics such as age and body-weight (which affect drug dosages) through to more complex factors such as occupation, housing conditions and family situation, or other concurrent medical factors (e.g. a heart condition) or contra-indications that have a bearing on the particular problem the doctor is trying to deal with. Hence, the relationship between a particular doctor and patient is not just a kind of emotional or social bond, but a matter of building up background knowledge about the latter (and sometimes the former too). Changes and patterns over time can be picked up more readily in this way, and hence continuity in the relationship may be important, which is perhaps why patients often say they like a doctor who knows them well. Of course, that very familiarity can screen out perceptions and possibilities that the temporary locum may see. And one can see parallels in teaching.

What the doctor does may also be affected by a third set of contingencies, concerned not with the patient, but with medical *provision.* How much time is there? What kinds of investigation and treatment are available, when and at what cost? How can the situation be best managed? What role should other professionals (nurses, social workers, psychiatric services) play? The skill and expertise that the doctor and his or her colleagues bring to the situation may also influence the performance of the various functions. Certain possibilities — diagnoses, treatment options, counselling support — may be excluded simply because the expertise or equipment are not there. Cultural norms and social factors may rule out others. So what doctors do (functions) is likely to be affected by a wide range of possible factors (contingencies) related not only to the medical problem, but to the patient as a whole, and to the wider context of medical provision and even the society.

What teachers do is also potentially affected by a wide range of factors. In the model set out in Chapters 3 and 4, these will be grouped under four main headings: the why, what, who and where of teaching. These can in turn be further subdivided. For example, under the 'who' one might want to consider the students as a group, as individuals in that group, and also any external 'clients' who may have an indirect interest in what is going on: parents, employers, examining boards, government agencies, and so on. The 'who' also needs to include those who are teaching — the staff, oneself as teacher — since these are also factors that affect the situation. One may have a good plan for a course, but if the staff are not ready or available to carry it through, it is not likely to get far. One may even have good ideas about one's own teaching, but if for whatever reason one is unable to put them into practice — lack of time, confidence, skill, motivation — one will have to take oneself into account as one factor in the situation. Teachers are both outside and inside the frame.

The third question — *How do they do it?* — refers to the means of teaching. As noted earlier, those means or procedures can range from physical tools and equipment, through identifiable methods and procedures, to the more subtle approaches and ways of doing things that every profession develops. Again, the example of medicine is instructive. The doctor uses, or has at her disposal, a wide array of procedures for doing what she does. As noted in the previous chapter, these range from the verbal and physical through the biochemical, pharmacological, surgical and radiological to the newest techniques of computerized analysis or medical physics. The use of each of these kinds of procedures requires specific knowledge and skills, which the doctor or some other specialist has to acquire. Again, such a list helps one to understand some of the arguments that go on within medicine, about the use of drugs, the relative emphasis on natural or hi-tech procedures (for example in childbirth) or conventional versus homeopathic or alternative methods.

Like the doctor, the teacher has a repertoire of means at his or her disposal. These include all forms of educational hardware and software and the methods and techniques for using them. In Chapters 3 and 4, the procedures of teaching will be divided into the various stages involved in putting on a course, and the means used to deliver it. Putting on a course involves design, organization, enrolment, delivery, assessment, evaluation, and so on. Delivering the course may involve a combination of presentation, demonstration, discussion, practical work and the like: what are conventionally called methods. In further or higher education, one often has an entire session devoted to one method: a lecture, seminar, tutorial, laboratory experiment. In the schools, a single class is much more likely to involve a combination of such methods, with a mix of presentation, whole class work, small group work, and individual tasks.

As with medicine, the relationship between these methods and the functions of the teacher is not one-to-one. So much discussion of teaching is in terms of methods, and the putative advantages of one method over another, that it is important to assert that teaching is not just a matter of methods. One might just as well ask: is a spanner better than a screwdriver? Methods are methods of something. It is logically quite wrong to conceptualize an activity such as teaching purely in terms of its means, how it is done, because that leaves unasked the more basic question: What is being done? So in addition to asking what method, we need to ask: What is the method being used for? What is being done with it? Is it being used, for example, to perform the function that I referred to earlier, to *explain*?

If that is not the prime reason for using it, what is it being used for? What other functions may it perform? And why this method or procedure rather than another?

The answer to these questions will draw in certain contingencies. A method may be used because it is associated with that subject or level of work, because the students like it, because staff feel comfortable with it, because the rooms are adapted to it, because the institution teaches that way, because society expects it. Different methods become established and normalized in different settings. But it is important that we do not simply accept context, precedent or habit as an answer to the question, but go back to the functional issue as well: How does this method enable you to do what you do as a teacher? And what do you do anyway?

Even this brief analysis will have shown that the three questions — What do professionals do? What affects what they do? How do they do it? — are linked. The answers to one draw in the others. So the model for analysing professional work will be a three-dimensional one, rather than just a list of three questions. Teaching, like other professions, is a composite of instrumentality, contingency and procedurality, and these three aspects relate to one another. The three-dimensional model that will be set out in Chapters 3 and 4 should help us to hold these three aspects of the activity in relation to one another, sometimes in tension. Professional work involves keeping certain functions or roles permanently in mind, but those functions are always subject to the variability of circumstances, and involve a repertoire of possible procedures. This implies both continuity and flexibility. There has to be a steadiness of vision and purpose, but also sensitivity and skill and a willingness to adapt to the situation. It is this particular mix of attributes that gives professional work its peculiar feel. Teaching, like all professions, is a plurality, a composite, a mixed bag.

The point could be reinforced by referring to other professions. What do managers do? The classical management theory of Fayol and others (Harries-Jenkins, 1991, pp. 20–1) initially identified a number of basic management functions — command, control, coordinate — but these have since been refined and extended by the addition of other less explicit ones, such as the 'modelling' of desired behaviours (Tannenbaum and Yukl, 1992). However, the way such functions are carried out depends on the nature of the task/product, the structure and culture of the organization, and the characteristics of the environment in which they have to operate. This leads to a more contingent view of management, in which the optimum forms of control or communication, not to mention leadership, may vary from one situation to another (Fiedler, 1967). Likewise, the manager needs to possess a wide repertoire of means and techniques in order to carry out these variable functions. Some of these will relate to finance, some to information technology, some to actual plant and equipment, some to human resources. As with teaching, the effective manager begins to appear less like a paragon of identified competences, than someone who can keep certain fundamentals in view, continually read and re-read the situation, and deploy the right means and techniques at the right time — a much more complex animal. And the relative emphases on function, situation and procedure help to explain the different approaches to management education, with their varying emphases on general concepts and principles, case studies and problem-solving, and concrete skills and techniques.

Professions that result in concrete artefacts rather than changes of state or condition can also be analysed in the same three-dimensional way. For example, what do engineers do? The key functions are arguably to *design* and *construct*. However, as with the medics, other functions soon come to mind. Design has to be preceded by an *analysis* of the engineering problem. The engineering solution to that problem has to be concretized in an operational *plan* before the actual *construction* can begin. That construction will in turn need to be *managed*, in terms of physical, financial and human resources. Artefacts that have been constructed also have to be *maintained* and repaired. Their social and environmental impacts have to be *assessed*. The way the engineer goes about all these various functions depends on various contingencies: the nature of the project (which will include the general specification, the type of construction, the scale, time-frame), the context of the work (political, social and environmental factors) and the resources available (finance, organizational infrastructure, work-force, possibilities of subcontracting). To do all this, the engineer needs to deploy his or her repertoire of procedures: skills and techniques in mathematical analysis, computer-aided modelling and design, financial control, human resource management, and sometimes other organizational, negotiating and political (with a small 'p') skills as well.

The three basic questions I have identified thus seem to offer a viable general framework for analysing professional disciplines, although the working out of a model in each case is a complex task, which has only been sketchily attempted here. Professional disciplines are instrumental, and this raises questions about role and function; they are contingent, which requires some analysis of situational variables; and they are procedural, which implies a repertoire of means, skills and techniques. But the whole point is that professional work involves the integration of these three aspects. It is not enough to think of it simply in terms of general or underlying functions, otherwise the performance of such functions may be inappropriate to the situation, and ineffective in terms of concrete skills and techniques. Nor is it enough to focus purely on the situational variables. That can lead to a preoccupation with the specific and particular in which the general plot is lost. And an emphasis purely on procedure risks reducing the analysis to a matter of techniques and technologies, without any reference either to context or to underlying function.

Different professions may be prone to different over-emphases at different times. Too great an emphasis on fundamental medical knowledge can leave the practitioner ill-equipped to analyse specific cases and situations, and unskilled in certain practical techniques. A preoccupation with case study in management or social work can lead to an ignoring of fundamental concepts and knowledge, and inadequate training in concrete skills. Engineering education seems to oscillate between an emphasis on basic engineering science, and an emphasis on design and applications; either can be dysfunctional if pushed too far. A legal education that consists mainly of the analysis of cases and precedents may underplay both the importance of general legal concepts and concrete legal skills. The perennial arguments that go on within professional education are testimony to the difficulty of getting the balance right (Kennedy, 1987).

Teaching has manifested all these possible imbalances at different points in time. The rather academic approach to teacher training in the 1960s and 1970s, which leaned heavily on the foundation disciplines of philosophy, history, psychology and sociology, tended to disregard the analysis of classroom situations, cases and problems, and teachers, it seems, often felt ill-prepared to cope with the actual business of teaching and the management of classes. The pendulum has now swung the other way, and the concern with the specifics of classroom management has tended to drive out general ideas and concepts, to the extent that theory is notable mainly for its absence. Historically, much teacher training has always been seen in terms of routine methods and skills, to the detriment of either functional or situational analysis. Paradoxically, contemporary competence-based approaches, which claim to be highly practical, show an operationalist disregard for what teaching is basically about (function) and how it should relate to context (contingency). These issues will be discussed again in the final chapter; here it is enough simply to stress the need for a balanced concern with the three dimensions of professional work that I have identified. Indeed, one of the advantages of this model is that it should help us to hold these different aspects of teaching permanently and steadily in view, and thus make it less prone to the pendulum swings or sudden lurches of policy or practice which, as argued at the beginning of this book, betray an underlying theoretical weakness in the discipline.

Chapter 3

Analysing the Course

The model that will be set out in this and the next chapter did not emerge fully fledged from the conceptual analysis of professional disciplines in the previous chapter. As described in the Preface, it developed gradually out of a combination of such reading and thinking, and work with practitioners in the teaching and training fields over the last ten years or so. That work has been documented in a number of occasional and previous publications (Squires, 1982, 1988, 1990) and culminated in the publication of a comprehensive training package for use in courses and work-shops (Squires, 1994). That package has been used quite widely by myself and others with a wide variety of groups, both in the UK and abroad, and has proved a very useful means of testing and refining the model in practice.

The way in which the model developed is hardly important here, but several points should be made because they may help to explain where it has come from and how it should be viewed. As pointed out in the Preface, my work has been in the fields of post-school education and training, and the model is likely to reflect, consciously or not, that provenance. The ways in which it may relate to the schools sector will therefore be specifically discussed at various points in this and the next chapter.

Secondly, the fact that I have had a foot in both the education and training camps has no doubt affected my approach. Like many educators, I think I brought a degree of prejudice to the training field when I first became involved in it, but I have learned a great deal from working with trainers and managers. The field of training has, I think, become much more interesting because work in a modern economy has itself become more complex and fluid, and contemporary training programmes are often a very long way from the drill-like stereotype that teachers (and educational philosophers) often had of them in the past.

Thirdly, my background in continuing education and my research on informal learning in particular (Gear, McIntosh and Squires, 1994) make me very aware of the fact that a great deal of self-directed and self-organized learning goes on outside the education and training systems altogether. This has perhaps made me view the main features of the educational system — institutions, curricula, teachers, exam-inations — with a certain provisionality, a certain detachment. Teaching has to be associated with learning, but learning does not always have to be associated with teaching. Behind much of what I say about teaching stands, as it were, the ghost of the autodidact.

Finally, it goes almost without saying that a model such as this should be treated as just that: a model. Whatever one may think about the various paradigms reviewed in Chapter 1, the net effect of such an analysis must surely be to underline just how difficult it is for us to get a purchase on this complex activity we call teaching. So the usual health warnings associated with models must be issued. They are representations, not 'reality'. They can blind as well as illuminate. In disaggregating a totality, they risk losing synergies. They need to be seen as dynamic, not static. And they should be sucked gradually, not swallowed whole.

The Macro Model

The macro model is set out in Fig. 3.1, with a brief glossary explaining the various headings. The glossary is not intended to be exhaustive, but merely to begin to flesh out the terms, and where possible suggest synonyms that readers may find relate better to their own work. The language of teaching varies somewhat from level to level and sector to sector, not to mention country. It is up to readers to consider the terms in the light of their own experience, and if appropriate come up with alternatives that suit them better.

As indicated earlier, there are three dimensions that correspond to the three basic characteristics of professional work: functions (instrumentality); variables (contingency); and procedures (procedurality). The Macro Model poses these three questions at the level of the entire course or programme; the Micro Model set out in the next chapter relates to the single class or teaching session, and nests within the Macro Model. By 'course' here is meant a substantial, organized educational event, in any sector or setting, which may last anything from a day to several years, which may take place on-site or at a distance, and which may use any of a wide range of resources and methods. The three basic questions are thus:

What do courses do?
What affects what they do?
How do they do it?

We can spell out these questions more fully as follows:

1. What do people get by going on a taught course that they would not get if they learned independently, under their own steam, by themselves? (functions)
2. What kinds of things affect the planning and delivery of taught courses? What factors do teachers and students have to take account of? (variables)
3. How is a course provided? What are the various tasks or stages involved in actually putting on and running a course? (procedures)

I shall explore each of these questions in turn. In doing so, it is important to remember that each of them can be addressed from the perspective of the teacher or the learner. The model is not just a model for teachers; it is a model for students insofar as they may want or need to take on some of the job of teaching for themselves — what is often referred to as 'learning to learn'. And in the case of informal self-directed learning, it will be the learner who has to take on the whole responsibility for planning and delivering the 'course', of self-teaching himself or herself: a kind of internalized curriculum. The functions are ones that have to be fulfilled, performed or carried out for learning to take place. Who fulfils them — teacher, learner or others, or some combination of these — is a secondary, though no less important question.

Figure 3.1 The Macro Model

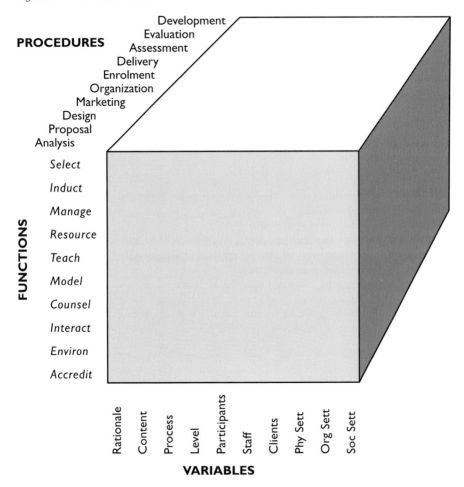

MACRO MODEL: GLOSSARY

Macro Functions
SELECT: ensure appropriate match of participant and course
INDUCT: introduce, provide initial overview of course

MANAGE: organize all the elements and activities of the course
RESOURCE: equip, supply materials, equipment and facilities
TEACH: perform functions or roles expected of teacher (see Micro Model)
MODEL: act as role model, represent, embody, enact
COUNSEL: support, guide or advise in relation to learning problems and choices
INTERACT: communicate and relate within the learning group
ENVIRON: create physical/social environment conducive to learning
ACCREDIT: validate learning through publicly recognized credits or qualifications

Macro Variables

RATIONALE: broad aims, goals, ends, purposes
CONTENT: subject-matter, discipline, field, topic, theme
PROCESS: generic or transferable strategies, skills or approaches
LEVEL: official level or standard of course in relation to public qualifications
PARTICIPANTS: course members, learning group, class
STAFF: teachers, lecturers, tutors, facilitators
CLIENTS: external stakeholders or interest groups
PHYSICAL SETTING: venue, campus, site, location of course
ORGANIZATIONAL SETTING: host organization, institution or agency
SOCIAL SETTING: society, economy, culture, subculture

Macro Procedures

ANALYSIS: initial framing of course, needs analysis, target group analysis
PROPOSAL: outline proposal, plan or specification
DESIGN: detailed plan or design of course
MARKETING: negotiation/research re potential learners, publicity, recruitment
ORGANIZATION: administration, scheduling, practical arrangements
ENROLMENT: intake, admission, registration
DELIVERY: implementation, running, putting on of course
ASSESSMENT: testing, assessment or examining of participants' learning
EVALUATION: formative or summative analysis of effectiveness/success of course
DEVELOPMENT: further or future development of course and teaching

Macro Functions

Where to begin? I shall start with the functions, because these address what is arguably the most basic question of all: What does a course do? (It is worth noting that all the functions are *verbs*: things that have to be done.) Without some answers to this question, we have no way of distinguishing teaching from any other occupation or profession we might choose to look at. Of course, some functions may cut across professions: for example, one might argue that doctors, teachers and engineers all have to manage their respective activities, and it is perhaps no accident that the language of management has come to permeate all three fields. But the particular list of functions that we build up for each profession goes a long way towards defining its peculiar nature and purpose, to identifying what it is about.

One could start with one of the other two dimensions. That might reflect a personal preference for beginning either with identifiable procedures or with the situational contingencies with which one has to deal. That inclination to explore procedures or variables first might reflect a deeper orientation to the nature of the work, a way of viewing and addressing it. The prior analysis of functions may suit those of a more logical, rational frame of mind, who like to abstract these basic concepts from their context, whereas the discussion of variables might reflect a preference for seeing things situationally, embedded in their field. Such preferences might in turn stem from deeper, philosophic or methodological stances (rational enquiry as against naturalistic analysis) or perhaps even relate to underlying cognitive styles (for example field independence/field dependence [Witkin and Goodenough, 1977]) although such ideas are rather speculative. But they do underline the fact that people can address the model in different ways, and such differences may be more than accidental. Moreover, such preferences might also manifest themselves in the language used: terms such as function, variable and procedure sound rather drily rational (although I hope to show that they are not) and some people might prefer words like role, context and means. All that can be said here is that wherever and however one starts, it is important to end up in the same place: with an integrated, three-dimensional view.

The same point applies on a smaller scale to the lists of headings in each dimension. They are in the form of lists because they have to be laid out along each dimension in a serial manner; but that does not necessarily imply a logical or operational sequence, or an order of importance. I begin with *selection* because it is something that typically happens before the course actually starts; but the problems of selection, that is of the match between learner and course, course and learner, may continue well into the course, when people may have second thoughts about, or feel confirmed in, that initial decision.

However, there is nothing to stop someone beginning at the end, with *accreditation* — the validation of learning through some publicly recognized certificate — because one might argue that this is often the driving and shaping force of the whole enterprise, for the student or teacher. Accreditation can have wash-back effects on the other functions in the list, including selection; who chooses or gets chosen may be deeply influenced by the prospects for ultimate success, both in terms of individual expectations and institutional performance indicators. Someone else might want to begin with the *environ* function, on the grounds that the most basic thing a course can or should do is to create a world in which learning is prioritized above everything else.

Such differences of emphasis and starting-point have been a normal feature of class work on the model; people go at it, and about it, in different ways. One therefore needs to treat the headings as provisional not simply in terms of what they are, but where they sit on each dimension; and the model might itself vary perceptually from its standardized, cubical form, with subjective bends, bulges, elongations and distortions, and some parts magnified above others. In other words, the standard format is open to topographical variation, and playing with the model visually can be a useful exercise, which brings to light differences of perception and interpretation.

Select, Induct

To return to *selection*: one of the problems that faces the autodidact, the person who decides to learn independently, is to know what is right for him or her. Suppose that someone decides to learn some basic economics, perhaps to help with running a small business. Where should he or she start? Go down to the local library or bookshop? But what are the right books? Are they pitched at the right level? Do they deal with the right topics? And in any case, is economics what is really needed? Does the person really have to delve into macro-economic theory? Wouldn't micro-economics be much more relevant? Might not the person in fact be better off finding some material on business studies, which would include some economics along with other aspects of business, and place it in that context?

Or take the case of someone who wants to learn computing. She could buy some of the computer magazines in the local newsagent, and leaf through them. They might give her some basic advice, but a lot of what they contain makes sense only if one knows something about the field already. She might contact a mail order firm or go into a local store. But what kind of computer does she need? What is she going to use it for? What is word-processing exactly? What is a spreadsheet or a modem? What is the real difference between a Mac and a PC? Does it matter? Even if she does buy a machine and some software, she may find that she cannot understand the manual, which is full of incomprehensible jargon ('booting up' and so on).

So she decides to enrol on a course. But is it the right course? This is where the concept of selection comes in. Selection implies a kind of matching: the course should be right for the student, the student right for the course. One of the basic functions of education (and training) is to ensure that the relationship between need and provision is an appropriate one, in terms of the aims, content, level and style of what is offered. These kinds of issues begin at school: children, teachers and parents need to make choices at various stages about what the pupil will study, and what he or she will give up. Those questions become particularly sharp during late adolescence and early adulthood: what GCSEs, what A levels, GNVQs, or NVQs, what degree or diploma. But they are questions that continue right along the lifespan, even if their consequences for life-chances become less dramatic as time goes on.

The importance of this function of selection can be clearly seen if people get it wrong. They can waste months or even years of their lives. And if selection is not right, then a lot of the other macro functions will be affected. However well taught a course is, and however good the learning environment or learning resources, if the person does not want to be there, the whole experience will be a profoundly negative one, for teacher and student. However, the pattern of and responsibility for selection may vary. Modular systems incorporate a series of choice points, which increases the frequency of decisions, but also makes those decisions less irrevocable. In other cases, self-selection by the students may be more important than selection by the provider; it is worth noting that open access courses are not actually non-selective, but merely shift the selection decision to the learner. In many training situations, selection is actually carried out by a line manager, rather than the trainer or trainee, and people can end up going on courses for all the wrong reasons, as well as the right ones. In my experience, trainers often pick out selection as a particularly problematic function, over which they have little control.

One can see also how the process of selection may be affected by a number of variables. Rationally, people's decisions about selection should reflect their *rationale* for following the course. The *content* and *level* of the course are other obvious variables. But some of the other headings may also affect decisions. The influence of *clients* (such as a parent or line manager) has already been mentioned. People may want to know what the student *group* will be like before they decide to join a course. Schoolchildren may want to be in groups with their close friends. Adults may want to know if the group will be older or younger than them, or mainly men or women. (Gender differentiation is very sharp in some cultures, where, for example, adult literacy classes are entirely segregated). Both children and adults may be influenced by the *staff*: who is teaching the course. The *physical* location may rule out courses for some people (too far, difficult to get to, unsafe) and the *organizational* setting may seem either remote or familiar in terms of cultural distance. Selection decisions are thus not made wholly on purely educational grounds in terms of aims or subject-matter; various other factors may impinge. The same can be true from the institutional end. Recourse by admissions tutors to terms such as personality, motivation, attitude, background, fluency or more colloquial equivalents can signal a wide variety of selection considerations, which go well beyond the strictly rational or sometimes even justifiable.

Let us imagine that the selection decision has been made: both institution and applicant have decided that the match is an appropriate one. This establishes, in effect, a basic contract of expectations, that each will do what they have to do to make the process work (although this 'invisible handshake' may actually be absent in some cases). The first step in fulfilling this contract involves *induction*, the next function on the list. Induction means finding a way into the course and the teaching–learning process. Induction may be carried out formally by the institution, less formally by staff, or informally by peers. It may deal not only with the organization and content of the course (what it covers, when, in what order, why) but the ground-rules of teaching and learning (how it will be conducted), the pattern of assessment (often an initial anxiety) and the general ethos and norms. Indeed, induction can relate to almost all the variables in the Macro Model: the rationale of the course; its content, process and level; the participants and staff; the physical and organizational settings. Once again, we see how a function has to be analysed in relation to not one, but a number of variables and procedures.

In some cases, it will be more accurate to speak of negotiation than induction. Where the participants have a good deal of say about a course, this early process will be one of working out together a set of mutually agreed plans and procedures, rather than introducing applicants to a given curriculum or environment. That might be the case, for example, in some non-vocational adult education courses; it is much less likely to occur where there is a qualification (accreditation) of some kind in view. Whatever the balance of power and responsibility, it is important to recognize that induction may have its implicit or tacit elements as well as overt formalities. It may relate to the 'hidden curriculum' (Meighan and Siraj-Blatchford, 1997; Snyder, 1971) as well as the formal one. There may in fact be contradictory or subversive messages (this is what *really* happens) as well as official ones. And although we associate induction with the period before, at the beginning of, and early on in a course, it may in fact continue for some time. The need to 'find a way in' does not suddenly end.

Again, the nature of this function becomes clearer if we think about the situation of the autodidact. One of the difficulties of teaching oneself is precisely that of finding a way into the subject-matter or topic, knowing how to approach it or go about it. Once that becomes clear, it may be relatively plain sailing; but subjects, like all cultures, have their tacit side, which is not overtly spelled out, and hence may be difficult to grasp. There is a fallacy of transparency about the curriculum, which assumes that everything about a subject can be made clear and obvious to the learner: that subjects are wholly explicit cognitive structures. Recent studies of disciplinary cultures have, however, shown just to what extent subjects have an unexpressed, implicit or even veiled aspect that is difficult even for practitioners sometimes to explicate (Becher, 1989). Induction addresses that problem.

Manage, Resource, Teach

The next three functions — *manage, resource, teach* — can be taken together. As pointed out earlier, the list of functions does not imply a particular, linear relationship between them and, as I shall argue, differences in the ways people relate one function to another may signal different views of and emphases in teaching, just as they do in medicine and other disciplines.

The first function can be illustrated with some negative examples. When learners complain that they cannot cope with a course, they may be referring to the content and sheer difficulty of learning it: the maths itself, the economics itself, the foreign language itself. Learning can be hard. But often they are referring to other things: the lack of clear aims, structures or boundaries; the feeling that the course does not really hang together; the fact that one cannot get hold of information, materials or people when one needs them; the peaks and troughs in workload; the fact that the course makes unreasonable or inappropriate demands; that the staff do not liaise with one another; that assessment deadlines bunch together; that one cannot cover the material in the time; that the day-to-day arrangements seem haphazard; that the actual class is not well managed.

In simple terms, we are saying that the course should be well designed, planned and run. All the elements and activities that go to make it up should come together, and this is what we mean when we state that one of the basic functions of a course is to *manage* learning. If the learner cannot cope, it can be because the course is unmanageable. But it may not always be that simple. If the structure and boundaries of the course are not clear, it could be because the subject really *is* fluid and open-ended. The fact that there is too much to cover may be a consequence of inescapable external professional requirements. The fact that the assessment deadlines bunch together may be caused by institutional regulations, not the teacher. And whose job is it, anyway, to manage the course? To what extent is it the learner's responsibility rather than the teacher's or lecturer's? Whereas staff in a secondary school may assume the main responsibility for planning and managing their pupils' learning, the approach in further education is typically more hands-off. University lecturers leave students to their own devices to a considerable extent, on the grounds that they shouldn't spoon-feed them, because to do so would inhibit the development of the autonomy that is one of the basic aims of higher education. And the whole burden of self-management falls on the independent learner who is working entirely outside the formal system.

A course is a complex operation, involving locations, schedules, resources, people and activities. It is at least as complex as many production or service processes in the outside world, and so like them it needs to be managed. But how it is managed, who takes responsibility for managing it, and when and in what ways, are questions that can be answered only in the light of the variables listed along the bottom of the model: the rationale, the content, the level, the organizational setting and so on.

The management of a course is in part the management of its *resources*, and this brings us to the fourth heading. When somebody enrols on a course, he or she expects to be provided with the wherewithal for learning: the materials, textbooks, software, equipment and facilities needed to study that subject or topic. Again, this function of a course can be illuminated by comparing it with the situation of the independent learner, the autodidact. Textbooks may be difficult to get hold of, or expensive; and even if they are available, it is hard to know if they are the best ones for the job. The recent explosion in the publication of learning packages and software has made such materials much more accessible than in the past, and thus independent, self-directed study has become an option in cases where it simply would not have been before. And such materials are increasingly being used as part of all kinds of taught courses, blurring the previously sharp distinction between face-to-face and distance education, on-site and off-campus provision. But the very growth in such a market makes the problems of choosing such materials more acute. And in subjects that require the extensive use of equipment, workshops or laboratories, independent study is virtually impossible. So another of the basic functions of a course is to provide the resources for learning. And just as one might complain that a course was badly designed or managed, so one might complain that it was under-resourced or poorly resourced. Such a problem is more likely to occur in courses that require expensive and up-do-date equipment, but it can relate sometimes to basic library and computer provision, not to mention textbooks. However, resource problems in this country are as nothing compared to those in many developing countries.

Our imaginary student will thus expect to be supplied with the wherewithal for learning, and to have that learning managed to some degree. However, the learner will usually have a more specific expectation as well: that he or she will be *taught*. One can imagine a course that simply provided the learner with a study guide and learning materials and then let him or her get on with it, with minimal teacher contact. Traditional correspondence courses were like this, and developments in technology combined with pressures on staff–student ratios could point in the same direction. In most cases, however, the learner — the student, trainee, pupil — expects to be taught.

The word 'teaching' is habitually used in both a broad sense, to encompass all the activities of a teacher in and outside the classroom, and in the more specific sense of what the teacher actually does during the class. It is being used in this second, narrower sense here, and the whole of the Micro Model in Chapter 4 is concerned with unpacking what that involves. Here I shall simply use 'teaching' in a common-sense way to mean that there will be someone there to aid the learner with his or her learning on a regular basis. This says nothing about the style and methods of teaching, which might range from the didactic to the non-directive, nor about the relationship between teacher and taught, nor whether the contact is face-to-face or at a distance. It simply indicates that, unlike the autodidact, the learner is not left on his or her own. But what does the taught pupil or student get that the autodidact does not?

Again, one has to draw in the variables. The expectations of teaching will depend on a number of things. First, the *rationale* of the course — its general goals, justification, purposes — may affect what the teacher does. If the aim of the course is to transmit an authoritative body of knowledge, that will imply a rather different expectation of teaching from that where the main goal is to develop students' capacity to think for themselves. What the teacher does and is expected to do may also vary from *level* to level; there is usually a shift in role and style between GCSE and A-level. The role of the teacher will certainly be affected by his or her organizational context, and probably also by the wider social setting. Whereas in the schools the teacher carries a complex mixture of expectations that involve the social, pastoral and personal as well as the purely pedagogic, in some technical or professional courses the teacher's role may be much more circumscribed. And cultural differences come in here too. Whereas in this country or the United States we might expect teachers to develop some 'rapport' with their students, the relationship is much more formal and remote in other cultures and settings. Even across the Channel in France, the function of teaching is more strictly pedagogic, with less responsibility for disciplinary, pastoral or extra-curricular matters. I contrast this with the comment a further education lecturer here made to me about her role *vis-à-vis* her students: 'I'm there for them'. A lot is contained in that simple phrase.

The function of teaching is thus a complex and varying one, and assumptions that we make about it in one culture and setting need to be very carefully tested in different ones. Again, however, the function can be clarified by comparing it with its absence. The independent learner has to do without. So what do students gain by having access to a teacher? What do teachers do for them that they could not do for themselves? If the teachers were taken away, how would they be missed? Would they be missed? It is a good question to put to teachers or intending teachers.

In this analysis of the functions of courses, I could plausibly stop here. I have said that courses should select their participants carefully, induct them effectively, manage the learning situation, provide the necessary learning resources, and deliver the whole through teaching. This might seem like a reasonable, if still debatable, set of answers to the question: What do courses do? However, to stop at this point would be to miss out some of the more elusive but equally important functions of courses. I shall look in turn at five more of these: the idea that courses should *model* or exemplify what is to be learned; that they should offer *counselling* on learning or related problems; that they should enable learners to learn through *interaction* with one another; that they should constitute a dedicated learning *environment*; and that they should *accredit* the learning that results from all this.

Model, Counsel

The reference above to the role of the person of the teacher in the teaching process leads naturally on to a discussion of *modelling*. The word is being used here not to mean the creation of analytic models (such as this model) but in the social psychological sense of learning through the observation and imitation of significant others. The main source of this idea is Bandura's work on social learning theory (Bandura, 1971, 1986), which initially emerged out of work with children but which has since been related to a wide variety of contexts.

The phrase 'role model' is now familiar, but it is important to realize that modelling can be of approaches, procedures and ways of thinking as well as of social roles. In fact virtually any kind of learning can take place through modelling if there is exposure to a respected exemplar (not necessarily in the flesh) and the opportunity to imitate, practise and internalize that behaviour. Social learning theory shares with behaviourism some common features, such as the emphasis on reinforcement, but is otherwise distinctive in its emphasis on the embodied and often embedded nature of human learning. Bandura's later work has gone on to explore related themes, such as that of 'self-efficacy', which relates to the learner's self-concept and sense of confidence and competence (Bandura, 1986).

The importance of modelling in a course stems from the fact that pupils and students may learn a good deal not just from what teachers say, but from what they do and indeed what they are. The distinction between teaching and modelling is not clear-cut: much depends on how broadly one defines the teaching function. But it is important to identify modelling as a distinct function and heading in order to draw attention to what is a pervasive but sometimes unconscious and even denied process in education. Teachers may not see themselves as models, and may even reject the very idea as pretentious or paternalistic, but it is difficult for learners not to be influenced by the living example set before them. Much of our experience, learning and memory is not verbal and semantic, but non-verbal and situational: people loom large in our life-world. And that remains true even in the mainly verbal or symbolic world of education.

The importance of modelling can also be seen negatively, where what teachers say is at variance with what they do. Argyris has pointed up the difference between espoused theories (what people say they think) and theories-in-use (what their actions reveal about their thinking) (Argyris, 1982, pp. 82–106). The teacher who espouses the idea of dialogue with students may in fact close down divergent or dissenting points of view very quickly. The lecturer who believes in feedback may give back essays late. The research-orientated professor may in fact spend a lot of time helping students with their problems. And so on. One can distinguish between the curriculum on paper and the curriculum in action, and the latter includes the behaviour of staff, which may provide positive, negative or contrasting models for the course participants.

Indeed, one might push the argument further and say that some forms of teaching are based not on conventional forms of instruction at all, but on a public modelling process. The university lecturer may break many of the rules of conventional teaching (forget names, lose his place, go off on tangents, mumble, and so on) but nevertheless give the students an insight into, and enthusiasm for, the discipline: the *doing* of physics, history or economics. The students, in this case, are voyeurs in a positive sense; they are let in on an otherwise hidden or private process, and the role of the teacher is to externalize what is usually internal, to explicate what is normally left implicit. One should not push this argument too far, but it probably explains some of the apparently incompetent but actually effective teaching that goes on in universities. However, this kind of modelling approach depends on the students playing a major role in their own teaching; we are back to the question of division of labour, and the implicit contract between teacher and taught.

Courses can also offer *counselling* as distinct from teaching. This may be carried out by professional, designated counsellors, but ordinary teachers and lecturers often fulfil this function also in a less formal way. Counselling here can be defined as guidance and support in relation to learning problems, or problems that affect the learning process. We are thus talking about educational, rather than personal or vocational counselling, although there is often an overlap between the three. As with modelling, much depends on how the teacher sees his or her role. Some staff feel that they are not competent to, or should not be expected to, counsel students. Others see it as a natural and necessary extension of their primary role of teacher. Terms like tutor, supervisor and coach often carry some expectations of informal counselling.

Two, by now familiar, points can be made. The first is that counselling is a function of teaching but not necessarily of the teacher. Others — friends, colleagues, workmates — may perform the role (peer-counselling or co-counselling) and there is an expectation that maturity or adulthood brings with it some capacity to sort out problems for oneself: self-counselling. That does not of course mean that adults do not run into major problems that require such guidance and support: they do, and the fact that they may be better at hiding such problems and presenting their normal public face can make the problems all the worse. The second point is that we can, as usual, relate the counselling function to a wide range of variables in the model both in terms of the need for and provision of it. Counselling problems may stem from the rationale or ultimate aims of the course ('I feel I'm going down the wrong road'), difficulties with course content and the level of work expected, relationships with other students or staff ('I don't get on with them') and the context of the institution ('I don't really feel I belong here'). The provision and process of counselling may also be affected by a range of things. The institution and wider culture may be tough-minded or tender-hearted. Staff may or may not see it as their business. The group may or may not take responsibility. (An African student remarked to me once that counselling problems in her country tended to be dealt with by the student group rather than individualistically 'in the Western way'). As with the other headings discussed here, what may seem at first sight to be an invariant, across-the-board function has to be related to not one, but a number of possible variables.

Interact, Environ

The mention of the group leads us on naturally to the next heading, *interaction*. One of the things learners can get from attending a course is interaction with the other participants. Indeed, they may sometimes value this more than their contact with staff. Here again, the contrast with the autodidact is stark. He or she usually works in isolation, and family or friends may soon tire of attempts to share his or her current enthusiasms. Indeed, the sharing or not-sharing of the learning experience can on the one hand create a bond with other learners, and on the other drive a wedge between the student and other people, including spouses, friends and colleagues.

As with the other functions, the responsibility for facilitating interaction in the learning group may be shared between the teacher and the members. However, the teacher can play a key role in creating opportunities for such interaction even if he or she does not always manage or lead it. Spaces and tasks can be devised that allow students to work together in pairs, trios or larger groups. Shared practical activities, such as projects and field trips, can be very effective in promoting and cementing this kind of interaction. It is useful also for teachers to know something about the dynamics of small groups, and to have some of the skills needed to manage them.

But why is interaction important to learning? What does the autodidact lose in terms of learning, as distinct from human company or social buzz? After all, interaction is not necessarily good in itself, and its benefits have to be weighed against those of other learning situations, in which, for example, an authoritative exposition can be delivered quickly and effectively to a large group, or where the learner can work individually at his or her own pace to his or her own agenda, without interruption or distraction from others. However much we may warm to the idea of student interaction, we should not take its value for granted.

There is first of all a simple mathematical aspect to this. With 2 people there is 1 possible interactive link, with 3 there are 3, with 4 there are 6, with 5 there are 9, with 12 there are 66. The number of possible interactions thus increases dramatically with the size of the group. But how important are those possibilities? Again, it depends. If one imagined a group in which everyone was doing exactly the same routine task — which might be a verbal one like learning some vocabulary, or a psycho-motor one such as learning to type — in exactly the same way, it would not matter much whether the learner was doing it alone, or in a group of 20 or 200. Interaction begins to become important where the learning task involves the acquisition of meanings and understanding rather than such routinized learning. That process is well captured in the title and content of Abercrombie's classic *The Anatomy of Judgement* (1960), which describes the use of small group discussion in the teaching of scientific concepts and ideas. It is not for nothing that the emphasis on small group interaction, in the form of seminars, workshops or problem-classes is strongest where the educational rationales concern the development of thinking, interpretation and understanding.

However, as usual, more than one variable comes into play. There may be individual differences in the preference for working with others or working alone; some people may like the stimulus, cut-and-thrust or support of a learning group; others may find such interaction intrusive, threatening or simply a waste of time. Wider norms and patterns may also affect the situation. The institution *qua* institution may or may not value such interaction in itself, as a reflection of a more general emphasis on, say, teamwork and communicative skills, or in the negative case of a more individualistic, competitive model of achievement. In cultures where the teacher is accorded magisterial authority, interaction among learners may be regarded as unimportant; what matters is the direct transmission from teacher to taught. And the physical layout of the learning setting can obviously affect interaction, both at the macro level of the campus and the micro level of the classroom.

All these factors can affect the importance and fulfilment of this function, and in some cases it may not be prioritized. But we cannot leave it out, because to do so would be to ignore the social nature of much learning: the fact that it occurs not just with individuals, but in and through groups. Meanings are held by communities and groups, not just individuals. And the rather individualistic mode of education that has developed in the West should not blind us to the fact that in some cultures — in parts of Southeast Asia for example — the group is central, and the maintenance of 'harmony' is regarded as a key responsibility of both the teacher and student. That this pattern coexists in some cultures with a highly didactic, authoritative model of teaching just goes to show that we need to think very carefully about the *social setting* before attempting to generalize about this or indeed other functions, such as counselling, which may also be culturally inflected.

The penultimate heading in this list of the functions — *environ* — exists as a verb in French (*environner*) but not usually in English, but I shall have to Anglicize it here because there is no adequate alternative. To environ, therefore, will be used to mean to create, provide and maintain a physical and social environment that is conducive to learning. The importance of this can be established by considering two environments that, in quite different ways, are not at all conducive to learning. The first is the stereotypical uncontrolled school class: a high noise level, the teacher unable to get or keep attention, a lot of other things going on, in fact anything but teaching and learning. The other situation is the beleaguered adult learner, trying to study despite lack of time and space, frequent distractions or interruptions, competing priorities, and a dearth of interest or support from family, colleagues or friends. The first example suggests why classroom management is such a key theme in schoolteacher education, the second why adult educators often place a good deal of emphasis on creating a sense of solidarity and identity within the class, a little micro-world that the students can be assured of at least for two hours in the week.

Environ is one of the broadest functions in the model, and could be criticized as a kind of catch-all heading, designed to sweep up everything that has not been covered by the others. However, it is important to include it for several reasons. First, as we shall see in the next chapter, the list of micro-functions is quite close to, although by no means identical with, some of the characteristics of 'direct instruction', which emerged from American research in the 1970s and 1980s (Rosenshine and Meister, 1995). These are important, but, I would argue, too narrow on their own, and it is essential therefore to set them in a wider instructional context, which includes notions such as modelling, counselling, interaction and environment.

Secondly, although it is difficult to adduce hard evidence on the topic, there is plenty of anecdotal support for the idea that the learning environment, in a generalized sense, matters to the learner. The broader environmental aspects of learning tend to be stressed in humanistic psychology (see Rogers, 1983). One concrete example of this is the emphasis placed in higher education on contact between staff and students outside the class (Pascarella and Terenzini, 1991, pp. 620–2). Such informal contact is an aspect of the learning environment that goes beyond overt, timetabled teaching. Much autobiographical writing on education also often refers, positively or negatively, to the general learning environment: the experience or feel of the school, college or university as a whole (see Haselgrove, 1994; Marris, 1964). Such experience is a composite of physical and human elements: the buildings, the layout, the social facilities and even mundane things such as car-parking, and the fabric of human relationships between staff (not only academic but technical and support) and students.

Even if we recognize the general importance of an environment that is dedicated and conducive to learning, what can we do about it? One practical consequence is that student feedback should go beyond direct teaching to pick up these wider experiences, and has therefore to ask the broader questions about the learning *setting*. The other message is that teaching and learning do not end at the classroom door; phenomenologically, they are part of a total experience, embedded in its context. Just as we often associate teaching with the teacher, we also associate learning with the place. And the place is a composite of the physical and the human.

Accredit

My discussion of the first function — *selection* — involved some reference to the last one — *accreditation* — but something more needs to be said about this. Accreditation means the recognition and validation of learning and achievement through the award of public and legitimate qualifications or credits of some kind: certificates, diplomas, degrees, credit units, grades or some other form of accepted currency. Accreditation does not refer to the process of assessment (which is a heading in the third, Procedures dimension) but to its end-point.

Some courses and programmes are not accredited, and do not lead to any such certification, in which case this function is simply absent. That might be the case with some non-vocational adult education courses that are followed mainly for personal interest and pleasure, and not in order to get a piece of paper. Other courses may simply offer a certificate of attendance. Accreditation may also be irrelevant in non-formal education, which is often concerned with community development rather than individual achievement, and obviously does not exist at all in informal learning, although retrospective recognition of this may be possible through APEL (Accreditation of Prior Experiential Learning). However, the great bulk of educational courses at every level from primary through to postgraduate end up with some form of accreditation.

It might be objected that this is not really a teaching function at all, since it is not an integral part of the teaching–learning process, but a form of educational and social labelling resulting from it. Certainly, accreditation plays an important role in the labour market and more generally in social stratification and mobility (OECD, 1977). But it has to be included in any list of course functions for two reasons. First, it is probably the only function of the ten over which the teacher/institution has a complete monopoly. With all the others, the learners can play at least some part, in self-selection, peer-induction, self-resourcing, peer-teaching, and so on. Students can do many things for themselves, but they cannot (or should not) award themselves certificates. This fact throws an interesting light on the nature of the ultimate control exercised by educational institutions. Paradoxically, their real power lies not in their central or official function, which is to teach, but in approving and legitimating learning. Thus the independent learner might reach a level of competence or achievement similar to that achieved by a student on a taught course. The difference between them would lie not in what they had learned, but in the recognition of it (Evans, 1992).

One can begin to see why assessment and accreditation are so central to education, and why they often dominate the design of curricula and the behaviour of teachers and students. This is the second reason for including it. Accreditation — the necessity for it, the demand for it, the process leading to it — may drive the rest of the activity, exerting a powerful tidal pull on other functions such as selection, teaching and interaction. For example, it is difficult to decide whether the current impetus towards modularization in further and higher education stems from the curricular logic of course units (building-blocks, student choice, flexibility) or the inexorable spread of a standardized currency of course credits (120 credits = 1 year) (Squires, 1996b).

As with the other functions, we need to look at accreditation in the light of the relevant variables. The social setting may be particularly important here: the premium placed on educational qualifications is so high in some cultures as to lead writers to speak of *The Diploma Disease* (Dore, 1976) and *Education Versus Qualifications* (Oxenham, 1984). But the nature and structure of qualifications may be affected by other variables too. The institution may be delimited in terms of the kinds of qualifications it prepares for or awards, for example GCSEs, NVQs, A-levels, degrees. The demand for qualifications from students will influence the teaching process. We have already noted the wash-back effect on selection. The public, external level of the course will be largely defined in terms of its accreditation.

And one has to look no further than the UK system to see the historical importance that accreditation can have in terms of the development of curricula and teaching. The British system has often evolved not by putting on new courses or building new institutions, but by creating new frameworks for accreditation: in the nineteenth century, the Royal Society of Arts (RSA), the City and Guilds of London Institute (CGLI) and the University of London external degree; in the twentieth century the system of national certificates (ONC/D, HNC/D) the CNAA and now the NCVQ. Such frameworks have shaped entire sectors and generations of educational activity. Accreditation rules.

Interpreting the Functions

The analysis of the macro functions is now complete. But before we go on to look at the next dimension of the Macro Model — the contingencies or variables — it is necessary to make a few general points about this list of functions. First, as noted earlier, they are all verbs: something that courses do or should do for learners that learners might find it difficult or impossible to do on their own. In this way they express the instrumentality of teaching. Unlike the Micro Model, where there is a body of research related to most of the functions, the macro functions that I have set out above seem to be largely 'commonsensical' although in some cases (such as modelling, counselling and interaction) there is a substantial literature on them. But the underlying logic all along has been the implicit comparison between the course participant and the independent autodidact. By not taking courses for granted, by continually posing the question of what people get from going on them that they would not get studying or learning on their own, I have come up with a list of putative general functions. Of course, as noted above, such functions can become dysfunctional if they go wrong, and in some cases the participant learner might be worse off than if he or she had never enrolled on the course at all.

The functions raise a number of questions that can usefully be put to practitioners. The first is: Do you agree with the list? Would you leave out any of the ten headings? Would you add any more? The current list has evolved mainly through work with practitioners, and has stabilized sufficiently to warrant making it public in this way. But that does not mean that it is set in stone, and the search for additional functions can generate interesting discussions about the nature of teaching and what it is that courses actually do.

A second and more complex question is: How do you see the relationship between the headings? I have already made the point several times that the list does not imply any particular order of priority or operational sequence, although it seems logical to begin with selection and induction and to end with accreditation. But one has to be careful about 'logic' in this context. One interesting exercise is to ask practitioners to draw diagrams of the relationship between the various headings, using whatever format they wish — flow-charts, mind maps or Venn diagrams. These can be used to display relationships of various kinds — linear sequences, one-way or two-way relationships, hierarchies, networks, subsumption or overlap. Such exercises tend to throw up a wide variety of representations. For example, some diagrams show a number of separate clusters (rather like the groupings in this text). Some have a core of two or three overlapping functions. Some subsume all the other functions under a 'key' one. Some impose linearity, others do not. (The same exercise throws up similar variations with the micro functions in Chapter 4.) What does this mean for the model?

Logically, if all the functions are on the same dimension, they should all be fundamentally of the same category or kind. I have argued that they are all aspects of the instrumentality of teaching: what teachers do. However, there is room for differences of interpretation and emphasis even at this basic level. All we can say is that teachers should at least consider each of the functions, otherwise they may omit some important aspect of their job. However, the amount of emphasis they place on a given function is ultimately a matter of judgment for them. The purpose of the model is to ensure that their judgment is a considered one; but it stops well short of prescribing what it should be. Hence, a teacher might conclude that selection and accreditation were nothing to do with him, or that the idea of modelling ran counter to his personal values. Thus the model begins to look more heuristic and less prescriptive than it may at first sight.

The third question that one can put to practitioners is: Whose job is it, anyway? Each of the ten functions can be set out on a spectrum of teacher–learner responsibility, and people asked to place themselves on it. The results (which again tend to vary considerably with both teachers and students) can be used to open up discussion about the relative roles of teacher and learner, and the implicit or explicit contract of expectations. It is important to reiterate here, therefore, that the functions are functions of teaching but not necessarily the teacher; they may be taken over and internalized by the learners, individually or collectively. Again, the model is agnostic on the desirability of this, and people's views will likely reflect the rationale of the course, the nature of the content, the characteristics of the participants and staff, and the wider organizational and social contexts. In other words, most or all of the variables. It depends.

It should now be clearer what the model attempts to do, and what it does not. It does not give answers to specific questions about what decisions to take in particular circumstances. But neither is it merely descriptive, because it selects a relatively small number of aspects of teaching, places these in a particular kind of relationship and says: Make your decisions in the light of these. At its heart, therefore, lies the notion of professional judgment.

Macro Variables

I have analysed what courses do. What affects what they do? The answers to this second question form the second, horizontal dimension of the model. They comprise four groups relating to the why (rationale), what (content, process, level), who (participants, staff, clients), and where (physical, organizational and social settings) of the course or programme. Although the 'when' of courses could be treated as a separate variable, it has proved easier to subsume this under the other headings, since there are various different aspects of time and timing.

The groupings have a certain common-sense logic, but do they have a stronger empirical basis? There is of course an extensive literature connected with aims and objectives, content and process, student variables, teacher characteristics, institutional settings and the social contexts of education, which it would be impossible to review here. However, where there are studies that are particularly relevant to the headings, they will be referred to. It is worth noting at this point that the model as a whole has some affinities with the categories identified by Shulman in his discussion of teachers' knowledge bases (Shulman, 1987). Four of these — knowledge of ends, knowledge of content, knowledge of learners and knowledge of contexts — correspond largely though not completely to the why, what, who and where. Shulman's curriculum knowledge corresponds somewhat to the third dimension (Procedures) discussed in the next section. The main difference between the two schemes lies in Shulman's 'pedagogical content knowledge', which as Grimmett and MacKinnon (1992) point out is of a different order to his other headings. Pedagogical content knowledge refers to knowledge or know-how about the teaching of certain kinds of content (as distinct from knowledge of the content itself). Thus the physics teacher has to know about the teaching of physics, not just about physics, and knowledge of the latter does not guarantee the former. Grimmett and MacKinnon suggest complementing this with 'pedagogical learner knowledge', on the argument that knowledge about learners is not the same as knowledge about the teaching of learners. My model differs in two ways. First, it attempts to identify general functions of teaching in a way that the other authors do not; and secondly the model implies that teaching involves the integration of all aspects of the three dimensions. Thus, in Shulman's terms, pedagogical content knowledge needs to be complemented not only by pedagogical learner knowledge but also by 'pedagogical context knowledge': how one goes about teaching in particular settings.

Rationale

The first heading is *rationale*. This refers to the broad aims or goals of the course; the same heading in the Micro Model will refer to the more specific objectives of a lesson or class; the difference is simply one of scale. It may seem strange at first sight to treat aims as a variable. In many models of teaching, particularly of the rational planning or systems type, aims are the point of departure for the whole process. First one decides what one is trying to do, then the rest (strategies, resources, timing, implementation) follows, referring back to the aims in the evaluation.

In fact, the third dimension of this model — the Procedures — can be regarded, with some caveats, as a course planning sequence, which begins with an initial needs analysis, moves on through design and organization, into implementation, evaluation and development. However, that sequence has to be carried out with reference to the underlying functions and situational variables; it does not stand *in vacuo* as it does in the conventional systems model. An aspect of the *proposal* and *design* stages is the formulation of general aims or goals; but the nature or substance of those aims (i.e. the *rationale*) will itself constitute a variable affecting the process. Some courses have a very clear rationale, others do not; some are preplanned, others are evolutionary; some have a single rationale, others have multiple or even conflicting ones; some have short-term aims, others have long-term ones. The nature of the rationale will thus affect the nature of the course, the performance of the functions and the procedures of course planning.

It is perhaps this variable more than any other that dramatizes the full contingency of the model. Rational planning assumes that one has a clear, unambiguous point of departure; it can tolerate ambiguity and complexity in the means, but not in the ends. But the contingent model removes even that bit of *terra firma*; aims themselves are variable in timespan, character, clarity, specificity and stability.

Another way of looking at this is in terms of the difference between a curriculum model and a teaching model. Curriculum models tend to begin with aims and objectives, move on to content, and treat teaching as a means of delivering that curriculum. By contrast, a model of teaching such as this treats the curriculum, including aims, as a variable affecting the basic process of teaching. The two approaches illuminate education in different ways, but it is worth remarking that models of teaching *per se* are actually fairly rare. As Anderson notes, it is important to distinguish between models of learning, models of teaching and learning, and models of teaching (L.W. Anderson, 1998). This model is the third.

The variable of rationale will surface again in the final chapter, where I shall comment on the apparent lack of emphasis on it in current teacher-training regulations. Its importance lies in the fact that it ties the process of teaching into the whole wider debate about the aims of the curriculum and the purposes of education, and therefore to aspects of educational philosophy. In so doing it also alerts one to the possibility that the way one intends to achieve those purposes (the process of teaching) may variously reinforce, amplify, distort or undermine them.

Content, Process and Level

The next three variables — *content, process* and *level* — can be taken as a group, since together they constitute the 'what' of teaching. In education, the word 'content' is actually quite ambiguous. It can refer to everything that the student experiences as part of a course, or it can refer more narrowly to the subject-matter. It is being used in the latter, narrower sense here, because it is important to identify process and level as aspects of a course that need attention in their own right, and do not simply get subsumed under something else. However, as we shall see, the three concepts are interrelated in various ways.

In the first place, the analysis of content involves some fundamental epistemological questions. How do we organize knowledge? What constitutes a discipline or field? How does one discipline relate to another? (Hirst, 1974; Phenix, 1964). However, teachers and students rarely confront these issues in quite so abstract a form; usually they are embedded in curricular realities or choices (Squires, 1990, pp. 37–73). For example, certain university subjects may be grouped together to form a Faculty of X, whereas in the institution down the road they are grouped differently in a School of Y. Funding bodies may distinguish between laboratory-based and library-based courses, but this rather blunt demarcation may not accommodate all subjects well. The broad arts/science divison is widely used, but engineers might feel unhappy about being subsumed under the latter. And there seem to be some subjects that don't quite fit anywhere. Law might be grouped with the social sciences or other professional fields, but is often treated as *sui generis*. Mathematics is usually housed in the science faculty, but in fact relates to a wide range of other subjects. Philosophy is typically regarded as one of the arts, but could equally be seen as belonging everywhere and nowhere. (One interesting exercise that throws up a lot of these issues is to present students with a list of, say, twelve subjects, and ask them to assign these to two groups, then three, then four.)

Content questions also arise at an even more practical level, in the design and delivery of courses. One member of staff argues that the subject-matter has to be taught in a particular order, while another disagrees. One examination board considers it essential to cover A, while another gives the option of doing A or B. Some people think that there is too much emphasis on coverage, and not enough depth. Disciplines seem to have their own cultures, and their members behave in some ways like members of a tribe (Becher, 1989).

The content variable thus raises many issues. Here, however, the key question in terms of the model is: How does content affect the functions? How might the content of the course affect selection, induction, resourcing, teaching, modelling and so on? Content might affect selection in terms of the criteria used in admitting students. Some kinds of content may call for particular skills or aptitudes, others may require a good grounding in the subject, others again evidence of general ability. Induction into the course may be partly induction into the culture as distinct from the structure of the subject: its assumptions, norms and styles. Different kinds of content will require different kinds of resources (books, equipment, software, facilities). The style of teaching may reflect the nature of the content: the process of teaching mathematics, involving a lot of board work, may be different from that of teaching literature, which may involve a lot of discussion. Modelling may be more important in professional subjects than in more general or academic ones. The possibilities of student interaction will depend on the extent to which the content involves the transaction of meanings.

Content — the subject-matter of the course — thus emerges as a potentially major variable in the analysis of teaching, and it is no surprise that it plays such a key role in the training of teachers and in many curriculum decisions. But what about the next variable, *process*? The content/process distinction was a key element in much curriculum writing in the 1960s, and the classic formulation of it remains Bruner's statement:

> We teach a subject not to produce little living libraries on that subject, but rather to get a student to think mathematically for himself, to consider matters as an historian does, to take part in the process of knowledge-getting. Knowing is a process, not a product. (Bruner, 1968, p. 72)

With hindsight, we can now see this as an expression of a particular curriculum movement, which stressed enquiry and discovery rather than mastery of facts and concepts, and which has over time provoked a swing of the pendulum back to an emphasis on 'basics' and subject knowledge. Nevertheless, the distinction remains an important one because we cannot, in fact, talk about content without talking about process also. Every time we set a question for an assignment, test or examination, we are involved in process, usually through the verb: list, state, identify, define, compare, apply, analyse, evaluate. These verbs indicate what it is that the learner has to do with the content, and the difference between two *levels* (as we shall see below) may be the difference between two verbs rather than two topics: describe X, analyse X, evaluate X. Words such as 'know', 'understand' and 'cover' are actually quite vague, and tell us little or nothing about the *kind* of thinking and learning that is required in a particular course.

This in itself is not controversial. What is, as so often, is the question of emphasis and priorities. Is it better to learn a lot of information in a form that can be listed, stated and identified; or to learn less but to be able to analyse, discuss and apply it? The age-old debate about breadth versus depth is an expression of this. It would be fine if there were time for both, but usually there is not, and there are choices to be made, on both the teachers' and students' side.

However, process may go beyond the scope of the particular subject that is being taught and learned, in the form of core or generic skills. Such skills typically relate to oral and written communication, numeracy, and computer literacy, although they may extend into less concrete areas such as social skills, teamwork, problem-solving, and self-management. Such skills are typically justified in terms of their relevance to learning, thinking or working, or some mixture of these, and the need for all students, irrespective of their subject of study, to acquire them. It is a view that has been influential in the post-16 sector for the last decade, but is also affecting higher education now as well.

This kind of argument raises a number of thorny problems. First of all, are these 'skills' really skills in the usual (though admittedly vague) sense of the word? Do not some of them seem more like capacities, qualities or characteristics? Secondly, what evidence is there that they really are 'transferable'? The research evidence is equivocal, with the view that learning transfers relatively widely through high-level general strategies or procedures contrasting with the counter-argument that much of it is in fact domain-specific, an issue that will surface again in the discussion of expertise in Chapter 5. And how does one teach transferable skills? If one embeds them in a content domain, are they really generic? And if one teaches them on their own, do they not become rather abstract? There is no room here to go into any of these issues; they are raised simply to make the point that 'process' is not a simple matter, and its relationship with 'content' is problematic.

How might process as a variable affect the functions of courses? The most obvious effects are probably on the management and teaching of the course. An emphasis on discovery, thinking and problem-solving will have implications for the scope and sequence of the curriculum; for example, one criticism of modular courses is that they impede this kind of developmental process, and encourage a short-term test and forget approach. The nature of the process can also affect the style of teaching in ways that will be explored in the next chapter. But process may have more subtle effects on the nature of the interaction among the course participants, and the kind of learning environment that is created. If all the emphasis is on the memorization of facts or acquisition of routine skills, the environment will tend to reflect this, and critical thinking or open-ended discussion may be suppressed or discouraged.

The analysis above implies that the next variable — *level* — is really a combination of content and process. Higher level courses will be ones that cover more content and involve more complex forms of process. The undergraduate course is not only broader and more extensive than the A-level one; it puts a greater premium on high-level behaviours such as analysis, application, interpretation and critical thinking. The substructure of factual information is assumed. However, it is important to identify level as a distinct heading for several reasons. One is that people use it as a way into discussions of content and process that they would not otherwise broach. Few people will have read Bruner, but everyone knows about key stages, NVQ levels, A-levels, Level 1 modules, and so on.

Another reason is that there may be more to level than meets the eye. For example, higher levels of education and training may assume a shift in the balance of responsibility between teacher and learner towards the latter. This can affect not only the function of teaching, but other functions such as induction, modelling, and counselling. And it is important to identify level as a separate variable because it ties the whole macro model into the public structures of accreditation. The way that a course is accredited indicates the level it is at; indeed such accreditation will largely be in terms of its level. Likewise, the initial selection of the student will often be in terms of a required level (five GCSEs, two A-levels, an upper second class honours degree). Level in education is at once a wholly familiar and yet highly complex concept. It can be quite difficult to explain what it is that makes one course higher or more advanced than another. The ease with which we use the term masks some difficult questions. But whatever its meaning or meanings, it is unthinkable that it should be left out of any list of factors that affect what teachers do. In the formal education system, level is one of the facts of life, and its salience in the schools seems to be increasing with the spread of national systems of testing and assessment.

Participants, Staff, Clients

The next set of variables concern the 'who' of teaching. One of the hoary old debates in education opposes subject-centred teaching to student-centred teaching, but the purpose of the analysis here is to move beyond that. Teaching involves various aspects — the why, what, who and where — and concern with any one of these needs to be complemented by an awareness of the others. In this way, hopefully, a more balanced and steadier approach can be achieved, which avoids fruitless dichotomies or longer-term swings of the pendulum. Thus the preceding analyses of rationale, content, process and level need to be followed by some discussion of *participants, staff* and *clients.*

The most obvious of these variables is the *participants.* Here, I am concerned with their general characteristics, rather than the detailed nature and dynamics of the group and its members, and as before the question will be how and in what ways they affect the performance of the course functions. Size is probably the first issue: How big is the group? This can have obvious consequences for the provision of resources (numbers of books, computers, laboratory or workshop benches, seats). It may also affect the way they are taught, in terms of the pattern of large group, small group or individualized instruction. Sometimes a change in numbers means that an existing pattern of teaching — seminars, for example — can no longer be sustained, and the whole approach has to be re-thought.

Sheer size, however, may be less important than homogeneity or heterogeneity. If the group is homogeneous in terms of background, ability, level, experience, and so on, it will usually be easier to teach than if it is diverse. Such diversity will certainly affect teaching, but it may also affect the management of the course, with the need to create several tracks or pathways within it. A diverse group will also interact in a different way from a homogeneous one, and various sub-groups, cliques or little subcultures may develop. That in turn will affect interaction. Of course, the nature of the group is itself partly a function of selection, but those who run courses are not always wholly in control of this, and may have to work with whoever is enrolled.

Other broad group characteristics may have an impact on functions. Age range, gender balance, ethnic origin and first language may affect the processes of teaching, modelling, counselling and interaction. It is impossible in the abstract to specify what group characteristics will be important; for example, a wide age range may matter in one kind of course but not another; language differences may matter more in some subjects than others. However, what is important is that teachers ask the question: How does the nature of this group affect the functions? This puts the group on the agenda, so to speak, and avoids the dangers of taking it for granted as simply another class, form or year.

It may seem odd to include *staff* as one of the variables that can affect the functions of courses. Surely it is the staff who would use this kind of model and therefore stand outside it or above it? That would be to ignore one of the salient, and sometimes unspoken realities of education. What happens or does not happen on courses is often due not to rational planning or curriculum design, but to the persons, personalities, enthusiasms, energies, expertise, prejudices, habits and sheer bloody-mindedness of the staff. In a rational world, we fit the staff to the course; in the real world, it is sometimes the other way round.

This is a consequence not just of the fact that education is a labour-intensive activity, but that its very process entails delegating a lot of control to those at the chalk-face. It is very difficult to centralize or standardize teaching, because so much of what happens is specific, localized, private and often hidden — and will always remain so. There are arguments about whether teaching has all the characteristics of a profession — including a unique knowledge-base and a regulating professional body — but it certainly possesses the characteristic of professional autonomy in great measure. The teacher in her classroom may be a bit less autonomous than the doctor in her surgery, but is probably more so than the engineer, social worker, or architect in their domains.

As noted earlier, there is a substantial body of research on teacher characteristics and their impact on learning, although the general findings of this are rather bland and not very illuminating. Teachers should be enthusiastic, approachable, organized and knowledgeable (see Fontana, 1995, pp. 384–7). However, to get some insight into the ways in which teachers can actually affect the planning and delivery of courses, one has to turn to more narrative, autobiographical or literary accounts (Clandinin and Connolly, 1996; Gudmundsdottir, 1997). Here, we see the living teacher, not simply as a human resource in a system, but as a person who can affect virtually every aspect of a course. Selection can depend on the individual judgment of the teacher, and the induction carried out by one teacher may be very different from that done by another. Teaching reflects the individual's approach, modelling and counselling even more so. And teachers constitute a large part of the environment of the course.

Apart from putting the question on the agenda — how do we as teachers affect the course? — what can be said about this? The problem is not a technical or organizational one: it is not difficult to create opportunities to discuss these matters. The obstacle is psychological, even existential. Teachers identify with what they do; they typically regard their teaching as an extension and expression of themselves, and hence any analysis of it becomes an analysis of them. They are thus often defensive about and resistent to analysis and criticism. There is an interesting contrast here with the performing arts. Actors, dancers and musicians also identify strongly with what they do, and regard it as in some way an expression of their being. But there is also in the arts a tradition of direct, concrete, frank and sometimes brutal criticism; the director at the end of the play, the conductor in rehearsal, may not mince their words.

What is the difference? Perhaps the sense of playing a role, distinct from oneself, is stronger in the arts than in teaching. Or perhaps it is the concern in the arts to get 'it' right, it being the performance, act or artefact. The artist is, according to the rhetoric, in the service of his or her art, and good intentions, sincerity and trying hard are ultimately irrelevant. Why do we not see teaching as 'it' in the same way? After all, the teacher is performing a function and the professional discipline is concerned ultimately with doing, making, producing or creating something. The model addresses this question directly. If we do not have a coherent way of thinking and talking about teaching, we cannot conceptualize it as 'it', as something that is ultimately outside or beyond us. So we tend to assimilate 'it' to 'us' or 'me'. However, the model (and other such models) should give us precisely that: a way of thinking and talking about teaching that sees it as an 'it' in which we play a large role, but which is nevertheless not the same as 'us'. Such a view is likely to run into the powerful identification of teacher and teaching, which is most obvious in, though by no means confined to, the schools, and is a feature of the art paradigm discussed in Chapter 1.

It will have been evident that I have not followed the current fashion of calling everyone who receives a service a client, referring to the recipients of education as pupils or students, because that describes the particular nature of the service they get, and sometimes as learners (as the complements of teachers) in the generic, psychological sense. Who then are the *clients* of courses? The term is being used here to describe any third parties outside the course who may have an effect on it. Since that effect is likely to be a generalized one on the course as a whole, rather than on the minute-to-minute detail of teaching and learning, the client variable appears in this Macro Model, but not in the Micro Model in Chapter 4.

Clients may affect courses in a range of ways. Their influence may result from expectations that are brought to bear on the course, through the behaviour of teachers or learners. The most obvious examples of this are parents in the school sector and employers in the post-school sector, whose expectations may influence what teachers and learners do. Such expectations might, for example, affect the teaching process or the learning environment: parents (and employers) might want to see a disciplined, practical approach to the work, which emphasizes its importance for future jobs or current occupations.

Other third parties have a broad, regulatory effect. The prime example here is examination boards, who lay down syllabuses and programmes, but one should also include professional bodies, who may specify certain requirements for the accreditation of courses, and agencies such as the NCVQ, which has had a powerful influence on vocational and technical courses. More general educational regulations emanating from government would also come under this heading. These may affect not only the aims and content of courses (the national curriculum) but their assessment. The broad influence of funding and funders is also important: he who pays the piper may not call the precise tune, but is likely to have some ideas about what constitutes good music.

Other clients or stakeholders are less easy to classify. Suppliers of educational materials — publishers and producers of software — clearly have a direct influence on the resourcing of courses. The local community may have an influence, through boards of governors and trustees, as can the mass media in highlighting educational issues. The churches retain a strong influence in some cases and in some countries, and political interest-groups or parties can have a general if more diffuse effect. The police have an interest in what goes on in schools, for example in terms of drug education and petty crime.

Again, it is difficult to identify who the main clients will be in the abstract, since much will depend on the nature of the institution and the course. The important thing, as before, is to place the question on the agenda: How do our clients affect our courses? Such a question can identify stakeholders and modes of influence that do not always come immediately to mind. And then the question needs to be tested against the various functions. What do they affect? Do they influence the process of recruitment and selection, who gets in and who doesn't? Do they affect the level and type of resources? (Does private support supplement public funding; if so, does that influence things?) Do they impinge on the management of courses? The actual teaching process? The learning environment? The business of accreditation? The last in particular may turn out to be important, since it is accreditation that in many ways provides the link between the educational system and the external client world. It is the pressure point; and many groups, organizations and individuals may have an interest in pressing it.

Physical, Organizational and Social Settings

I have now looked at the why, what and who of teaching, and the list of variables is completed by the 'where': the *physical, organizational* and *social settings*. Whereas formal teacher training typically deals with the first three types of variable, the where sometimes receives less attention, perhaps because it is assumed that the best way to come to grips with it is on and through the job. The physical, organizational and socio-cultural embeddedness of teaching may be experienced powerfully at first hand, in the concrete realities of rooms, schools and departments, and their wider locations. But it is important to flag these variables along with all the others, because they are just as important and potentially just as influential in the way we teach. Often they appear as constraints on what we would like to do: the lack of space or facilities; the niggle of regulations or the rituals of the institution; the indifference or pressures of the community. But the setting of our work can have very positive aspects too; part of the trick is to know how to exploit and use them.

These three final headings also appear in the Micro Model; here I shall be concerned with their broad impact on the course as a whole, rather than on the fine detail of teaching and learning. Thus in terms of the *physical setting*, I shall focus at this stage not on the actual teaching space — the room, furniture, fittings — but on the physical location and nature of the teaching site: the school, building or campus. How might this matter, and what functions might it affect? Here are some examples. If a site or campus is in an accessible place, rather than a remote or possibly dangerous one, more people may apply to join courses, and this will affect selection. The physical layout of the site will affect the interaction among students; for example, those who are located in a separate campus or annexe will usually find it more difficult to socialize with the others, and may develop an insular culture (a feature of some medical and art/design faculties in universities). The physical character of the site will be an element in the general learning environment. That is not to say that run-down buildings and purely functional settings may not have a good ambience; sometimes paradoxically they acquire a strong identity. But in general, a pleasant site will make the course a more pleasant experience; social and recreational facilities matter to most students.

The physical site may also send out more subtle non-physical signals. The annexe in a college may generally be regarded as not the college proper, and its denizens, staff and students, as second-class citizens. Rather grand buildings can suggest in physical form an intimidating treatment meted out to learners on their courses, and physical complexity can mirror students' psychological disorientation. Teaching takes place in a place, and just as we sometimes find it difficult to dissociate the experience from the teacher, we may associate it strongly with the setting. The smell, feel and sounds of the place are all part of the phenomenology; the experience comes as a package.

There is usually not much a teacher can do about the physical setting at the macro level, whereas he or she can often create a particular ambience in the room that is used, with posters on the wall, particular arrangements of the furniture, and so on. At the level of the site or campus, the physical setting is a given. But what about the *organizational setting*? On paper, at least, that is a variable that we ourselves can modify, since we are part of it. The reality, however, is that many teachers and lecturers experience the organizational setting as something that is almost as difficult to alter as the buildings themselves. It seems like a given, a reality that we have to work with, through, around or sometimes under.

The first step, however, is to analyse. Which functions of courses are affected by the organizational setting? It might be easier to ask which are not, because the organizational context penetrates virtually every aspect of what happens on a course: selection, induction, resourcing, teaching, and so on. The only possible exceptions are those aspects of courses that are determined mainly outside the organization (sometimes selection, frequently accreditation) and those that are so private or tacit that the organization cannot get any purchase on them. Some aspects of teaching and counselling are relatively tacit or hidden, as is perhaps the process of modelling; and the interaction among the learners may to some extent be independent of the organization where it takes place: students and pupils sometimes create their own subcultures.

If the organizational setting is as pervasive as has been suggested, then the lesson is that we have to think about it even harder than we do about the other variables if we are to understand and influence it. That means getting involved. This has implications for the way we think about courses. The curriculum development literature of the 1960s and 1970s presented the process sometimes as a rational planning one, sometimes as a negotiated, evolutionary one, but nearly always as a purely *educational* one, in which curricular and teaching–learning considerations dominated the agenda (see, for example, Stenhouse, 1975; Taba, 1962; Taylor and Richards, 1985). The last two decades have managerialized teachers and lecturers at all levels and in all sectors. Curriculum development now seems like a quasi-educational, quasi-managerial, quasi-political (small 'p') activity, which demands skills that go well beyond the traditional domain of curriculum and teaching. Planning, budgeting, quality assurance, negotiating, contracting, bidding: all these are now part of the process. Somehow the lines between management or administration on the one hand, and course planning and teaching on the other, have become blurred, and we have to operate in a hybrid world that demands a complex mixture of skills. It would take me well beyond the scope of this book to ask why this has happened; all that I can say here is that the organizational variable now looms very large indeed for most lecturers and teachers.

It is time to move on to the final variable. The sociology of education is sometimes described as being concerned with the 'three Ss': selection, stratification and socialization. All of these may have a bearing on courses: selection in terms of that particular function, socialization in terms of the teaching–modelling–interaction process, and stratification primarily in terms of accreditation and its consequences for social labelling, mobility and life-chances. But the impact of the *social setting* on a course can be addressed more directly and simply by asking the question: would the course be different if it were taught somewhere else? In a different part of the city? A different part of the country? A different country?

Again, it is difficult to suggest what those differences might be in the abstract, but some examples may help. To begin with, selection occurs at different stages and in different ways in different educational systems. French higher education is generally regarded as less selective than British at entry, but more so during the undergraduate stage, with much higher wastage rates. The resources available for learning can vary from one institution to another, and even more dramatically from one country to another. As regards structure, modular-credit courses are more common in some systems and sectors than others, which tend to be relatively linear (Squires, 1989). The teacher is accorded more authority in some systems and cultures than in others; that affects the teaching process, and probably modelling too. As noted earlier, the pattern of counselling may reflect cultural norms, with more or less emphasis on individual or group approaches. Attitudes to education can vary from one community or sub-culture to another.

Much of this is commonplace and may not seem of much immediacy to the working teacher or lecturer. And in the next chapter I shall look at ways in which the social setting may affect the teaching–learning process in its detail, for example in the pattern of relationships and communication in the class, the perception of roles, and the use of language. At the macro level of the course, we may have less pressing reasons to think about our social setting. However, the very fact that we often tend after a while to take this setting for granted means that we need to counteract this deliberately by raising the question: Would your course be different in a different place? And which of the functions would such changes affect? The initial selection of participants? The level of resourcing? The style of teaching? The interaction among the learners? The general learning environment? The structure of accreditation?

If the course functions do remain largely unaffected by changes in the social setting, it might be because the differences between those social settings are not in fact so great. But a more likely reason is that the 'where' is outweighed by the who, what or why. 'Contextualization' has become a kind of mantra in educational thinking, leading to what might be called the contextualist fallacy: that environments always determine the systems and processes that are located in them. But it is not always so: other variables — rationale, content, participants — may in fact be more significant than the social one, and override it. Although universities clearly vary from one country to another, there is also the notion that they should be essentially the same wherever they are. Likewise, it is claimed that some subjects, such as mathematics and science, exhibit a kind of universality. The influence of one variable on the functions of courses thus has to be set against the influence of all the others.

Sometimes several variables will pull the same way, but often they will pull the course in different directions, and teachers and learners have to work out their compromises or trade-offs between them. It is the plurality of variables that, along with the plurality of functions and procedures, makes teaching so complex to ana-lyse and so difficult sometimes to do. It is not enough to think of one thing, or even two or three; we have somehow to hold in mind and often in tension a whole array of considerations. It all makes the art of the juggler look quite simple.

Procedures

The third dimension of the Macro Model addresses the third of the three basic questions: How do they do it? How do teachers put together and put on a course? The suggested answers are that they *analyse* the need for the course, work out a *proposal* for it, *design, organize* and *market* it, *enrol* the participants, *deliver* the course, *assess* the learning and *evaluate* the teaching, and use the findings to *develop* the course the next time round. These could be regarded as the normal stages in putting on a course, but the word 'procedures' has been used instead in order to avoid implying that the events always come in this particular order, one after another. Clearly, one may be engaged in some activities (marketing) at the same time as others (organization) and evaluation should be seen as something that informs the ongoing process (formative) rather than being left just to the end (summative). Some readers may prefer to think of these headings in terms of Stages and to construct a flow-chart of the activities, or to wrap the headings round in a planning cycle that returns to where it began. But that chart or cycle is likely to vary from course to course. Like the functions, the procedures are also affected by the variables.

On its own, this dimension would look rather similar to the rational course planning cycles that one typically finds under the heading of the systems approach described in Chapter 1. The individual headings can also be subdivided: design, for example, into objectives, syllabus, activities, materials and assessment; organiza-tion into facilities, equipment, materials and staffing; evaluation into diagnostic, formative, summative and follow-up. One can thus construct a detailed operational framework and sequence for the planning and delivery of courses. In fact, this is exactly what a competence-based approach would involve. Each of the ten head-ings would be 'progressively desegregated' to the point where it yielded precise performance criteria for the various competences. One could thus build a com-petency model of teaching simply by taking this one dimension and dividing it into its detailed elements.

The difference between this model and the typical systems or competence approach lies in the existence of the other two dimensions. The *procedures* have to be seen as the means whereby the basic *functions* of the course are fulfilled, and done so in the light of the *variables*. However, before I discuss the relationship between this dimension and the other two, I need to say something about the list of procedures.

Analysis, Proposal, Design, Marketing

The headings can be roughly grouped into three: those that precede the course, those that happen during it, and those that come after. The first thing that has to occur is some initial *analysis* of the need for and potential of the course. That initial stage is a crucial one in the training field, where it typically involves a systematic training needs analysis (TNA). Without this, there is no way of relating training to the needs of the organization or its members, and there is a sizeable literature on this aspect of training alone (Buckley and Caple, 1992, pp. 73–110). For many teachers, by contrast, such analysis is a given: the need for the course is determined by a public agency such as a ministry of education, public examination board or professional body. Even if it is not, the needs analysis may be less rigorous than in the training field, and amount to little more than a belief that the course might be a goer or a good idea, or reflect the interest of staff in putting it on. The importance of the *proposal* stage will also vary. With many school sector courses, this is effectively out of the hands of the individual teacher and often the school as well. In other sectors, the proposal may range from a brief, back-of-the-envelope job through to a fully worked out and costed application that has to run the gauntlet of several committees. Getting proposals to and through the relevant decision-making procedures can be an art in itself, which demands organizational and political skills quite different from those involved in the actual design or delivery of the course. Indeed each of the procedures demands rather different skills, and this again underlines the composite nature of teaching: it is not one thing, but many.

Once the proposal is given the green light, the serious work on *design* and *marketing* can begin. The former has been covered extensively in the educational literature (see the dated but still useful bibliography by Richards, 1984). There is a wide variety of models of course design or curriculum development, but all of them involve putting together the various aspects of the course — objectives, syllabus, methods, materials — so that they form a coherent whole. Design is an important early stage in the whole planning process, but it can continue through the later stages, if the course is modified in the light of its implementation. It is not necessarily a pre-set, once-for-all business. Planning may need to be balanced against evolution, decisions with negotiations, scripts with spontaneity.

The idea of *marketing* may seem alien to many teachers and lecturers, but is becoming less so as education moves into a more competitive arena. As writers on the subject typically point out, marketing is not simply a matter of advertising or sending out publicity, as some educators tend to think; it actually involves building a relationship with actual or potential customers, which attempts to match what one has to offer with what they need or can be persuaded that they need. Again, this may require skills that are very different from those conventionally associated with the role of teacher or even course planner, and again it is a stage that may be more or less relevant to the individual teacher or lecturer, depending on his or her role and context.

Organization, Enrolment, Delivery

The analysis, proposal, design and marketing stages precede the actual operation of the course. The next three headings — *organization, enrolment, delivery* — are associated with its implementation. *Organization*, here, refers to the organizing of the practical, administrative, operational aspects of the course: working out time-tables, booking rooms, ordering stock, preparing materials, checking facilities, lining up staff and examiners, administering budgets, arranging this and that. It is important to give these often mundane tasks their own heading, because unless they are done properly, the best designed and marketed course will come to grief. The job of doing or overseeing these things may fall to one or more members of staff, and in some cases to an administrator or secretary, but whoever carries them out needs to do so well. These are the nitty-gritty of the course, which will affect the concrete experience of the learners in many small ways and some larger ones as well. And obviously the task of organization does not stop when the course starts; it underpins its operation right the way through, and sometimes beyond as well.

The *enrolment* of the course participants may also begin some time before the course actually starts, or it may happen at the first session; much depends on the situation. It is important to distinguish between the function of selection, and the procedure of enrolment. Selection is what teachers do; enrolment or admission is how they do it. Selection involves trying to arrive at an appropriate match between provision and learner; enrolment involves the actual setting of admission criteria, the design of enrolment forms, the processing of enrolment information, the carrying out of interviews, the provision of pre-course guidance, the dispatch of pre-course information and joining instructions, and the initial registration on the day. Like organization, it is in many ways a very practical and routine activity, but it matters a great deal to the incoming student because it is his or her first contact and transaction with the institution. And like organization, it may actually continue during the programme, if there is a series of curricular choice points, as there is in modular systems.

Again, the complexity of the enrolment process depends very much on the context or situation. It can range from the simple signing on and payment of a fee in a non-vocational adult education course, through to a rigorous multi-stage selection procedure in, say, a university degree course. In the school sector, it may be concentrated in the initial reception years, but even then the transition from one school year to another has elements of enrolment at the beginning of each, in terms of the flow of information and the preparation of and for the incoming pupil or student.

Everything that has been said so far has its ultimate rationale and purpose in the actual *delivery* of the course: the teaching and learning. Much of the detail of this is dealt with in Chapter 4 in the Micro Model: the methods used, the classroom variables, the underlying functions of it all. Here, just a couple of general points will be made. First, it is important in the delivery of courses to look at the communication among the staff who deliver it. Unless the course is a completely independent, free-standing one, it will be necessary to keep an eye on how it is going in relation to whatever else is happening at the same time. The reason for this is that although courses can be planned, they are not wholly predictable. They acquire a dynamic and ethos of their own, which can affect the initial plan in all sorts of ways. Content may be covered more or less quickly than was envisaged. Groups may gel or fall apart. Materials may or may not prove adequate. Teachers may fall ill. The content of what goes on in the classroom may curve away from the original agenda. Assessment may produce surprising or problematic results. And so on. A course is not just a paper exercise, but a living thing. It is not the script for a play, but the play itself, acted out and to some extent improvised by all those involved. It is therefore essential for all staff to keep a continuing, watching brief on what is happening.

That in turn involves getting continuing feedback from the learners. One of the most important aspects of delivery is the quality of contact between teacher and taught. The experiential nature of education — after all, classes are something that we live through — means that the nature of that experience may differ from person to person and in particular from staff to students. Giving and taking a course can be very different experiences, even though they occur in the same room at the same time. Even one's physical position in the classroom can alter one's view of events. What one experiences depends partly on what one knows about the situation, and the teacher often knows more than the learner, for example in terms of the 'script' that he or she has planned for the next ten minutes or two weeks. Phenomenologically, even the perception of time may differ, since that depends partly on one's perception of tasks, and the tasks of the teacher and learner are very different. All this makes it even more important than usual to stay in touch, to make a conscious effort to keep track of the situation for all concerned. This may sound rather abstruse, but in fact it comes down to quite simple things like creating some time and opportunity to talk about things that go beyond the immediate learning task; to provide openings for people to express their feelings, expectations, anxieties or enthusiasms; to open up the possibility of a commentary on what is happening. Sometimes this implies a degree of contact outside the classroom, but it can happen in it as well.

Assessment, Evaluation and Development

The next heading — *assessment* — refers to the formal, often official assessment of pupils or students that occurs in most school-based and many post-school courses, rather than the informal process of giving feedback on learning that occurs as an inevitable part of the process of all teaching (see the Micro Model). Formal, structured assessment may occur during a course or at the end of it, and may involve a variety of methods, ranging from in-class presentations, quizzes and tests, through essays, assignments and laboratory reports, to seen and unseen examinations and longer projects or portfolios. There is an enormous educational literature on testing and assessment, and this reflects its importance in the formal educational system. It also looms large in prescriptions for teacher training in the UK, reflecting the importance it has in current educational policy. I will obviously not attempt to summarize this vast field here, but simply make two points, in relation to the two other dimensions.

First, to which functions is assessment related? What is it a means of doing? The most obvious answers are initial or interim selection and interim or final accreditation. It is important to ask this rather simple question, because there is a danger that otherwise assessment comes to be taken as a fact of life, and not itself assessed. Why is it actually necessary to test, assign, examine and so on, and to record and make public the results? Selection and accreditation represent the linkages of education with the external social and economic world. But assessment can also be closely related to the internal teaching function, in ways that will be explored in more detail in the next chapter. It can be seen both as a means of teaching, and an obstacle to it. It can relate to the interaction between learners, in terms of encouraging individual competition or peer-learning. And it also constitutes part of the teaching–learning environment: a defining element of what the learner experiences. Again, we might view this in a positive or negative light, as something that gives rigour and seriousness to the enterprise, or as something that skews real learning and gets in the way of good teacher–learner relationships.

Secondly, the methods and pattern of assessment will depend on a number of variables, and it is important to think these through. Does the nature of the assessment reflect the broad rationale of the course, or does it in some way run counter to it? Does this particular content have to be tested in a certain kind of way? Are certain types of assessment associated with this level of work? If so, why? How do the participants feel about the methods of assessment? Are staff competent to handle those methods? Are there physical constraints on assessment, for example in terms of facilities and equipment? Are there institutional pressures that affect the choice of methods and the way assessment is carried out? Do social norms influence the methods we use? Perhaps because of their symbolic and actual importance, certain patterns of assessment can become reified and even deified to the point where any questioning of them is regarded as a kind of heresy. What the model reminds us of is that we must always look at how we teach in relation to what we are doing, and the contingent situation we are doing it in. Assessment, like all our other methods and procedures, needs to be thought through in relation to the headings on the other two dimensions.

The performance of the pupils or students is one measure of the success of a course, but *evaluation* usually attempts to give a more comprehensive and analytic account. Even if the students have done well (or badly), it is not always clear what we should attribute this to. It could be due mainly to their initial selection, to the resources they have been provided with, to the teaching they have had, or to the interaction and environment that they themselves have created: we cannot simply assume that good or poor performance results directly from good or bad teaching.

Evaluation attempts to understand such causes, relationships and effects, and also to go beyond performance to look at, for example, student satisfaction with the course (which might affect future attitudes to the subject and to education) and sometimes also subsequent effects. As with assessment, there is a large literature on models and methods of evaluation in education (and training), which I will not attempt to get into here (but see the useful list of questions framed by Nevo, 1986). The important point in terms of the model is that evaluation is an essential stage in putting on a course, because it yields feedback that can affect other stages, such as design, organization and enrolment, and can give us valuable information about the various functions. Thus evaluation can tell us things about induction, resourcing, counselling and the general course environment that might not be obvious to those who are teaching. As noted earlier, evaluation may occur during the course, in which case it can help to shape it, or come at the end, in which case it represents a final judgment. Post-course or follow-up evaluation is rare in education, but important in the training field, where the ultimate measures of effectiveness relate to the impact of the course on the individual's performance in the workplace and its contribution to organizational success (Kirkpatrick, 1987).

Evaluation provides grounds for the *development* or redevelopment of the course. It may be that little needs to be altered, but if changes do need to be made, they may entail development of the curriculum, staff or organization or all three. Curriculum development involves changes in the content, methods and materials of the course; staff development means the retraining of existing staff or acquisition of new staff; and organization development involves changes in the structures, procedures or norms of the organization. Together, these three forms of development form a triangle of possible types of change, which are often related. Indeed, making changes in the curriculum without re-skilling the staff to deal with them, or retraining the staff without adapting the organization to accommodate them, can lead to ineffectiveness and frustration. Teaching is an embodied and embedded activity.

A great deal more could be said about each of these elements or stages of course production. The purpose here has simply been to sketch out the main headings, so that they can be related to the other two dimensions of the model. As with the other headings, these should not simply be taken for granted. There are various ways of conceptualizing the planning and provision of courses, and various terms that can be used. The important thing is that people feel that the terms they use are adequate to describe what actually happens in their own case and in their organization.

Procedures, Roles and Skills

The last point raises several others about the list of headings. The first is that the allocation of responsibility for the various tasks and stages will depend on the institutional setting of the course. In a small organization, or one where the running of courses is devolved largely to individuals, a single person may be responsible for everything from A to Z, analysis through to development. He or she will have to design, market and organize the course, enrol, teach and assess the students, and evaluate the result. This kind of one-man band is quite common in non-vocational adult education, and in small training consultancies. In larger organizations, however, responsibility for the various stages may fall to different individuals or to teams, or even to different departments or sections within the organization. And in some sectors of education the analysis, proposal, design and assessment stages may be carried out at national level, in which case the role of the school or college teacher is essentially to organize and deliver the course. This will be particularly true in hierarchical systems, where there is a strong top-down decision-making process.

The role of the individual teacher or lecturer may also change over time. The junior member of staff may initially be tasked simply with delivering and assessing the course, and have no other responsibilities or powers. After a while, he or she may begin to take on some additional, mainly administrative roles: organizing the practicalities of the course, enrolling the students, perhaps taking care of marketing and publicity. As he or she accumulates more experience, and moves up the institutional ladder, he or she is more likely to take on the more strategic and senior tasks of analysing, proposing, designing and evaluating; sometimes to the point where he or she actually does very little direct teaching any more. Thus the scope of the person's responsibilities may gradually widen out over time to span the whole dimension.

This is a familiar enough pattern, but what the headings in this model help to illuminate is the extent to which these different tasks actually demand different kinds of capabilities and skills. The classroom skills that one needs to deliver and assess a course are not necessarily the same as the managerial or analytic skills one needs to organize or design it; and those skills in turn are rather different from the quasi-political skills one may need to formulate and see through a proposal. Marketing requires specialized skills, as does evaluation. We cannot assume that because a teacher or lecturer has learned how to do one thing well, he or she will automatically be competent to do something different, even if it relates to the same course. Teaching, in this light, again appears as a composite activity, demanding a range of knowledge, skills and capacities, and the process of continuing professional development is often that of extending a person's initial competence into these newer and rather different areas. Such professional development also has to take account of the fact that individuals may prefer or show a talent for certain tasks rather than others. The good chalk-face teacher may not make the best designer or evaluator, and *vice versa*, because the nature of the activities is rather different. Similarly, some people may have a penchant for, or hatred of, administration and organization; others may take to, or be repelled by, the politicking that accompanies decision-making about course proposals or evaluation.

These comments have already exemplified some of the ways in which the tasks and stages of course provision may be influenced by the course variables. A great deal may depend on the organizational setting of the course, in terms of finance, structures, procedures and norms. Indeed, it is usually at the macro level of the course, rather than the micro level of the teaching session, that the organizational context has its greatest impact. Once one gets down into the detail of teaching and learning, its influence often recedes to become a background factor. The staff who work in that setting are another potentially important variable in the provision of the course: it is they, after all, who have to carry out the various tasks and stages indicated in the headings: not only delivery and assessment, but also other tasks such as design, marketing and evaluation have to be interpreted and implemented by real, living members of staff, with their own motivations, preoccupations, strategies and skills. Beyond this, the social setting may also influence tasks such as the marketing of the course and the enrolment of students; the initial analysis will almost inevitably have to explore this wider context. The physical setting may have a bearing on the organization of the course: what is available, what can be done where, with what facilities. Design and delivery will have to refer to the rationale, content, level, participants and clients.

Thus, though not all the tasks and stages of putting on a course will be affected by all the variables in every case, many of them will be affected by several, rather than just the most obvious one. The headings in the model, and the possible intersections between them, continually raise the question: What about this? What about this? The model thus presents a totality of possible links, relationships and effects from which the practitioner can select those that seem most relevant at the time. The same is true of the relationship between procedures and functions. In our natural preoccupation with the practicalities of planning and delivering a course, we must not forget what the point of the whole exercise is to perform the basic functions of a course as effectively as possible in the light of the variables. Thus the various stages and tasks can be checked against the function headings. Is this design likely to produce a manageable course? Will it help to create good interaction? Does this enrolment process achieve the kind of selection we want? The kind of induction? Does this form of organization make the best use of our resources? Does this delivery provide not only good teaching but appropriate modelling and counselling? How do the methods of assessment lead to appropriate accreditation? How does the whole process of provision create a good learning environment?

What this means is that we cannot judge the performance of the various procedures in isolation. We might want to say 'this appears to be a well-formulated proposal' or 'this looks like a coherent course design' or 'this seems a well-organized course' because we see evidence of care, thought and application. But ultimately, our judgment can only be made in relation to the underlying functions of the course in the context of those particular variables. The proposal might be well formulated but in fact going down entirely the wrong road; the very coherence of the design might in fact pre-empt the development of new learning; good organization might coexist with an unfriendly learning environment.

The various procedures of putting on a course each involve their own characteristic skills and procedures, just as, at the micro level, do the various procedures of teaching. To that extent, we can look at them in terms of their own, intrinsic tasks and skills. But they are tasks of something, and that something is teaching. We must not mistake the how for the what. The key difference between this model of course provision and many others is that here the tasks and stages of running a course are laid out, not in isolation, but in relation to the two other dimensions. The three dimensions of the model form a necessary whole, and we cannot divorce any one from the others.

It should also be clear by now that the model can be used not only by teachers, but by learners as a means of analysing their learning situation, in terms of the functions they have to perform, the situational variables that affect them, and the course tasks they need to carry out. The learner, too, needs to consider the functions, and the variables that may affect them. As noted earlier, we can prefix many of them with 'self' or 'peer': self-selection, peer-induction, self-managment, self-resourcing, peer-counselling. And the notions of interaction and environment clearly involve the learner. Self-accreditation is the only no-no.

Even the procedures, which at first sight look like a purely institutional or professional matter, can involve the learner. In fact, it is precisely these kinds of things that self-directed learners, working outside the formal system, have to sort out for themselves: to analyse what kind of learning would be best for them; to set themselves aims or targets; to organize their time and their resources; to design their learning; to get started; to teach and assess themselves; to evaluate how it has gone; and to apply those lessons the next time round. As with everything else in the model, we should not necessarily identify teaching with teachers. We are concerned with the process, rather than who carries it out.

We can now move on to the Micro Model, which is concerned with analysing teaching at the level of the class or single session. Just as a single class happens within the wider context of the course, so the Micro Model nests within the Macro Model. The broader functions, variables and procedures set out above will continue to have a bearing on our analysis. But we need to turn up the level of magnification to get at the fine grain of what goes on in the classroom, lecture hall, workshop or laboratory. Since the form of the model will be the same, reflecting the same three underlying questions, I shall not need to spell out its logic again. We can thus cover the ground more quickly. But most of the headings will be different, reflecting as they do the detail, rather than the broad canvas, of teaching and learning.

Chapter 4

Analysing the Class

The Micro Model, as its name suggests, deals with what goes on minute by minute and even second by second in the classroom, workshop, laboratory or wherever else teaching is taking place. It offers a way of analysing these events and interactions in terms of what the teacher is doing (functions), what affects what he or she is doing (variables) and how he or she does it (procedures). While the list of variables is similar though not quite the same as in the Macro Model — referring to the why, what, who and where of teaching — the function headings are quite different, and the third dimension (procedures) relates to the familiar methods that classroom teaching involves, rather than the tasks and stages of putting on a course that were dealt with in the last chapter. The Model is set out in Fig. 4.1, and as with the previous model, a glossary is provided to help indicate the meanings of the headings, although these can only really be fleshed out in the text of this chapter, and readers might want to add some alternatives of their own.

As before, I shall take each dimension in turn, explaining the headings and the reasons for using them, and then show how the three can be related to form an integrated, multi-dimensional view of teaching. Since the general arguments for this kind of model have already been rehearsed, they will not be repeated here. The underlying logic is the same and would be the same if, for example, one developed a generic educational management model that subsumed the macro, course model. The management of education — involving another professional discipline — also has its functions, variables and procedures. The basic approach can thus be applied to the various levels of educational activity, and the Micro Model should be seen as 'nesting' within the Macro Model.

MICRO MODEL: GLOSSARY

Micro Functions
MOTIVATE: stimulate, interest, arouse, energize
AUDIT: diagnose, identify prior or baseline knowledge and expectations
ORIENTATE: establish direction, purpose, objectives, agenda
INPUT: impart, inform, transmit
EXPLAIN: clarify, amplify, interpret, relate
EXPLORE: enquire, discover, debate
REFLECT: encourage meta-cognition, meta-affect, meta-learning
TASK: drill, rehearse, exercise, practise, activate

Figure 4.1   The Micro Model

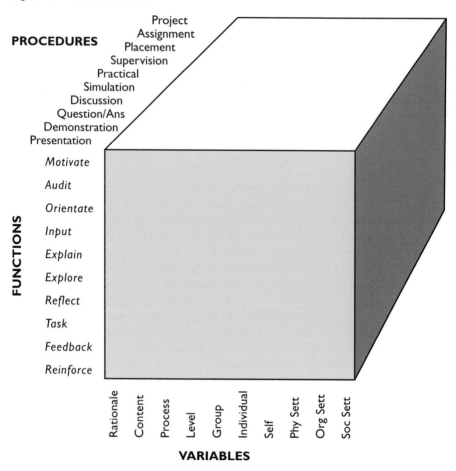

FEEDBACK: comment, criticize, appraise, debrief
REINFORCE: confirm, establish

Micro Variables
RATIONALE: objectives, outcomes
CONTENT: subject-matter, topics, themes
PROCESS: strategies, approaches, skills
LEVEL: difficulty, complexity
GROUP: participants, members
INDIVIDUALS: learners, pupils, students
SELF: teacher, lecturer, tutor, facilitator
PHYSICAL SETTING: learning space, classroom, facility, venue
ORGANIZATIONAL SETTING: department, school, faculty, institution
SOCIAL SETTING: society, economy, culture, subculture

Micro Procedures

PRESENTATION: talk, lecture, briefing
DEMONSTRATION: performance
QUESTION AND ANSWER: exchange, dialogue, quiz
DISCUSSION: small group session, seminar, case study
SIMULATION: role play, game, in-tray exercise
PRACTICAL: workshop, laboratory, skill session, field trip
SUPERVISION: tutoring, coaching, mentoring
PLACEMENT: work-shadowing, apprenticeship, work-based learning
ASSIGNMENT: homework, exercise, reading, essay
PROJECT: long essay, report, study, dissertation

Micro Functions

The idea that one should try to define what it is that teachers do to bring about learning in (and outside) the classroom is so obvious that it hardly needs stating. Indeed, it is difficult to write about what goes on in the classroom (or lecture hall, workshop or laboratory) at all without some reference to the putative roles or functions of teachers, and the classic literature on pedagogy over the ages has addressed this issue, more or less explicitly. The question — What do teachers do? — is never far away in discussions of teaching, even if it is not framed in quite the analytic, functional terms being used here. However, the attempt to arrive at a systematic account of teachers' functions belongs mainly to the last three decades, and mainly to American rather than British studies.

Much of the early work was done in the 1970s in the context of an 'instructional systems' approach to teaching and training. As noted in Chapter 1, much systems writing operates at the general level of course design and development (on a par with the macro model), but in the end such an approach has to get down to the concrete, nitty-gritty realities of what goes on in the classroom if it is going to be of practical use. One of the first modern, systematic attempts to do this was Gagné's identification of nine 'instructional events' (Gagné, 1965, 1975), a foundation that was subsequently built on by him and other writers (Gagné, Briggs and Wager, 1988; Reigeluth and Curtis, 1987). Gagné is probably best known for his theory of conditions of learning, which states that learning is not a single, unitary phenomenon, but rather an umbrella concept that covers a number of different kinds of behavioural or cognitive outcomes, each of which requires its own internal and external conditions. However, in parallel with this, he also developed his ideas about basic instructional events, which have to occur for learning to take place in relation to any outcome. This list of instructional events shows the influence of earlier work by him and others in the training field, some of which goes back to the Second World War. By the fourth edition of *The Conditions of Learning* (Gagné, 1985), the list had become linked not only to outcome variables but to student variables, though not to setting variables.

A second and rather different approach to the identification of teacher functions also developed in the United States in the 1970s and 1980s, under the general heading of 'process–product' studies (see Brophy and Good, 1986; Rosenshine and Stevens, 1986). The context this time was not military or industrial training, but an interest in the impact of teachers' behaviours on pupil achievement in the school system, in particular the practices of what appeared to be effective teachers. The resulting findings came to be labelled as 'direct instruction'. It is not easy to summarize this field of research; Rosenshine and Meister (1995) distinguish between five different meanings of 'direct instruction', some of which are negative (e.g. teacher-dominated). However, it is worth citing Brophy and Good's original conclusions on this work, even if they now seem somewhat over-generalized:

> students learn more efficiently when their teachers first structure new information for them and help them relate it to what they already know, and then monitor their performance and provide corrective feedback during recitation, drill, practice, or application activities. For a time, these generalizations seemed confined to the early grades or to basic rather than more advanced skills. However, it now appears that they apply to any body of knowledge or set of skills that has been sufficiently well organised and analysed so that it can be presented systematically and then practised or applied during activities that call for student performance that can be evaluated for quality and (where incorrect or imperfect) given corrective feedback. (Brophy and Good, 1986, p. 366)

There are more recent examples of attempts to analyse teaching in terms of basic functions. Schuell (1992) identifies 12 'learning functions', which in some ways recall Gagné's list, but also show the influence of contemporary information-processing theory. He stresses that the functions may be carried out in a variety of different ways, and that they may be initiated either by the teacher or learner; both points which are entirely congruent with my own model. In this country, Entwistle has compiled another list of teaching functions in higher education, which shows some similarities with the one presented here (Entwistle, 1992). Gagné's, Schuell's and Entwistle's lists are set out side by side for comparison in Table 4.1; Entwistle views all the functions after the first two as supporting student learning in two main ways by 'structuring knowledge to provide a "map" of the subject domain' and 'facilitating and managing the student's interaction with that structured knowledge' (1992, p. 57). No attempt has been made here to relate the three schemes to one another, but they offer both interesting similarities and differences, and can be compared to the list of functions set out in Fig. 4.1.

In recent decades however, research on teaching in schools and higher education has on the whole moved away from attempts to identify the general pedagogical functions of teachers, to a naturalistic, ethnographic or phenomenographic approach, which is concerned with the experience of the classroom and reflection on that experience (Calderhead and Gates, 1993; Elliott, 1993; Ramsden, 1992). The whole style and language of research has shifted, to the point where the very word 'function' would be antipathetic to many researchers, suggesting something hard, mechanistic and schematic. The emphasis now is on discovering the textures and meanings of teaching and learning as they occur. However, within this research

Table 4.1   *Teaching/learning functions*

Instructional events *(Gagne, 1985)*	**Learning functions** *(Schuell, 1992)*	**Teaching functions** *(Entwistle, 1992)*
Gaining attention	Expectations	Orientating
Informing learners	Motivation	Motivating
of the objective	Prior knowledge activation	Presenting
Stimulating recall	Attention	Clarifying
of prior learning	Encoding	Elaborating
Presenting stimulus	Comparison	Consolidating
Providing learning guidance	Hypothesis generation	Confirming
Eliciting performance	Repetition	(Structuring)
Providing feedback	Feedback	(Facilitating/Managing)
Assessing performance	Evaluation	
Enhancing retention	Monitoring	
and transfer	Combination, integration	
	synthesis	

tradition, a new attempt to identify what teachers do or should do has emerged in the field of higher education. The stimulus for this has been the mainly European and Australian research on 'student approaches to learning', which has explored differences between students in the way they conceive of the learning task and process, and in particular the difference between a surface approach, which sees learning mainly in terms of memorizing and reproducing, and a deep approach, which sees it in terms of understanding and constructing meaning (Entwistle and Marton, 1994; Marton, 1977; Marton, Hounsell and Entwistle, 1984). More will be said of this work later; here, however, what is relevant is that it has spawned some parallel research on teachers' conceptions of and approaches to teaching (Gow and Kember, 1993; Prosser, Trigwell and Taylor, 1994). What do university lecturers think their role is? What is teaching to them? Is it mainly the transmission of information, or has it to do with developing concepts and ideas? And to what extent are these functions the responsibility of the lecturer or the student? To what extent are they internalized by the learner? There are clear affinities here with our earlier discussion of the location and attribution of functions: Whose job is it anyway?

A detailed analysis of these three lines of research would occupy too much of this book and risk unbalancing the treatment of the three dimensions of the model. Each line has of course been open to criticism. Gagné's work is now rarely referred to outside the training literature, and the process–product studies have been attacked for failing to take account of the contextuality of teaching. The intensive, small-scale studies that typify phenomenographic research raise issues about generalizability. The identification of the ways in which teachers can help bring about learning — whether we call them events, functions, strategies or approaches — goes to the heart of teaching, and is the most problematic aspect of any model.

All that can be said here is that these three lines of research — instructional systems, direct instruction and approach to teaching — have informed the list of micro functions that will now be set out. However, as with the rest of the model, the main source of these has been the work with practitioners over the last ten years, rather than the research literature. The latter has been used mainly as a way of checking and evaluating what was emerging from the practical work. There is in fact a substantial degree of congruence between the two kinds of sources, but there are also differences, which will be discussed below.

As in the Macro Model, the functions in the Micro Model are all verbs; they are things that have to be done, performed, fulfilled or carried out by the teacher, the learner, someone else, or a combination of these people. And as with the Macro Model, it will become clear that the list is not simply a linear one, and that the relationship between the various functions is an issue in itself. Indeed, the way teachers or learners relate and structure the functions will tell us something about their view of teaching and learning, their 'personal theory'.

Motivate, Audit, Orientate

The first function is to *motivate*. Even if people have the capacity to learn, that capacity will remain latent — merely an unrealized potential — unless there is the volition to go with it. Again, if we think of the autodidact, we can see the importance of this function. One of the key problems that the independent learner faces is that of summoning up and sustaining the motivation to study. People need to want to learn, and therefore the first function of the teacher is arguably to enhance that desire. Motivating can range from the specific gaining of attention for a particular piece of teaching, to the more generalized encouragement or enthusing of learners for a range of learning tasks. It may appeal to intrinsic factors (curiosity, interest, a sense of achievement) or extrinsic rewards, such as good marks, peer approval or desired employment. And although it is important in the initial decision to embark on learning, it also needs to be sustained over time. Motivation can dip in the middle of a course, or change with changing personal or educational circumstances. And teachers or teaching can demotivate students who are initially well motivated.

As with many other functions, this one is often seen most clearly in its absence. Many's the time that teachers say things like 'he doesn't seem to try', 'they're not interested', or 'she simply isn't paying attention'. The reasons for the lack of motivation may be highly complex, and relate to a number of variables: the rationale for the class or lesson, the content, the process, the group, individual factors, the teacher's approach, the influence of the setting, and so on. Motivation, like the other functions, is an embedded, contingent one, and part of the subtlety of teaching lies in teasing out the various things affecting it in any given case. So although the teacher has a general function to motivate, that function may manifest itself in all sorts of different ways. It thus goes beyond a particular 'instructional event' in Gagné's terms, although it may be related to the kind of teaching method or technique being used. Some methods may motivate learners better than others in certain circumstances.

It is useful to see motivation, particularly with adult students, in positional rather than absolute terms. It is not so much a question of wanting or not wanting to learn, as of giving learning priority over the other things that may compete for time, energy, interest or pleasure. In that sense, motivation can be seen in terms of the economist's notion of a preference function. However, if we assume that that preference is there, the next question concerns the general direction of learning, and this leads on to the next two functions, *audit* and *orientate*. Audit is the process of analysing existing or prior learning and experience so that new learning can take account of it; it tries to establish the baseline, or entry behaviour. That process may be particularly complex (and important) in a mixed or heterogeneous group, and there may be various ways of doing it: through formal tests, individual interviews, group discussion, initial brainstorming.

However, audit is important not only at the beginning of teaching. It may be important to continue to explore learners' existing conceptions of the world, derived from prior experience and common-sense knowledge, so that they can be related to, and sometimes challenged by organized knowledge. For example, children's or adults' 'naïve' scientific concepts and models can persist and coexist with what they are learning formally about physics and chemistry, without ever fully engaging the latter. It is important, therefore, to take time to explore the implicit or personal theories that people may have about the content of their subject at various stages in a course. This point applies equally to teacher training.

Where audit looks back to what the person has previously learned, *orientation* looks forward to what he or she is going to learn. It involves establishing some sense of where the learning is going, in terms of outcomes, expectations, priorities and boundaries. It helps to define mutual expectations and purposes. Conventional teacher training emphasizes the need to articulate such directions, and one can often hear the lecturer or teacher doing this at the beginning of the session: 'I want to cover three things this morning . . .'. Depending on the situation, such orientation may be laid down by the teacher, or negotiated with the group or individual. And it may be more or less tight: some sessions will be framed in terms of specific objectives, while others will proceed according to the loosest of plans. Again, it depends: on the nature of the course, the subject matter, the group, the organizational context and so on. The detailed lesson plan is not necessarily an appropriate framework for teaching; something more evolutionary and improvisatory may be needed, although one must be careful not to use the latter merely as an excuse for lack of preparation. Open-ended teaching, with its multiple possible pathways and directions, requires more preparation than the preplanned linear script, not less.

The need for audit and orientation stems from the cognitive requirement that learning makes sense: that people can relate one thing to another. Again, as with motivation, these two functions are often recognized most clearly in their absence: the piece of teaching that starts off without any attempt to establish where people are, or what they know, or that makes assumptions about baseline knowledge that are true for some members of the group but not others; or the piece of teaching that plunges straight into the business, without any preamble; or which jumps from one topic to another without any apparent logic or rationale; or ends just as abruptly.

Most teachers, even if they are not trained, are at least dimly aware of the need to orientate their students, and make some attempt to do so ('say what you are going to say, say it, and say you said it'). However, they are often much less careful about auditing their students' prior learning, perhaps because they are in a hurry and want to get on with things, or because they assume that the educational system is more consecutive than it really is, or because they think it is up to the learner to make the connections anyway. But a journey involves coming from as well as going to, an origin as well as a destination.

Input, Explain

The next two functions — *input* and *explain* — can be taken as a pair. It is difficult to find quite the right term for the first, but I shall use 'input' here to mean imparting or transmitting information to the learner. Its contemporary, colloquial use in this way implies an input–throughput–output model of teaching and learning, which takes little account of the interactivity of the process, and is thus rather crude. But since teachers and lecturers spend a good deal of their time imparting information — telling or showing, in traditional terms — we need some way to describe this. Information is being used here in the broad information-processing sense, rather than to mean simply facts; it can refer to anything the teacher imparts or transmits. The prime purpose of such inputs is to put across or get across the substance of the course. However, it is important to remember that some information is transmitted non-verbally, through visual or aural means such as videos or tapes, through demonstration of the content, for example in a laboratory or skill setting, or even through the enacting or embodying of what is to be learned. In this last case, we cross the fine line between teaching and *modelling* (cf. the Macro Model).

A good deal of inputting is also done indirectly, through prescribed reading or software. Even if a teacher never gave a lecture or a talk, she would still be 'informing' her learners if she gave them handouts and notes, directed them to certain texts, or made available certain software packages. One must be careful therefore to distinguish between the *function* of input, which can be performed in various ways, and the *procedures* of presentation, demonstration and assignment. Just as the function can employ a variety of procedures, so the procedures can be used for a variety of functions: a presentation can be used to motivate and orientate students, and even to provide collective feedback on their work, as distinct from imparting content.

Inputting is a function of teaching because teachers, on the whole, know more about the subject-matter than the learners, and part of their job is quite simply to impart this knowledge or know-how to them. That implies an authoritative, but not necessarily authoritarian view of teaching. Teachers teach partly by virtue of their expertise in their field of study, whereas students or pupils will usually (though not always) be relative novices or apprentices. Thus, although inputting may seem a rather simple and even routine aspect of teaching, it is important not to undervalue it. In order to inform their students, teachers have themselves to be well informed, and be able to select and order that information in ways that will be clear and accessible to their learners.

At the same time, there are reasons for thinking that teachers often over-emphasize this function, at the expense of other, more facilitative and interactive ones. After all, teaching time is limited, and the relative priority given to the various functions is a key aspect of one's approach. There is the question, first, of how much learners actually retain of the information that they are supposed to absorb. The right balance between general concepts and specific detail, or between content and process is itself a contingent, teaching decision, and one can see how the pendulum may swing too far in either direction. However, teachers in schools, let alone further and higher education, do seem to spend a good deal of time simply transmitting information in class.

Secondly, although one can encourage students to gather information for them-selves rather than simply give it to them, the fact remains that many forms of input are relatively passive in terms of student learning. There is little encouragement for the learners to do anything with the information other than register and memorize it. And thirdly, in some situations, the learners may know a good deal about the subject-matter themselves, in which case the teaching time might be better spent in some kind of *exploration* or *reflection* (see below) rather than simple transmission of content.

The efficacy of inputs also depends heavily on how well learners understand what is being imparted, and this leads on naturally to the function of *explaining*. Explaining is often used in a loose, general sense to mean the exposition of a topic: thus the teacher may say that she explained the origins of the First World War in a lecture. Here, however, I am using the term in a tighter sense to mean the teacher's response to a learner's problem. Explaining, in this sense, refers to what the teacher does when a learner says 'I didn't follow that' or 'I don't understand what you mean' or 'Could you go over that bit again?' Explaining thus involves not simply imparting something, but relating two things: the script of the teacher's or text's exposition and the comprehension of another person. Whereas inputting is essen-tially one-way, explaining is inescapably two-way. To the teacher who says 'I explained X in my lecture' the response is: How do you know?

As noted earlier, explaining is one of the most commonplace functions of teaching, but also one of the most subtle. How do we explain? How do we respond to someone's question or confusion or incomprehension? As noted before, one can hear teachers employing various procedures when they need to explain something. And although explaining is thought of as a thing that one person does for another (and not just in educational but in common-sense terms), it can be seen as an internalized process as well: trying to figure something out for oneself. Yet again it is important to emphasize that the functions are functions of teaching, but not necessarily of the teacher. One of our key aims might be to get students or pupils to internalize the business of explaining, or share it with one another.

Up to this point, teaching has been treated as a relatively defined and delimitable activity. Even the two-way process of explaining is bounded by what is necessary to 'understand' the topic. Once something has been explained or self-explained, the task is notionally complete. By contrast, the next two functions — *exploring* and *reflecting* — are both open-ended. The difference between them is that the first points outwards to the content, and the second inwards to the learner.

Explore, Reflect

It is perhaps here that the list of functions departs most obviously from those that emerged from the work on instructional systems and direct instruction, which tend to a more closed or convergent view of education. *Exploring* goes beyond *explaining* in that it involves an open dialogue or discussion about the topic in which the agenda and the boundaries are no longer set by the teacher or the syllabus. The purpose is no longer simply to ensure that the learner understands what is being taught, but to investigate together the possibility of new approaches, interpretations and meanings. This openness is perhaps most obvious at the higher levels of education, and is a fundamental attribute of research, but it can occur at many levels and in many settings. Discovery learning may no longer be quite so fashionable in the schools as it was, but it has its place as a way of encouraging such exploration at an early age. How else do we show children the possibility of different interpretations, approaches, meanings — what Bernstein once called 'the ultimate mystery of a subject' (Bernstein, 1971, p. 57)? How else do we make problematic some of the information we impart, and enable people to question what is presented as fact or given? How else do we challenge what is taken for granted? Exploration is one of the characteristics of education that helps to distinguish it from training, which has a more restricted agenda. Even where open-ended methods — brainstorming, for example — are used in training they tend to be used in the service of a bounded objective. Education, however, is defined partly by its very lack of boundaries — something that is implicit in the venerable concepts of dialogue and enquiry.

The other open-ended function — *reflect* — relates not to the content but to the learner. It implies that teaching involves not simply enabling learners to accomplish specific tasks and to master specific contents, but to develop their capacity to do so cumulatively over the longer term. There can be few teachers who do not see it as part of their remit to help their learners to develop in this general way, even if it is difficult sometimes to pin down what such 'development' actually means. We are embroiled here with notions such as learning to learn, meta-learning, meta-cognition, or learning to think, and ultimately with concepts of cognitive, personal and professional development (Gibbs, 1981; Nisbet and Shucksmith, 1986; Squires, 1990, pp. 123–50; Weinstein and Mayer, 1986; Wilson, 1981). Reflection is not the only element in the process of development, but it is a key one. Through reflection, people make their own thinking, feeling and learning the objects of thought and learning. Reflection involves the internalization of the teaching–learning process, and thus develops the capacity to become an autonomous lifelong learner who does not need the constant input and direction of a teacher or curriculum.

Although exploration and reflection are difficult notions to pin down, and are sometimes two sides of the same coin, they would be even more difficult to omit from any list of teaching functions. Without them, the process of teaching becomes a purely convergent, non-cumulative business, geared to the defined agenda of the moment. In my experience, discussions of the two functions tend to start off with: But what do they mean? However, it is precisely that question that is important in opening them up, and with them the often deeply held beliefs and expectations about the longer-term purposes and processes of teaching. One might argue that reflection is in fact a meta-function that is a consequence of or spin-off from all the other functions in the list. However, it is useful to place it alongside the others because it highlights the question of priorities. How much time does the teacher or learner devote to reflecting on the process of thinking and learning as against the more immediate demands of all the other functions? How often does he or she pause to turn the discussion back on itself, to question the strategy or debrief the process? How much cognitive or personal space does he or she create? There are real, operational choices to be made here. (One frequent comment I have met on Return to Study courses for adults is that people never had any time or opportunity at school to think about how they learned or approached their work; they just got on with it.) Equally, exploration is often curtailed in order to cover the ground ('I'm afraid we haven't got time to go into that now') and put on the back burner as everyone focuses on the immediate assignment or the looming exam. Time, as noted earlier, is a fundamental variable of professional work, and the various functions often have to compete for their slice of it. In a pressurized situation, it is no surprise that these longer-term or more elusive functions often get marginalized.

Task, Feedback, Reinforce

An influential and useful line of research has defined teaching and learning in terms of tasks that the teacher sets and the learner performs (Blumenfeld, Mergendoller and Swarthout, 1987; Doyle, 1986; Doyle and Carter, 1984). Such tasks have not only a certain content but a certain form: one has to write an *essay* on *Far from the Madding Crowd*, do an *experiment* on heat loss or a *report* on estuarine development. The student is thus faced with formatted content, rather than content in the abstract. Such tasks might range from in-class presentations or tests, through conventional academic assignments and practical skill exercises to longer-term projects.

Setting, organizing, supervising and appraising such tasks occupies a major chunk of the teacher's time, and thus constitutes a key function of his or her work. Indeed, it is useful to regard teaching and learning precisely in terms of 'work' in this way; it helps us to see what the concrete experience actually involves for teacher and student. One of the things that the autodidact finds difficult to do is to set appropriate tasks for himself or herself. Again, however, it is difficult to find the right word for this function. In the training package version of the model (Squires, 1994) the term 'exercise' is used, but while people do understand this, it sounds rather old-fashioned. 'Activate' carries the sense of involving learners in doing something for themselves, but seems rather inhuman. 'Practise' is familiar, but has rather routine connotations associated in particular with skill learning.

In the end, the least bad option seems to be *task* (as a verb) as long as this is not confined to closed or predictable activities. It carries the general sense of working through or trying out some piece of learning, which may be of a cognitive as well as perceptual-motor kind. Thus an essay, class presentation, lab report, assignment or even project might be a form of task just as much as a skill session or language exercise. The essential point about this function is that it involves someone (usually the teacher) setting up a situation in which the learner can operationalize or concretize his or her own learning, if necessary repeatedly. Such situations are, however, of little benefit if there is no *feedback* on how the learner has performed. Merely carrying out the task may teach the learner something — he or she may internalize the feedback in the sense of realizing that this or that did or did not work — but the real value of the learning task comes in the modifications that the learner makes in the light of some appraisal of his or her performance. And while that appraisal may be internalized, and may come from peers, it often comes chiefly and officially from the lecturer or teacher.

What the learner needs is information: about his or her interpretation of and approach to the task, how well it was carried out, how good the outcomes were, what alternatives there might have been, what might be changed next time around. Often this information is encoded and encapsulated in a mark or grade, but by no means always; so, as we have seen, the term *assessment* has been reserved for one of the formal procedures of a course, rather than this ubiquitous and often informal function of teaching. What we are talking about here goes well beyond simple criticism to include discussion, advice and judgment about what has been done and how. And while the feedback function is most obviously associated with particular learning tasks, it may also be more generalized, as when a teacher discusses a student's work and progress at various points in a class or course.

The final function in the list is *reinforce*. Reinforcement is one of the fundamental behaviourist concepts of learning, and indicates the need to ensure that what has been learned has not simply been accomplished once, but has been confirmed or established in the learner's repertoire. Teachers can do this in two main ways: repetition and reward. Each of these helps to strengthen the structures and connections involved in the learning, the first cognitively, the second affectively. When a teacher recapitulates or synthesizes what has been learned at the end of a session, he or she is using the first strategy; another way of doing this is to assign follow-up work (exercises, practice, application, revision) that will take the learner through the learning task again. Where the nature of the follow-up task is rather different, the teacher may be attempting to reinforce transfer of learning to cognate tasks or situations.

The other way to reinforce learning is to associate it with some kind of affective reward: attention, interest, praise, good marks, or something else that the learner finds pleasurable. The current dominance of cognitive theory has tended to underplay the importance of reinforcement in learning, on the argument that the essential factor in most learning is the acquisition of meaning and understanding. This may be true of the higher level cognitive learning that is characteristic of higher education; after all, meaningfulness and understanding are intrinsically pleasurable.

However, it is worth noting that reinforcement is a key element in contemporary theories of neural networks, which could be seen as a newer form of behaviourism (see Alexsander and Morton, 1990). It remains an important function because, like motivation, it affects the will to learn: volition. The difference between the two is that where motivation relates mainly to the intention of learning, reinforcement relates to the outcome. A student may be stimulated, encouraged, enthused and even inspired to begin learning; but if the results of his or her endeavours do not bring some sense of confidence, security, pleasure or reward, that will to learn may well be eroded. The teacher who simply offers feedback without any reinforcement may find that the student's motivation is beginning to flag. Conversely, effective reinforcement may help to turn around an initial lack of enthusiasm or interest. The learner may come to see that it is all worthwhile after all.

Reinforcement can also come from elsewhere. One's peers can reward one in various ways: with their attention, interest, respect or praise. People outside the immediate learning situation — parents, employers, colleagues — can also reinforce what one learns. One of the most effective ways to reinforce learning is to use it or apply it outside the class. This may be less often the case in the school sector, where such use is often deferred, but it can be a potent factor in further and higher education. Once the learner sees that the learning has actually equipped him or her with new capabilities, it ceases to be associated purely with education. Indeed, a common problem in the training world is that what people learn on their training courses is not in fact reinforced in the workplace, because they have little or no opportunity to put it into practice. Indeed, they may be actively discouraged from doing so. For example, the 'canteen culture' in the police service can negate some of what recruits are taught at the training centre. Or colleagues in a commercial company can make life difficult for the employee who comes back from a course wanting to introduce some new procedure. There are parallels with in-service training for teachers. The structures of reinforcement can affect us more than we sometimes want to admit.

Interpreting the Functions

Several points can be made about this list of micro functions. First, as with the macro functions and perhaps even more so, they raise the question: Who is responsible for them? Who performs them or carries them out? I have already stressed several times that the functions are functions of teaching, but not necessarily of teachers. The model is in no way a teacher-centred or teacher-driven one; one can easily prefix the functions by 'self' or 'peer': self-motivation, peer-motivation, self-audit, peer-orientation, peer-input, self-tasking, peer-feedback. Depending on the aims and context of teaching, this internalization of the functions by the learner or learners may be expected or encouraged. In that case, the role of the teacher may become the more oblique one of managing these functions: seeing to it that they are fulfilled by somebody, rather than trying to perform them all directly himself or herself. In some cases, for example in some forms of postgraduate or continuing education, even that ultimate responsibility may rest with the learner, and he or she will draw on and make use of the teacher or lecturer merely as one resource among others.

As I described earlier, one way of exploring this attribution of responsibilities is to present teachers and/or learners with a pro forma, which sets out each function as a spectrum ranging from total teacher responsibility to total student responsibility, and ask them to place themselves on each spectrum. Such an exercise illuminates not only the expectations of students as individuals, but allows individuals to compare their position with that of the group as a whole. It can also bring to light any mismatches between the expectations of teachers and students as to who will be doing what, and form a useful basis for discussion. This kind of exercise also helps us to get a handle on the important but elusive notion of 'active learning'. The idea that learning is essentially something that one does, rather than something that happens to one, is one of the few points of general consensus in educational psychology, although the interpretation of activity differs, with behavioural, cognitive and humanistic psychologists all giving it their own particular gloss. At its most superficial, the notion of active learning implies overt activity: learners visibly doing something in or outside the classroom, such as writing, making things, talking to one another. At a somewhat deeper level, active learning implies mental activity: not just sitting listening or viewing, but doing something with the information in one's own mind: relating, comparing, interpreting, applying, transforming. Such 'activity' may or may not be observable at the time. The concept of active learning is also associated with the concept of learning tasks referred to above: learners are active when they are engaged in such tasks, and therefore (it is argued) one should try to maximize the amount of time they spend on them, and cut back on situations that allow or induce passivity.

One problem with all these approaches is that they can end up focusing on the form rather than the substance of the idea. The essence of active learning is that the learner is engaged in and takes some responsibility for the process of learning. However, the degree of responsibility will depend on the situational variables, and may differ from one function to another. In one situation, the teacher might provide strong orientation, but leave the performance of the learning tasks very much up to the learner. The teacher might impart most of the information, or leave it to the learners to get hold of it themselves. The teacher may offer plenty of feedback, or deliberately refrain from doing so in order to engage the learner in self-appraisal. We need to avoid the simple dichotomy of thinking that teaching and learning are either active or passive. The fact that we have identified ten different functions of teaching implies that it is a composite, not unitary activity. In general terms, it is important for the learner to be engaged actively in the process; but that general strategy has to be translated into each specific function with subtlety and care, and not simply as a blanket approach.

The composite nature of teaching implies that learning too is a composite, multiple activity. There has been at times an unfortunate tendency in learning theory to try to explain the whole process in terms of one or two key concepts. Thus contiguity and reinforcement in behavioural theory, structure and strategy in cognitive theory and self-concept and meaning in humanistic theory have variously been presented as the key elements in the learning process, with the implication that any other factors or conditions are secondary. It is difficult to account for this reductionist drive. Historically, it may have something to do with the powerful example of the physical sciences, with their emphasis on theoretical elegance, in the early twentieth century when educational psychology was first developing. (It is interesting to speculate what the comparable effect of the current life and environmental sciences, with their rather different paradigms, would have been on an embryonic field of educational psychology.) It may also reflect the fact that different learning theories have actually focused on different types or aspects of learning — the original point made by Gagné in his *Conditions of Learning* (1965). Or it may simply reflect the human need to simplify. Whatever the reason, the position taken here is quite different. It is that learning, like most human and social phenomena, is a pluralistic, multi-factorial and rather messy business. If we want, as teachers, to help bring it about, we need to bear in mind not one or two or three but many factors: to keep our eye on a number of balls at the same time.

The list of micro functions also raises several more practical questions, which we need to address before moving on to the next dimension. First, is the list comprehensive? Is it complete? I have tried, in explaining each function, to give some reasons for its inclusion, although the discussion has necessarily been brief: most functions would merit a chapter to themselves, and there is already a substantial literature on most of them. The references to previous and related research at the beginning of this chapter suggest that there is at least some justification in the literature for including them, beyond the long and iterative process of work with practitioners that has yielded this list. But that does not mean that the list should be presented as a given. The whole purpose of the model is to engage practitioners in thinking about their teaching, and it is therefore important that they bring to it their own priorities and perceptions. Much useful analysis can come out of the question: Are there other functions? To give three concrete examples: a schoolteacher argued that the development of *rapport* was a basic function, an adult educator thought that *transform* should be included, and a trainer said that one of his functions was to *persuade.*

There are other ways, too, in which practitioners can engage the headings. One simple but effective way is to ask them to focus on the problematic ones, for example to pick out the two or three that they feel work least well in their own situation. Sometimes a group pattern emerges from this, in which case the discussion can widen out to look at situational factors that may explain this. But individual differences can be just as illuminating: why is it not the same for you as it is for me? Such discussion can then move on to the more practical question: what, if anything, can be done about the problem? And who can do it? An action plan may emerge.

A more complex but even more probing question concerns the relationship between the headings. The list, as presented here, is simply a list. As with the list of macro functions, it implies no particular priorities, structures or sequences. The question 'What are the most important functions for you?' will often initially bring the bland response that they are all important. But further probing will usually unearth differences of emphasis. One person will argue that the two most obviously affective functions — motivate and reinforce — are the key, since it is they that sustain continuing, lifelong learning, which should be the ultimate aim of all education. Everything else should therefore take second place to the building and maintaining of the individual's will to learn. Another person will see exploration as the linchpin concept, with everything else merely contributing to it; after all, what else is education about? A concern with audit may reflect a concern to value the learner's existing knowledge and skills, and signal a more student-centred approach. Problem-based learning is likely to place the task at the centre, with other functions such as input and explanation deriving from it.

The relative emphasis on input and explanation may also tell one something about the person's attitudes to surface and deep learning. This distinction, which has been developed by a number of Swedish, British and Australian researchers over the past 20 years, has proved an influential one in higher education (Marton, Hounsell and Entwistle, 1984; Ramsden, 1992). Surface learning is concerned mainly with memorization and reproduction, and deep learning with understanding and meaning. Although the distinction in terms of student approaches or orientations to learning is new in the context of higher education, it was in fact prefigured some years ago by Ausubel's distinction between rote and meaningful learning (Ausubel, 1963). Over time, the distinction has become less purely binary (with the addition, for example, of strategic learning) and also more contextualized, with student approach to learning seen increasingly as a response to the teaching and in particular the assessment environment (see Biggs, 1993).

In terms of the list of functions and the model as a whole, the distinction becomes both more complex and more relativized. Surface teaching and learning is indicated by an emphasis on the transmission and reproduction of information (orientation and input). However, deep learning begins to break down into a number of more specific aspects: not only explaining/understanding, but open-ended exploration, the relationship with prior learning and experience (audit), and the more general development of meta-learning and thinking (reflecting). And it is worth noting that the conceptualization of learning by some writers on adult education goes beyond the binary deep-surface distinction developed in higher education, to encompass notions of consciousness-raising (Freire, 1970) and perspective transformation (Mezirow, 1977).

A further complication enters with the variables dimension. The deep-surface distinction is arguably domain-specific, related to cognitive rather than affective or psycho-motor learning. Indeed it is difficult to see how the distinction can be related to, for example, Fitts's theory of skill learning, or Anderson's three-stage model (for an account of these and other models, see Patrick, 1992, pp. 41–54). The nature of the content is one of the variables that affects the approach to learning, and a largely psycho-motor or affective content implies a different gloss and emphasis on functions such as explaining, exploring and reflecting. Conventional models of skill teaching tend to emphasize guidance (orientate), practice (task), feedback and reinforcement.

It is obviously important to try to set this list of functions against other current lines of research in the field. However, as I pointed out earlier, it can be equally productive to ask practitioners to build their own 'theory' of teaching out of the functions: to construct a diagram, model or flow-chart that represents the relationships between them. This exercise can reveal major differences in the way people see teaching. In some cases, a kind of minimal model of direct instruction emerges, as follows:

Orientate > Input > Explain > Task > Feedback

This may represent what the person actually does, or reverts to when under pressure. (And we are all under pressure sometimes.) It also reflects the rather cut-and-dried approach to teaching in some more traditional systems. Motivation and reinforcement are left largely to the learner, and exploration and reflection are regarded as spin-offs or luxuries for which there is usually not time. Another model that sometimes emerges places reflection at the top of a hierarchy of functions, as being the most generic. Another model has a series of concentric circles, with task–feedback at the core. Whether the picture that emerges takes a linear, dualistic, hierarchic, concentric, Venn-like or some other form does not really matter. What is important is that one begins to get a sense of how that teacher (or learner) sees teaching, of how they represent it to themselves. And such representations provide fertile ground for discussion.

One other aspect of the micro functions needs to be explored before we move on. The reference above to 'rapport' raises the question of whether this should in fact be seen as a function of teaching. (Similar questions might be asked about other ideas such as the development of 'trust', 'communication' or a good classroom 'climate' or 'ethos'.) Certainly, the need to build some kind of rapport with pupils or students is part of the folk wisdom of teaching, not only in the schools, but in adult education and even in other more impersonal teaching settings as well, in further and higher education. But a cursory search of the indexes of the main texts on teaching referred to in this book found it listed in only one, Eisner's *The Educational Imagination*, in which it is seen as essential for entering into and understanding the experience of the child (Eisner, 1985, p. 69).

However much we might like the idea, it is hard to find solid evidence that good rapport actually enhances learning. One can speculate on some possible reasons why it might do so: less time is wasted on control and management of the situation, and so can be focused on actual teaching and learning; less defensiveness means more openness to learning; and somehow the tacit communication that goes on may be more efficient. And it is difficult to see how one can motivate or feedback or even explain without some degree of rapport with the learner. On the other hand, we have probably all had the experience of learning from teachers we did not get on with, or feel on a wavelength with, or positively disliked. (We may be able to dissociate teacher from teaching more as we get older.) Rapport is also attenuated in distance education, where there may be little contact between teacher and learner, and there is much less emphasis on it in more traditional teaching cultures, where 'respect' is more likely to be emphasized. Also, rapport is not peculiar to teaching. The tour guide, office supervisor or platoon commander also need to develop rapport, not to mention the actor or performer.

The reason why rapport has not been included is that strictly speaking it does not seem to be a teaching function. However, that does not mean that it may not be a pre-condition or concomitant of teaching in some circumstances. One may need to develop a good rapport in order to get through to teaching. Likewise, in a more general way, classroom management is a pre-condition of teaching in the sense that it creates a situation in which teaching can take place. But it is important to pre-serve the distinction between teaching (i.e. fulfilling those functions that facilitate learning) and those things that may enable or allow teaching in certain settings, if only because it permits us to pose the question: How much of the 35 or 50 minutes is the teacher actually teaching? The answer is unlikely ever to be all; but if the figure falls a long way short of the total, we have to ask why the teacher is not doing, or being allowed to do, what he or she is meant to do.

However, the issue of rapport also raises a more general question about the model. It is intended to be a model of teaching in the strict sense defined above. This may mean that it does not quite do justice to the human and social aspects of the situation, although headings such as 'environ' and 'interact' are potentially broad and inclusive, and the variables do draw in the group, individuals and oneself. I have excluded anything that I do not regard as teaching in the strict sense because to include them would compromise the basic purpose of the model; but the model itself may need to be located and embedded in the particular social situation in which the teacher is working. In this sense, teaching (like other professions) is not entirely a discrete activity, which can be cleanly separated from the other things that may be going on when we interact with other people. Professionals are, after all, human.

Perhaps the ultimate justification of the list of functions is that it offers us some purchase on the question posed some years ago by Hirst: how do we distin-guish teaching from other activities? (Hirst, 1973). Suppose that I go down to my local computer store to buy a PC. The salesman shows me several models and gives me some information about them. Is this teaching? Hardly. However, he not only tells me about them, but answers my questions and even asks me some of his own to see how much I know already. (By this time the manager is beginning to fidget.) Is this teaching? In fact, the salesman is happy to engage in a general discussion about the pros and cons of the new software, and speculate with me about future developments in the industry. Is this teaching? (By this time, the manager is hold-ing a lengthening queue at bay.) And being extremely thorough, the salesman asks me to try out some keyboard operations to see if I really have grasped what he is talking about, and corrects me several times when I get things wrong. Finally, when I do decide to make the purchase, he offers me a generous discount on the grounds that good users should be rewarded. (By this time, his manager has decided to sack him.) Is this teaching?

Conversely, we can ask at what point official 'teaching' turns into something else: entertainment, indoctrination, socialization, or mere classroom management. How much of the time do we actually teach in the strict sense defined here? (And we must not forget that our students may perceive things differently from us: we may think we are performing one function when they see a different one or none at all: a discrepancy of perception familiar from studies in illuminative evaluation.) The list of functions proposed above cannot provide a precise answer to these questions, but unless we can come up with some answer, unless we can unpack the activity in some such way, all we can say is 'I teach' and leave it at that.

Micro Variables

The list of variables is similar to that in the macro model, and grouped again in terms of the why, what, who and where of teaching, but scaled down to the level of the class or single session. Now, the *rationale* of teaching refers not to the broad aims of the course, but the more specific objectives or agenda of the class or lesson. The *content* is that which is covered in the single lecture, seminar, workshop or lesson, and the *process* the skills, procedures and approaches developed in and through that content. *Level* describes how the actual teaching is pitched, rather than its place in the formal hierarchy of public qualifications.

The headings for the 'who' change somewhat. The external *clients* disappear, since their influence is less likely to impinge at this level of detail. Instead we are concerned with the learning *group*, and the *individuals* within it. The broad concern with staff and staffing narrows down to a focus on *oneself* as teacher. It may seem odd to include oneself as a variable, but self-awareness is an important aspect of our knowledge about teaching, and this issue will come up again in Chapter 5 in the discussion of meta-cognition and self-monitoring.

Rather than the general location of teaching — the campus or site — the *physical setting* now means the actual teaching space: the classroom, lecture theatre, laboratory, workshop or studio. This space constitutes the experienced, concrete context of teaching, and may affect what we do in all sorts of practical ways, so it is important to think about it in some detail. The *organizational setting* may remain an important influence, but at a more microscopic level, for example in terms of our style of teaching, attitudes to pupils or students, and working relations with colleagues. The *social setting* continues to matter, but less in terms of the macro variables of system, structure and selection and more in terms of norms, roles, language and relations in the classroom.

I do not need to rehearse again the general arguments for relating functions and variables that were covered in the previous chapter, or to work through each one systematically. A few examples should suffice to illustrate how we can analyse these variables at the micro level. While there may seem to be one or two key variables in each case, we should remember that the analysis of the Macro Model often threw up other, less obvious ones. The complexity of teaching, and the many compromises and trade-offs within it, stems from the fact that, as noted before, the variables do not always all pull in the same direction, and we may face a conflict or tension between the demands of the content, the student, the organization and perhaps the social setting.

Motivation is a good place to begin, because it again illustrates the potential complexity and subtlety of the teaching situation. It is also a concept with a long and rich history (Biehler and Snowman, 1993, pp. 506–59; Lens, 1995). Our first thought might be that motivation is largely dependent on two things: the individual student's will to learn, and the influence of the teacher in enthusing or discouraging him/her. After all, we tend to speak of well-motivated and poorly motivated students as if these were intrinsic states of being, and we also acknowledge the potential gamut of the teacher's influence, ranging from the inspiring to the crushing or boring. But the kind of group he or she belongs to may also matter to the learner. A good, lively supportive group can lift one's motivation and sustain it; a hostile or negative group can have the opposite effect. Some students can stand out against the group or insulate themselves from its influence, but most do not. So we need to add a third variable in our analysis of motivation.

Surely, however, we should consider the why of learning — the *rationale* — in relation to motivation? Do the learners find that the programme meets their needs, their personal agendas? And what about the content itself, which might equally engage their interest or turn them off? Or it might be pitched too low to challenge them, or too high for them to master; in which case the variable of *level* will matter.

The setting can influence motivation as well. The room might be pleasant or dingy, well or poorly equipped, so stuffy as to send one off to sleep, or just about right to spend several hours in. One might feel welcomed, valued, supported by the institution (as distinct from this particular teacher) or not. And general social norms and expectations — about education, studying, working hard, getting a job, having a good time, not bothering — might also affect one's attitude.

In short, motivation might be affected by any or all of these variables to some degree. The lesson seems to be: we should cast our net widely in the analysis, and consider most or all of the headings, even if at first sight one or two seem to be the obvious ones. So we need to know something about the concept of motivation, and we need to have reflected carefully on our own experience and that of others, within the framework of the model. But we can also bring the learners in on it. After all, it is they who are doing the learning, it is their motivation that is the issue. The functions are and often should be shared functions; so there is every reason to use the model to enable students to analyse their situation, to become real partners in the learning enterprise.

If motivation may be affected by a wide range of things, what about *explanation*? (see Cruickshank and Metcalf, 1995). Surely that is a much simpler function, affected primarily by the individual learner's frame of reference, and the teacher's capacity to relate the subject-matter to it? Again, however, once we start to analyse the situation, other variables intrude. To begin with, the individual's understanding may be affected by the wider group. What is said in classes and seminars may contribute to it; likewise, students often turn to one another for help in trying to figure something out. (The student who works in isolation, perhaps at a distance, may be deprived of this, although 'cybercafés' are beginning to permit such on-line interaction.) But explaining has also to be related to what is being explained — the content — and the level at which it is being explained. The nature of explanation varies from subject to subject: what counts as explaining in maths or science may be rather different from the nature of explanation in history, and even within the latter, there may be different kinds of explanation (Leinhardt, 1993). Likewise, the explanation given to a primary school pupil is likely to be different from that which one will hear at sixth form or undergraduate level.

Organizational and social variables might also affect explaining in some cases. In authoritarian contexts, explanation may simply be reduced to: 'because it is'. Value-systems might rule out certain types of explanation as unacceptable or immoral. Organizations and cultures impose their own boundaries on what can be said and even thought. And we need to consider the possibility that what we regard unproblematically as rational, logical, historical or scientific is in fact culturally variable. This should not be taken as a simple argument for cultural relativism. One might believe, even after such an analysis, that there are basic epistemological commonalities between subjects or cultures, and that hence certain aspects of explanation are universal (for example in terms of concepts such as rationality, causality or evidence). However, it is one thing to arrive at such a position, but it is quite another to start from it. Thus the function of explaining, far from being a delimited interaction between teacher and learner, may be influenced by a wide range of factors.

The *task* and *feedback* functions may also be affected by a range of variables. I alluded earlier to the difficulty of finding the right label for the first, and the various possible terms suggest some of the ways in which learning tasks can in fact vary in terms of *content*. The word 'practise' is often associated with skill or motor tasks, usually in vocational and technical fields. It is also associated with the more routine aspects of language learning, indeed with anything that involves a degree of repetition of a standardized task, leading to a degree of overlearning, that is the capacity to run off the operation without conscious thought or control. But 'practise' is not the word we would normally use of more complex cognitive tasks: we do not usually talk about practising our ideas. The word 'exercise' can have a less routinized connotation — for example one can talk of exercising one's mind in relation to a problem — though the physical analogy is never far away. The original sense of the word 'essay' — from the French *essayer*, meaning to try or try out — is apt for some cognitive tasks, where the learning involves testing out one's ideas. In its broadest meaning, the word 'project' also carries the sense of planning and carrying through some kind of learning task.

The *task* function can thus vary greatly in terms of its content. But the nature of the tasks may also be affected by other variables: the rationale of teaching, the kinds of learning processes involved, the level at which they take place. The tasks will need to be appropriate to the learners both individually and as a group; for example, a teacher may set different tasks for different students if their interests vary or some are more capable or advanced than others. Too easy, and the task will bore them; too difficult, and it will throw them. Some practice will be individual, some will involve pairs, teams or the whole group. The nature, scope and timing of the tasks will also be affected by the physical setting, particularly in practical subjects: How many machines/workstations/terminals are there? How long will it take? Will people have to share or take turns? The availability of books may affect the setting and timing of tasks. And the general pattern of assignment-setting and marking will affect the pattern of practice too; the teacher who departs from the norm here will usually run into trouble with students and colleagues before long. The form of the tasks — classroom activities, quizzes, tests, essays, experiments — will be influenced by the prevailing pattern of work in the institution, and beyond that the system. American teachers tend to set tests much more frequently and regularly than British ones; in some systems oral tasks will be common, in others quite rare.

Even a function as fundamental and apparently general as *feedback* may be affected by a number of variables. Take *content*: whereas it is usually important to give immediate feedback in skill learning, in case bad habits become established, some delay in feedback in cognitive learning can sometimes encourage students to try to work out their own evaluations and judgments, and thus internalize the process. Teachers often vary the feedback they give to take account of the personality of the student: they will be more tactful with the sensitive student, more direct with the confident one. Sometimes feedback will be given to the group as a whole, sometimes individually. And the timing, frequency and depth of feedback will be affected by the prevailing pattern within the institution: the frequency of classes, the amount of contact with students, the length of courses. Social and cultural variables may affect the style of feedback as well, for example in terms of how much explanation there is of judgments or marks, and the general tone of comments.

I have explored how four of the functions — motivate, explain, task and feedback — may each be affected by a number of variables. There is not time, and it should not now be necessary, to argue the same case with all the others. Even brief reflection will suggest ways in which functions such as audit, orientation, input, exploration and reinforcement may be affected by various aspects of the why, what, who and where of teaching. The implication of this goes beyond simply saying that there are more variables affecting what we do than we typically think. It is that we need constantly to bear in mind the multi-faceted nature of our work, even if and when we tend to concentrate on one kind of variable. The subject-centred teacher needs to think about students also, the student-centred one about aims, content, process and level. Both need to reflect on the setting in which they work: the ways in which the physical, organizational and social environments influence what they do. And we all need to reflect upon ourselves: our presence, role, style and approach as a teacher or lecturer. It is partly this multiplicity that makes teaching messy and difficult. We have to focus on what we are doing at the moment we are doing it; but our background awareness has to include a wide range of very different kinds of things. And the most important variable or contingency of all — time — means that we often have to do what we can rather than what we would ideally like; in other words, we have to work with a simplified, stripped-down educational reality rather than the full complexity and subtlety that we know to be there.

The variables can be explored in quite practical ways. Among the activities contained in the training package based on the model (Squires, 1994, pp. 62–78) are the following: describe the ways in which your subject affects your teaching, and compare with this a colleague who teaches a different subject; imagine that you are suddenly asked to teach at a higher or lower level than you normally do; compare two groups that you have recently taught; use Kelly's repertory grid technique to analyse your constructs of a group of students (Bannister and Fransella, 1986; Kelly, 1955); write a pen portrait of yourself as a teacher; draw a diagram/ picture of your ideal teaching space; write a letter of advice to a friend who is coming to teach in your department just as you are about to leave it; and imagine that you have just been asked to go and teach in a different neighbourhood, region or country. Such scenarios and analyses can be used as a focus for small group discussion, and provide a very concrete basis for thinking about these aspects of one's work. And they inevitably draw in discussion of the functions and procedures as well. Paradoxically, this rather schematic framework yields the kind of detailed, practical analysis that is associated with the craft paradigm of teaching: specific, localized, embedded.

The model should therefore be treated not as a counsel of perfection, an impossibly comprehensive and complex ideal. Rather, it offers a framework within which we can interpret our situation, and work out our decisions and actions. This is sometimes in the knowledge that we have had to set some things aside: the niceties of a particular topic, the individual needs of a particular student, some longer-term aim or aspiration, some local regulation. However, the more experienced we are in performing this kind of analysis, the more expert we are likely to become. The model becomes so familiar that, rather like the experienced car driver, we begin to perform some of its operations — analysing the relationship between A and B, considering how X affects Y — almost without thinking. I shall return to that notion in Chapter 5; in the meantime we must consider the third and last dimension of the micro model, procedures.

Micro Procedures

In the Macro Model, the third dimension of Procedures referred to the stages or tasks involved in putting on a course. Here it refers to the methods and techniques of teaching a class or session. It is significant that we are coming to 'methods' last, because in many books on teaching they come first. Or to be more precise: in many textbooks on the subject, teaching is conceptualized in terms of methods, and indeed much public debate about it is couched in terms of methods. The whole of the preceding discussion should have made clear why one cannot begin with methods.

Methods are the means of doing something; they are the vehicles of the activity. But they are not logically synonymous with the activity. Methods are methods of something, in this case teaching, but we cannot reduce teaching simply to its methods, any more than we can architecture, engineering, nursing or social work.

First, we have to describe the nature of the activity, in terms of its functions and the contingencies that affect them; then and only then can we logically go on to see how those contingent functions are carried out, in terms of the procedures that are used.

The ten methods listed in the Micro Model represent those commonly used in post-school education, and which one typically finds described in texts on the subject (see, for example, Brown and Atkins, 1988; McKeachie, 1986). In the school setting, the typical class is likely to involve a mix of these methods, and indeed one of the issues in schoolteaching is the relative emphasis that should be placed on whole group presentations, question and answer, small group work, individualized tasks, classwork and homework, and so on. In most cases, there are alternative labels for each procedure, and readers may find these more familiar or comfortable to use. This does not matter greatly, and reflects differences of context and usage. It is the essential form of each method that matters. The list begins with two procedures that can be used with large groups, *presentation* and *demonstration*. These are both essentially one-way methods, although some forms of interaction and response can be built into them, through, for example, short quizzes, pauses for questions, or episodes of small group work. Usually, the smaller the group, the easier it becomes to have such interaction. Demonstration differs from presentation in having a greater visual or enactive element; it is about showing rather than just telling. It is worth remembering that there may be an element of *modelling* — acting out or exemplifying what is to be learned — in both.

The next heading, *question and answer*, is not usually regarded as a method at all in its own right, and in practice is usually associated with other methods, such as following a presentation ('any questions now?') or preceding some practical work ('before you get on with this . . .'). However, it is important to give it its own heading, for two reasons. First, it can account for quite substantial amounts of teaching time, both with groups and with individuals; it is not uncommon for a lecturer to spend five or ten minutes at a stretch posing or dealing with questions. Secondly, although questioning and answering are part and parcel of everyday interaction, and hence part of the common sense of teaching, they are in fact quite skilled and subtle procedures. There are various ways of framing and responding to questions, and as I pointed out earlier, the most obvious ones do not always lead to the most effective learning. Sometimes an open-ended rather than a closed question is needed to stimulate thinking and move beyond the simple, convergent response. Sometimes avoiding a straight reply — throwing the question back to the questioner or to others in the group, reframing it, linking it to something else — will generate more discussion than simply giving the student what he or she initially wants (Squires, 1994, pp. 88–90). Question and answer lie at the heart of the processes of explaining and exploring, and for that reason alone need to be highlighted. They should form an explicit part of the skill training of every teacher, just as much as giving a presentation or demonstration.

The next three methods — *discussion, simulation* and *practical* — tend by their nature to be used with smaller groups, although small in this instance can mean anything from five to over twenty. Where the group is at the upper end of that range, one usually has to divide it into sub-groups to get the necessary interaction, although the dynamics of practical work depend very much on the availability and nature of the equipment: some practical learning is purely individual. All three methods involve 'doing' by the learner; the differences lies along a spectrum ranging from the verbal, through the simulated, to the concrete or physical. Discussion may range from the formal seminar, based on a paper, through various kinds of structured discussion, to completely free-ranging, open-ended and sometimes leaderless discussion. Simulations may involve role-plays, games or computer-based simulations. The nature of practical work depends very much on the subject: laboratory experiments in science, clinical teaching in medicine, workshops in technical subjects, studio or rehearsal work in the arts, training sessions in sport.

The four final headings cover other methods, which tend to be individualized rather than used with small or large groups. *Supervision*, tutoring or coaching, typically occurs with one or a handful of learners, and is geared to individual work. It may involve an element of counselling as well as teaching. Supervision is often related to *assignments*, although the latter can refer to any kind of work that is set for students to do outside the classroom. *Projects* involve longer pieces of such work, usually for individuals but sometimes for groups. Having originated in science and technological fields, they are now a common feature of teaching across the whole of further and higher education, and consequently their nature varies from subject to subject. They all, however, require a fair degree of autonomy and self-management on the part of the student. *Placements* involve students going outside the educational environment altogether, to get a specific kind of work or social experience.

As noted above, this list is a fairly conventional one, and not too much should be made of the actual headings. Readers might want to amend them, to include ones that are typical of their own particular field: the mathematician may want to include problem classes, the geographer field trips, the musician performances, the lawyer case work. The list here is only a general one, a point of departure. Also, since there is an extensive literature on all these methods of teaching, there will be no attempt here to discuss any of them in detail. Their main features, and the skills and techniques they involve, are widely documented.

There is also a substantial literature on the growing potential and use of technology in relation to these various procedures. Earlier forms of educational technology were used primarily to enhance or replace one-way methods such as presentation and demonstration. Radio and audiotapes, film, video and off-air TV have now been used for some decades to present and demonstrate material to learners, and indeed can have distinct advantages over the conventional lecture or demonstration in doing this. The newer technology, however, goes well beyond such one-way traffic. The combination of media, computers and modern communications systems (such as ISDNs) allows many of the interactive features of other methods to be introduced. Presentations can now be followed up with question and answer sessions. Computer-based simulations and games can take account of the responses of the learner to the information presented to him or her. Telematics allows one-to-one real-time supervision to take place over thousands of miles, including the facility of showing and sharing documents just as one might in the same room. Interactive real-time networks can replicate some of the features of a group discussion. Students can send large chunks of projects by e-mail attachment, and tutors can respond with detailed comments on them. Technology, which initially seemed to depersonalize teaching, is now re-personalizing it again. This enables open and distance learning to fulfil better the macro function of interaction, and helps learners to create or recreate a learning environment of their own. While the new technology has stimulated hopes and fears in almost equal measure, there seems no reason to worry about its use in teaching as long as it is seen, like conventional procedures, in the overall context of teaching functions and variables. The model should thus help us to find the right use and place for communications and information technology, just as it does for traditional methods.

What does concern us here, in the context of the model, is (a) what we actually mean by a teaching procedure and (b) how this dimension relates to the other two. It may seem strange to pose the first question. Surely we all know what we mean by teaching methods? As noted above, a method is a way of going about something, doing something. Of course, much of our life is procedural in this way; we are constantly concerned with and involved in going about things and carrying out things. Common-sense knowledge is partly knowledge of procedures: what one does, what one doesn't do, how to get round the problem if one can't do it, and so on. The point about methods in teaching — or in any other profession — is that, as noted earlier, they go beyond this stock of common-sense know-how. They require something a bit more specialized, tailored to the needs of that particular occupation. Thus, although common-sense know-how will enable us to ask and answer questions, the process of question-and-answer in teaching requires something different, something beyond everyday expertise. Indeed, as noted earlier, where common sense would suggest that we reply to a question, the best strategy might be not to, to turn the question back on the questioner. Likewise, although we can all talk to other people, giving an extended presentation lasting 20 or 30 minutes to a sizeable group goes beyond the normal scope of our perorations, and requires some extra skills and techniques (such as structuring our presentation into several stages, varying the pace and tone, and maintaining eye contact with everyone).

The implication of this is that although our everyday know-how provides quite a good basis for methods of teaching, we need to acquire some additional skills related to each particular method. It is in this sense that we can speak of methods as 'technique': the dedicated and practised capacity to do something in a particular way. It is this that constitutes the element of craft and skill in teaching. I argued earlier that although we cannot regard teaching simply as a craft — the term is too limiting, too procedural — teaching does involve elements of craft skills. These are things that can be demonstrated, observed, imitated, learned, developed and refined, and in this they are no different from skills in technical and vocational fields, or sports and the arts. The good footballer or good musician has to practise, hard and regularly. Teachers may not have to be quite so rigorous in this regard, but they do need to take their skills seriously. This implies plenty of opportunities for observation and practice.

Why might teachers and lecturers not take such skills seriously? One problem is that professionals can look down on mere skill and technique, as something that is cognitively beneath them. To point out to the eminent physics professor that he is dropping his voice at the end of the sentence is — one may feel — to introduce a consideration that is trivial in terms of what usually occupies his thoughts. And 'skill' often has a dubious status in education: witness the lowly historical status of the vocational and technical in the British system.

Craft and skill are also important for a different kind of reason, which is most obvious in schools but latent everywhere. This is that most teaching takes place in social situations. In the Macro Model, I noted that in general terms a course has to be *managed* and should provide a good learning *environment*. These ideas acquire a much sharper focus at the level of the class. Methods and procedures are employed not in a vacuum, but in a classroom full of 11-year olds, a lecture hall seating 300, a busy workshop, or some other setting. There is a substantial literature on classroom management in relation to the schools, which stems partly from the work of Kounin (for an overview see Kyriacou, 1997, pp. 77–100) and a considerable emphasis on it in school teacher training. At the other end of the spectrum, writing on adult education has long stressed the social dynamics of the class, and the importance of developing rapport and building a strong group sense. The skills of the teacher, lecturer or tutor are thus not purely pedagogical, but social as well. As I noted earlier, the procedures we use are embedded in social situations, and it is difficult sometimes to say where the educational ends and the social begins. The skilled teacher sometimes seems to have antennae growing out of her head, which allow her to filter out signals from noise, and to pick up what is going on in all parts of the room — a kind of living GCHQ.

I need to stress the importance of craft and skill in teaching for another and more specific reason. The whole model set out in this book constitutes a refutation of the view that teaching can be seen merely in terms of methods. Teaching is not methods: methods are the means of teaching. But by the same token we must not dismiss them. They constitute one of the three dimensions, without which the model would be incomplete. It is not enough to know about teaching, to conceptualize and analyse it, to be sensitive to it and to reflect on it. In the end we have to do it, and that doing inescapably involves methods, techniques, procedures and skills. There is no alternative to buckling down to acquiring, practising and refining them to point where we can use them well.

However, the argument can be pushed further. Doyle (1988) has argued that methods go beyond the procedural in the sense that they are the 'enactment' of teaching. In fact, 'method' in the past connoted not just a particular technique, for example giving a lecture, but a whole approach to teaching, and it is in that sense that people talked of Socratic method, or the methods of Comenius, Froebel or Montessori. Method was linked to the notion of didactics, which was itself a broad concept, and the formal study of method predated the emergence of laboratory psychology. The distinction I have drawn between function and procedure means that I have adopted a somewhat narrower interpretation of 'method' here; most of the broader connotations are wrapped up in the various functions. However, Doyle's point is a valuable warning against too reductive an approach to our third question: *How do they do it?*

Methods are also important in a different kind of way, which relates back to the discussion of *task* in the micro functions. One of the merits of the concept of learning tasks is that it directs our attention not only to the content but to the form of learning: the fact that the student is not simply studying history, but has to do an *essay* on The Dreyfus Affair. An essay, of 2000 words, properly referenced, hand-written or typed, using one side of the page only, by Thursday morning: that is the requirement that the student actually faces over his or her pint of beer in the Union.

Methods of teaching are thus not purely transparent, not mere means: they format and concretize learning in certain ways. These formats become utterly familiar, almost second nature. One sign of this is the sense of shock all round when teachers decide to vary the format, and ask the student to do something different: not to write an essay, but to give a poster presentation or act out a role play. Whereas the content of teaching and learning is endlessly varying, the forms are limited and predictable. Content comes packaged in familiar ways, learning involves certain predictable routines: lectures, seminars, problem-classes, lab reports, essays, tests, projects, exams.

But what do these forms and formats do to the content? Do we end up 'essay-ing' novels, 'reporting' science, 'seminarizing' social realities, seeing history in terms of 50-minute answers? What is the novel? Is it the physical book? The text as we read it? The text as we discuss it? The text as we write about it? One does not need to go far down the deconstructionist road to raise questions about the way we structure our educational realities. And that structuring goes beyond teaching methods, to involve the institutional and professional forms we give them. Bodies of knowledge are also bodies of people. Economics is a subject, but it is also a department, a part of a building, a particular group of staff, signs on doors, a chair, conferences, journals, funding headings, research categories. The universe of knowledge is divided into faculties, schools, departments, research units, the physical expression of cognitive compartments.

We may seem to have come a long way from teaching methods, but the underlying point is the same. The means and forms of teaching structure and colour our perception of the whole activity; what we do is entangled with how we do it. One sign of this is the ferocity of arguments that can spring up about apparently trivial, practical matters, such as the format of lab reports, the required length of essays, submission dates, or some proposed change in assessment. The forms matter; procedures are never just that.

Procedures, Functions and Variables

Having looked at the procedures themselves, I want to explore briefly how they relate to the functions and variables. After all, the model is a three-dimensional one, an integral whole; the dimensions do not exist in isolation. The consequences of this for the way we think about procedures are quite radical. A good deal of discussion and research over the years has gone into comparisons between teaching methods. Such comparisons attempt to establish whether, for example, lectures are more or less effective than small group teaching, whether individualized instruction is superior to conventional class work, whether programmed learning or computer-assisted learning compares favourably or not with other methods.

The form of the model implies that at best such comparisons are misleading, at worst meaningless. The error lies in treating teaching as a single thing, a unitary process that can be carried out by this or that method. The model, by contrast, disaggregates teaching into a number of functions, so the question has to be: What methods are most effective for performing what functions in what circumstances? The idea that one method is simply better than another, *tout court*, goes out the window.

This makes the research agenda a good deal more complex, but hopefully more productive in the end. Instead of the older, simple comparative approach criticized by Dubin and Taveggia in *The Teaching–Learning Paradox* (1968) we should be able to formulate more focused empirical questions, and indeed this is the direction in which the research has already gone. Such questions investigate the use of certain methods in relation to certain functions and in the context of certain circumstances. Such limited parameters make it more difficult to arrive at broad generalizations about methods, but the hope must be that over time the aggregation of such studies through meta-analysis can move us forward. In other words, what looks like a more modest research ambition might in the end yield more than grandiose attempts to generalize across the board.

Two points should be noted about such research questions. First, they have to put functions first, and look at the methods in relation to them. This is only logical: the methods constitute forms or means of fulfilling the functions. This, as I have noted, reverses much of the conventional thinking, and helps to put the horse back before the cart. Secondly, it is quite possible that a particular method may be effective in terms of some functions but not others. For example, a lecture might be a good method of orientating or reinforcing learning — mapping out the field of study beforehand, drawing threads together at the end — but not so good in terms of transmitting detailed information, which one can get more easily from a text, and pretty hopeless in terms of explaining or exploring, which require interactive methods such as discussion and supervision. Small group teaching might be effective in terms of explaining and exploring, but not a very effective means of auditing prior learning (which may require something more individualized) or of inputting information. Learning packages or software might be effective in terms of auditing prior learning, orientating new learning, transmitting information and even (within limits) explaining problems, but incapable of meeting the less predictable needs of exploration and reflection. Project work might score well on many of the functions, but miss out on regular feedback because of the solo nature and longer rhythm of the work. Questions about motivation hover over all the methods: Which of them seem to engage the learners best?

That last question is still unanswerable in general terms, because much will depend on the way individuals and groups react to each method. And this shows why even the above questions remain too generalized: we have to bring in the third dimension of contingencies, because the use of each method will be affected by the why, what, who and where of the teaching situation. To begin with, subjects have their own norms and patterns in terms of teaching methods. Rightly or wrongly, these are believed to reflect the nature and demands of the discipline. As noted earlier, the mathematician may rely on a good deal of board work or OHP work. Language teaching may necessitate drills to be carried out in the class or the language laboratory. Science may require a lot of experimental work; engineering or architecture may involve projects. The pauses and silences in the English seminar might astonish the chemist. And so on. Whether these patterns really do stem from the nature of the subject is a moot point, but they do affect the choice and use of each method.

Methods are also, rightly or wrongly, associated with different levels and sectors of education. The hive of individual activity in the primary classroom, the whole class teaching in the secondary one, the workshop session in the technical college, the lecture in higher education, the group discussion in adult education: all these are to some extent stereotypes that may or may not match the reality or the need, but they influence the way people teach, because they constitute norms that individuals can find it difficult or impossible to go against. Practical considerations — the size of rooms, the access to equipment, the length and frequency of timetable slots, the opportunity for privacy with a student — equally affect the pattern of methods. Beyond these factors, there are others again, more elusive perhaps: the extent to which the methods enact the aims and objectives of the course (does lecturing develop critical thinking, do individual assignments develop teamwork?); the extent to which they reflect the ethos of the organization (authoritarian or democratic, collectivist or individualist); the extent to which they mirror or diverge from the norms of the wider society. People who try to import teaching methods from one culture into another can run into problems; if open-ended discussion or self-directed learning are not the general norm, they can seem very strange to the students.

It is the job of educational researchers to investigate the general relationships between functions, methods and contingencies, and if patterns emerge, these can provide useful guidelines for teachers and institutions in making their decisions about methods. But, ultimately, the practitioner has to operate not only in relation to the functions but in the context of the contingencies. The best method will be the best in the circumstances; and as Voltaire said, the best may be the enemy of the good. But in any case, the plurality of functions suggests that a plurality of methods will be needed. No one procedure is likely to fulfil all the functions effectively, so we will need to look for the best mix we can find.

Learning to Learn

In the emphasis on teaching methods, it is all too easy to forget what the learner is doing. For each of the methods listed in the Micro Model, there are complementary procedures or methods required of the learner, such as the following:

PRESENTATION: listening, note-taking
DEMONSTRATION: observing, listening, note-taking
QUESTION AND ANSWER: answer and question
DISCUSSION: speaking, listening, interacting
SIMULATION: observing, empathizing, acting
PRACTICAL: organizing, performing, reporting
SUPERVISION: speaking, listening, writing
PLACEMENT: performing, interacting, organizing, reporting
ASSIGNMENT: organizing, researching, reading, writing
PROJECT: planning, managing, researching, reading, writing

The list is by no means exhaustive, and one might want to add various learning methods and skills that reflect the particularities of the subject or level of work. Here, however, it is the general point that needs to be reiterated. Teaching is a collaborative activity in which teacher and learner play various roles. Even where most of the input and direction come from the teacher, the learner still needs to play his or her complementary part; and in many cases, the learner's role goes beyond this to become a shared or even dominant one. Learning to learn can be succinctly defined as the growing capacity to internalize and take over the model.

The model can thus be turned 'inside out'. It is as relevant to pupils and students as it is to teachers and lecturers, and indeed has been developed partly through work with them. It offers a comprehensive and coherent conception of learning to learn, which goes well beyond the typical emphasis in such work on learning skills or learning styles. It implies that learning to learn involves, first, involvement in and the gradual assimilation of the functions of teaching, both at the micro and macro levels. The learner not only begins to internalize the functions of motivation, audit, orientation, and input; he or she can take some responsibility for resourcing and managing learning, creating a learning environment, fostering interaction with others, and so on, not to mention selecting the right course in the first place. Secondly, the learner can begin to think about the variables that affect his or her work: the relationship between the formal rationale of the course and his or her own personal agenda; the nature and demands of the content and the process; the relationships with staff and peers; the impact of the various settings. Gradually, he or she develops the capacity to 'read' the learning situation, and take account of the factors that affect his or her work, in particular any that give rise to problems. Thirdly, he or she can develop the methods and skills that complement those of the teachers, and learn how to take notes, cope with large amounts of reading, communicate and interact with others, engage in practical work, structure and present essays and reports, plan projects, tackle tests and examinations, and so on. But these kinds of skills are unlikely actually to impact on the basic process of learning unless they are related to the functions and variables: to self, task and situation.

The tendency to see teaching purely procedurally in terms of methods has been paralleled historically by the tendency to see studying purely procedurally in terms of skills. The more sophisticated literature on the latter has been moving away from such a simplistic view for some time now. In line with that trend, this model offers a framework for thinking about learning to learn in a deeper and more comprehensive way than one finds in the typical study guide. There is little point refining our ideas about teachers' teaching if we do not do the same for students' learning.

Conclusion

The picture of teaching that has emerged from this and the previous chapter is an extremely complex one. It is not enough to view teaching in terms of one or even two dimensions, one has to take account of all three. And even the limited analysis carried out here has shown that the relationships between the headings on those three dimensions are numerous and often go beyond the more obvious ones that may first come to mind. Rather than a symmetrical array of intersecting headings — 2000 little boxes — the macro and micro models begin to seem like an infinitely complex web of connections, a network of densely textured relations and meanings.

In one way, this is reassuring, because it gives us some purchase on the real complexity of the activity. It shows why we are justified in seeing teaching as a professional discipline, comparable in the degree if not always the kinds of complexity that one finds in other professions. And it suggests why the various paradigms set out in Chapter 1 — common-sense, art, craft, competence and so on — are for various reasons inadequate. In another way, however, the picture is a daunting one. How can one begin to tackle such an activity? How can one bear in mind so many different things? How can people teach without such a model, as they clearly do? How on earth does anyone teach at all? A few final, general points should be made.

First, it is important to hang on to the functions. It is they, I have argued, which define the essence of the activity, just as the functions of the doctor define the essence of medicine. It is they which we can best relate to learning, although the research evidence is stronger in terms of some functions than others. If a function is not being properly fulfilled, it is either because it has not been adequately fine-tuned in relation to the variables, or it has not been executed skilfully enough in terms of procedures. But in either case, it is ultimately the function that matters.

Secondly, the model can be used both as a whole and in parts. As a whole, it offers a permanent, stable and reasonably comprehensive framework for thinking about teaching, for saying 'This is what I do.' It defines the scope of the activity, and acts as a kind of general aide-memoire or checklist, which should help to ensure that one at least considers all the various aspects of the situation. Most of the time, however, we are concerned not with teaching as a whole but with a particular problem or decision: how to approach this, what to do about that. We make our way through the particular. In these cases, we are much more likely to begin with a specific heading — selection, assessment, the group, project work — and think it through in relation to the other headings that seem to bear on it. So one does not have to deal with everything all the time, but the work on specifics progressively fills and fleshes out the understanding of the model as a whole. Rather like a person who goes into a dark room with a flashlight, one gradually builds up a sense of what is there by shining it now on one thing, now on another.

The other thing to be said is that although some of the headings in the model may initially be unfamiliar, there is likely to be very little in it that is actually new to most people. What is new is the way it is ordered and put together. So although the model is complex and detailed, the dominant sense is, in my experience, one of recognition, of a way of representing what (in some sense) is already known. The model offers a more formal, analytic language for talking about things that are often couched in the educational vernacular, if they are articulated at all. But the things to which it refers are, if not exactly common sense, at least commonly experienced, common points of reference.

This last statement opens up the wider question of what models such as this do or can hope to do. The model may offer a framework and a language for thinking about teaching, a heuristic device for analysing problems and decisions. But is that likely to make people better teachers (or learners)? How does such representation, articulation or analysis relate to what teachers actually do? We are back to the old issue of theory and practice.

Chapter 5

Theory, Expertise and Practice

This book has been concerned primarily with the ontology of teaching — what it is. The models set out in the two previous chapters can be seen as attempts to develop, in some detail, the general ontology of professional disciplines presented in Chapter 2 and to apply it specifically to teaching.

Jackson raises the question as to 'whether it is possible to define teaching ontologically — in a way that speaks of its true meaning or essence — without also getting entangled with a definition that is axiological — one that involves the meaning of "good " teaching' (1986, p. 94, n. 16). 'Good' here is being used in the sense not just of effective, but ethical. The discussion of the instrumentality of professions in Chapter 2 suggests why there can be no easy answer to this question. Of all the professions, education arguably carries the most obvious ethical load, since it is concerned with meanings and values through the curriculum. But even the process of teaching is usually thought to have certain ethical features that, for example, are commonly used to distinguish it from training, indoctrination or socialization. Interestingly, the notion of learning seems, by contrast, to be largely value-free, and the current shift in public discourse from 'teaching' to 'learning' (as in notions such as the learning society) raises questions about possible value shifts as well.

It could well be argued that this model does become entangled with axiological issues, particularly in the list of functions it sets out. The notion that such functions can be carried out not only by the teacher but by the learner and his or her peers also has ethical implications, in terms of authority, responsibility, autonomy and empowerment. However, the contingent nature of the model and the strong emphasis on situational variables means that it is difficult to draw direct ethical conclusions from it. A great deal depends on how much emphasis one places on the various functions, and that in turn depends largely on the situational variables: largely, but perhaps not wholly, since a complete absence of, say, explanation, exploration or reflection would raise questions about whether this still counted as teaching. As I have already said, there is no simple response to Jackson's point, but it remains an important one to consider.

This chapter will, however, be concerned with a second major question. What is the relationship between the ontology and the epistemology of teaching, between what it is and what we know about it? In this respect, the approach taken in this book is diametrically opposed to that taken in most of the current literature. There has been a great deal of writing in the last two decades on the epistemology of teaching — in terms of craft knowledge, teachers' knowledge-bases, the use of research evidence, the nature of professional judgment, and so on — but by and large such writing assumes the ontology of teaching to be unproblematic. We all, it seems, know what teaching is. By contrast, the assumption here has been that we have to establish an ontology of teaching before tackling the epistemological issues. In short, we have to be clear what we are talking about, before we can begin to say what we know about it.

Having attempted to set out an ontology of teaching, I will therefore move on in this chapter to explore the nature of our knowledge and know-how in this functional, contingent and procedural activity, and the kind or kinds of expertise that teachers as professionals have. I shall begin, if not quite at the beginning, then very near it.

Aristotle Revisited

The fact that teaching is still discussed in terms of theory and practice would be reason enough to go back to the origins of these concepts in Aristotle's work, even without the intrinsic interest of what he has to say about the nature of disciplines. Of course, Aristotle himself inherited these terms from previous thinkers, so they already carried with them certain resonances affecting his use of them. In particular, according to Lobkowicz (1967, pp. 6–8) the term *theoria* connoted ideas of spectating, which reflected its origins in the role of those who attended but did not participate in religious festivals or games, sometimes as official delegates of another city-state.

There are a number of obvious and less obvious problems in going back to source in this particular case. First, there are textual difficulties. Aristotle's works are rather less finished and polished than Plato's; indeed they have been described as lecture notes rather than finalized texts (Barnes, 1976, pp. 15–16). There are occasional repetitions and also doubts about additions or amendments by subsequent editors. The flow of argument is not always smooth and linear; sometimes the text appears to digress from the main line of analysis to tackle a related point, sometimes it returns again to a previous topic.

A second obvious problem is that of translation. The glossary of key terms in the Penguin edition (Thompson, 1976, pp. 367–70) typically gives two or three equivalents for the Greek, and some of these will be cited below. (To simplify matters, I have omitted the standard accents in transliterations of the Greek.) Over and above these obvious difficulties, there are the more subtle problems of interpretation. The mere fact that terms such as 'theory' and 'practice' have persisted in use over two millennia should alert us to possible shifts in their meaning over that time. We cannot simply assume that what we understand by them is what Aristotle meant. Related to this is the danger of abstracting such terms from the complex network of concepts to which they belong, taking them out of their intellectual context. Many of the other terms to which they were related — terms such as *sophia* (skill, wisdom) or *nous* (intelligence, intuition) — no longer have general currency, but this does not mean that they are unimportant in themselves, or in locating notions such as theory and practice within the wider system of thought.

The word 'system' brings up a third kind of difficulty. What Aristotle said is not just a matter of the content of particular passages, but of the general tenor and approach of his work (Ackrill, 1981, p. 4). There is a certain feel to it, a style of philosophizing, which is difficult to pin down in terms of specific concepts. One aspect of this is the relative importance he accords to certain ideas. Thus although he explicitly accords *theoria* a higher place than other kinds of thinking because it is closest to the divine, the amount of time and effort he devotes to other kinds of thought and activity give a somewhat different message: that they too have their value and place in the scheme of things, and should not simply be seen in relation to theory. Indeed, Randall argues that Aristotle makes no attempt to rank the different forms of thinking in terms of value (Randall, 1960, pp. 78–9). It should also be remembered that much of this analysis takes place in the context of a moral, rather than purely epistemological question: What is the good life?

With these cautions in mind, we can now turn to the issues. The bulk of the references will be to Book 6 of the *Nicomachean Ethics*, where Aristotle sets out his views on different forms of *dianoia* (thinking), but I shall also draw on passages in Books A, E and K of the *Metaphysics*, which also bear on the issues. And although it is not possible here to refer in any detail to other parts of his corpus of work, my analysis will attempt to reflect something of the extraordinary range of his preoccupations, and the fact, for example, that he concerned himself in other texts with the practicalities of politics and the arts. The references are all to the standard translation by Ross (1925).

One other prefatory point should be made. One's reading of Aristotle is likely to depend a good deal on whether one is focusing on the education system or the teaching profession. (The same would be true of the justice system and the legal profession, the health service and the medical profession, and so on.) Aristotle regarded education as a public matter which has important ethical, social and politcal consequences, and he had a good deal to say about it, particularly in Books VII and VIII of the *Politics,* where he enters into a detailed though unfortunately incomplete discussion of the curriculum, including the niceties of music and gymnastics. My focus in this book is on teaching. Since teaching is a central feature of education, it cannot but be ethically and socially dimensioned, but the task here is to explore how the process or profession of teaching looks in Aristotelian terms, and in particular in the light of his distinction between different kinds of knowledge or thinking.

Theoretical, Practical and Productive Thinking

The person who thinks of teaching, or indeed any other profession, in terms of theory and practice is likely to be in for two surprises when he or she goes back to see what Aristotle actually said on the subject. The first surprise is that one is apparently faced with a trichotomy rather than the familiar dichotomy. In the

Table 5.1   Forms of dianoia *(thinking, intellectual activity, discipline)*

Theoria (knowing, understanding)	*Episteme* (knowledge, scientific knowledge, deduction, induction)
Praxis (practice, action, doing)	*Phronesis* (practical wisdom, practical sense, prudence)
Poiesis (producing, making, creating)	*Techne* (art, craft)

Metaphysics (E, 1, 1025b), Aristotle suggests that all thinking (*dianoia*) can be divided into three kinds — the theoretical, the practical and the productive — and in the *Nicomachean Ethics* he devotes several pages to distinguishing between the last two (NE, 6, 1140a, b). Each kind of thinking has a different aim, and involves a different form of knowledge or know-how, as set out in Table 5.1.

A number of points need to be made about this classification. First, there are the problems mentioned above of the sheer translation of the terms. *Dianoia* is generally translated as 'thought' or 'thinking' but one also finds 'reasoning' (Randall, 1960, p. 76) and 'intellectual activity' (Edel, 1982, p. 388), and Ross uses both 'science' and 'knowledge' (Ross, 1949, pp. 20, 187). The term 'discipline', which is also sometimes found (see, for example, Barnes, 1976, p. 23) is perhaps justified by the fact that some of the examples Aristotle gives of the different forms of *dianoia* are what we, in modern terms, would call disciplines, but we cannot be sure that our notion of a discipline — which involves not only the epistemological but the institutional and professional structures we associate with, say, physics or history — is quite what he had in mind. The institutionalization and professional-ization of organized knowledge is a subsequent phenomenon, and our concept of a discipline is no doubt shaped by what happened in universities in medieval, Renaiss-ance and more recent times. Thus when we talk of Aristotle's classification of disciplines, we need to be careful about the connotations of that term.

There are similar problems with the other terms. Theorizing, for Aristotle, seems to have been a purely cognitive enterprise, aimed at knowing the world; and there is little or no sense that such knowledge might be applied in some way. *Theoria* is concerned with things that are non-contingent and cannot be otherwise than they are, though Reeve argues that contingency depends on the degree of 'enmatteredness' (Reeve, 1992, p. 78). *Theoria* is the domain of science, as Aris-totle understood it, particularly the natural sciences, but above all of philosophy. And although *episteme* is sometimes translated as 'scientific knowledge', the main thrust is deductive rather than inductive, hence the place of modern empirical or experimental science in this scheme of things is less salient than it would be for us (Urmson, 1988, p. 80).

Praxis is usually translated by its modern equivalent 'practice', but here again the sense is not quite the same. For Aristotle, it has to do with the moral dimension of action and behaviour. The highest expression of *praxis* is in politics, that is in the ways in which people live together in society, although it can be seen on a smaller scale in the life of a household, although Lobkowicz argues that this is a later addition (Lobkowicz, 1967, p. 82). Thus Lobkowicz sees the theory–practice distinction as, in one sense, between two kinds of life, that of the philosopher, who stands back from the world in order to know it, and that of the politically active citizen, who is heavily involved in social and political choices and decisions (ibid., pp. 3–5). The virtue of *praxis* lies not simply in its outcome but in itself, in the process of right decision and action; it is thus an intrinsic rather than instrumental value, a form of being good. It involves the ability to make right decisions in particular cases in the light of our general understanding of what is good; and the more general and comprehensive that understanding, the better. Good *praxis* is unlikely to come from a limited or narrow perspective on the world. Likewise, *phronesis* is a generalized wisdom or sense in dealing with the world, which illuminates and informs our concrete, specific decisions. It is concerned with the 'ultimate particular', but always in the context of the general. It is something that comes with experience and develops with reflection and deliberation. It is not a set of fixed principles, because it belongs to the domain of the contingent; indeed Aristotle warns us not to expect more precision in such matters than is possible. Interestingly, at one point Broadie (1991, p. 208) translates *praxis* as 'conduct', though in the sense of the morally dimensioned action, rather than external, socially sanctioned behaviour.

Poiesis is frequently translated as productive thinking, but the modern sense of that word is probably too narrow and mechanical for what is intended. The sense is rather that of a process that results in an artefact or outcome of some kind, although not all the examples Aristotle gives of *poiesis* are tangible: they range from what we would regard as craft or technology through medicine to music. The common factor, however, is that something results from the activity, and the emphasis is on that outcome rather than (as with *praxis*) the process itself. Moreover, that outcome is quite identifiable; *poiesis* refers to specific, delimited activities or domains, in contrast to the rather general ethico-political notion of *praxis*.

Equally, the term *techne* is probably broader and less routinized than would be suggested by our 'technical' or 'technique'; indeed 'know-how' or 'procedural knowledge' in the modern psychological sense might be a more accurate equivalent. To translate *techne* by 'craft' seems too limiting, to translate it by 'art' usually too vague; both terms are coloured by their own subsequent historical associations, craft by the concrete, craft guilds of medieval Europe, art by the romantic and expressive conceptions of the nineteenth century. Even in modern Greece, one is as likely to see the word *techniki* on the front of an art museum as on the side of an electrician's van.

Nussbaum (1986, pp. 94–121) discusses the concept of *techne* at some length, distinguishing between three kinds: *techne* that issues in an artefact (such as a pot or piece of furniture); *techne* that results in a change of state (such as medicine); and *techne* that leads to a performance (such as music or dancing). She argues that the term in all cases implies four characteristics: universality, teachability, precision and a concern with explanation rather than just operation. She also argues that the concepts of *techne* and *episteme* are closer than is often thought. This suggests that none of our possible modern equivalents quite fits the bill. However, it does point us away from the more limited connotations of craft or routinized notions of production to something that is cognitively complex and informed by its own kind of knowledge — characteristics that may be relevant to the modern concept of profession.

A further problem with the above, simplified three-part scheme is that it omits other kinds of intellectual 'virtues' such as reason and wisdom, which may play a role in the various kinds of thinking; the differences between the kinds of knowledge and know-how associated with each of the three are thus not as sharp as might appear here. The fact remains that, as noted above, we seem to be faced with a tripartite distinction rather than the familiar binary one. There has been a good deal of debate about whether the distinction between the practical and the productive is a primary or secondary one (Ackrill, 1981, pp. 142–43; Ando, 1965, pp. 175–207; Broadie, 1991, pp. 185–212). The two forms of thinking do have certain things in common. They both involve some kind of doing in the world, whereas theoretical thinking is directed purely at contemplation or knowledge. Unlike *theoria*, they are also both contingent, in the sense of being concerned with things that can be otherwise than they are. And in both practical and productive thought, the 'source of motion' lies in the person rather than in the phenomenon, whereas *theoria* is concerned with things that 'move themselves'.

However, there are also good reasons to avoid simply collapsing the scheme into our familiar duality. First, Aristotle, particularly in the *Nicomachean Ethics*, goes to some trouble to elaborate it, although the degree of emphasis on it seems to vary somewhat from place to place. Attempts to reduce the trichotomy to a dichotomy must also fall under the general suspicion of a retrospective reading: of imposing the way we think on the way he did. As Lobkowicz (1967, 1977) has pointed out, there is much in the subsequent history of ideas — early Christian, medieval, Renaissance, Cartesian — that reinforces dualism in our thinking: the distinctions between pure and applied, active and contemplative, spirit and flesh, mind and body. We have become very used to seeing the world in dichotomies and polarities, and it may be precisely this that makes it difficult for us to get our minds round what Aristotle proposed (see also Edel, 1982, pp. 339–40).

The second and even greater surprise for the modern educationist is that Aristotle does not talk about applying *theoria* to *praxis* or relating *praxis* to *theoria*. In other words, he does not see as a problem what many current writers on education and other professions see as a problem, namely the 'gap' between theory and practice. Indeed the main thrust of his argument goes in quite the opposite direction. For him, *theoria* and *praxis* are not two aspects of the same thing, but two distinct, different and autonomous modes of thinking and acting; and the same applies to *poiesis*, which is also, it must emphasized, a form of thinking, rather than simply an activity. Although Aristotle did have things to say about the relationship between thought and action, for example in the respective roles of intellect and habit in moral development (Burnyeat, 1980; Sorabji, 1980), Lobkowicz is quite emphatic on this point: 'the relationship between *theoria* and *praxis*, as the Greeks understood these terms, was precisely not that between abstract ideas and their concrete application or realization' (1967, p. 35), and again: 'the most significant thing that can be said about the Greek treatment of the relationship between thought relevant to action and action itself is that it cannot truly be subsumed under the heading "theory and practice". Productive thought to the Greeks was certainly not "applicable theoretical thought"' (ibid., p. 43).

Given our habitual association of the two, it is perhaps hard for us to grasp the full implications of this view. Insofar as educationists think about these things at all, there seems to be a common if rather hazy assumption that all forms of knowledge are somehow of the same kind, varying only in terms of how 'hard' or 'soft' and 'pure' or 'applied' they are. That certainly is the view of academic disciplines presented by Becher (1989, p. 12), who draws on a number of contemporary sources to arrive at his typology. The idea that there might be a number of quite different types of thinking, each of which has its own characteristic aims, processes, features and criteria for judgment, is quite hard to grasp; but this seems to be what Aristotle is saying. He is not just in the business of valuing practice or production *vis-à-vis* theory; he is suggesting that they are not even in the same ball-park. Or is he?

There is first a logical point. Insofar as the three are all forms of one thing — thinking (*dianoia*) — we would expect them to have something in common, that is the characteristics of a form of thought. We must not fall into the trap of assuming that the practical and productive do not involve thinking or knowledge of any kind. That each is a form of thinking is indicated by the fact that each, according to Aristotle, possesses its own kind of generality; neither is merely particular. That is why the practical — which one might regard as too concrete or embedded to stand alongside theory — is also regarded as a form of *thought*, with its own processes, its own generalities, its own *nous* (Kenny, 1978, p. 170). However, against this logical point must be set the general thrust of the writing, which tends to accentuate the differences between the three rather than their commonalities. In describing each of them, words like 'realm', 'domain' or 'sphere' come to mind; such images suggest a kind of autonomy of each form of thinking, which does not derive from or depend on the others.

Classifying the Professions

At first sight, this solves the educationist's problem. No longer does one have to worry about relating educational theory to educational practice, or bridging the gap between them. Since education is obviously about doing, rather than knowing or producing, it is clearly a practical discipline. The task then becomes one of working out the nature and characteristics of practical disciplines, and relating these to the particular business of teaching. This has been broadly the approach taken by Schwab (1969a, 1969b), Schilling (1986) Carr and Kemmis (1986, pp. 32–41) and Carr (1995, pp. 67–72). It is also the view of Kessels and Korthagen (1996), who, drawing heavily on Nussbaum (1986), see educational practice as depending primarily on *phronesis* (practical wisdom) and the related concept of *aisthesis* (situational perception) rather than *episteme*. Such a view provides a philosophical underpinning for the argument that teaching (like other professions) is best seen (and learned) in terms of reflective practice, of thinking about the experienced, situational specifics of the activity.

However, there are two problems with this argument. The first, already mentioned, is that Aristotle's notion of *praxis* is rather different from the modern concept of practice, in several ways. First, it is an autonomous concept, not one half of the kind of theory–practice dualism to which in most modern thinking it belongs. Even when contemporary educationists emphasize practice, they do so usually with reference to or as against theory, whereas with Aristotle *praxis* is a self-sufficient notion that does not need to be justified *vis-à-vis* anything else. Although some modern thinking rebalances the dualism, it typically remains dualistic. Secondly, the emphasis in *praxis* is on the process — living and acting well because of the intrinsic virtue of this — rather than on the desirable outcomes or consequences, as is usually the case with contemporary interpretations of practice, for example in education. Thirdly, Aristotle's *praxis* is a broad, ethico-political concept, concerned with how we live in society, not with a particular field of activity such as a profession. Indeed, it was the broad, political significance of the term that led thinkers such as Arendt (1959) and Habermas (1974) to want to rescue it for politics, against the potential and actual dehumanizing consequences of viewing politics as *techne* (see also Oakshott, 1962, pp. 6–13). However, even if we accept this view, that does not necessarily mean that *praxis* is an appropriate way of characterizing a specific profession.

The second major problem is that where Aristotle does refer to the equivalents of the modern profession, such as medicine or building, he in fact classifies them as productive, not practical disciplines, involving *techne*, not *phronesis* (*Metaphysics*, Z, 1032b). (And his father was a physician.) Again, we run into the problem of deciding what Aristotle actually meant by *poiesis* and *techne*, and some cautions have already been issued in this regard. But we should not underestimate the potential scope of *poiesis*, if only because Aristotle gave it parity of place as a form of thinking (*dianoia*), not just a set of skills or procedures; his view of medicine, for example, goes well beyond the merely procedural. The fact that, as we shall see, subsequent thinkers effectively relegated or lost this third component of the trichotomy should not mean that we do not honour Aristotle's intention in this respect.

Reeve (1992, pp. 186–7) argues that we can regard *phronesis* as an 'architectonic virtue', which is distinct from *episteme* and *techne* but may nevertheless draw on them and deploy them in the course of right action. Thus although the doctor's knowledge and skills represent forms of *episteme* and *techne*, these do not in and of themselves tell him how best to act as a doctor, how to order his priorities, and make his choices. *Episteme* and *techne* are thus drawn into the service of *phronesis*, but the latter is not reducible to either of them. That is a plausible model for a profession, although it implies a relationship between the three forms of thinking that goes well beyond what Aristotle actually said.

In one sense, the results of revisiting this aspect of Aristotle's work may appear rather negative or agnostic. To begin with, it has become apparent that there is no simple correspondence between Aristotle's terminology and modern usage. His *theoria* is a good deal more restrictive and more deductive than our theory; his *praxis* refers to the ethico-political domain, whereas our notion refers to virtually any kind of doing or action; and there are real difficulties in reconstructing what he meant by *poiesis* and the associated concept of *techne*. Although Carr (1995) and others have argued that education can be classified as a practical discipline in Aristotelian terms, the analysis here suggests that there are substantial problems with this view.

Perhaps we should not be too surprised at the difficulties of relating a twentieth-century phenomenon (the contemporary profession) to an ancient scheme of thought. The whole concept of applied science was largely absent from the Greek world (Lobkowicz, 1967, pp. 35–46). Even the concept of 'pure' knowledge may to some extent be a retrospective interpretation (Squires, 1990, p. 70, n. 6). Our notions of craft are coloured by the medieval guilds, our image of production by the industrial revolution. And the whole institutional and professional structuring of disciplines — which are bodies of people as well as bodies of knowledge — must affect the way we think about thinking.

However, in another way, the results of this brief foray into the past have been positive, even dramatic. It has freed us from the theory–practice dualism, at least as far as Aristotle goes. If the theoretical and the practical were to him two quite different kinds of thinking, then we no longer have to worry about the gap between them (because there is no gap) or about relating one to the other (because there is no relationship). It seems that we have been slaves to a dualism that never existed in the first place, and which in any case involved a third possibility. And most important of all: Aristotle suggests that there may be different kinds of thinking and knowledge appropriate to different domains. His is a pluralistic conception.

Of course, one does not throw off the past quite as easily as that, and the fact that the dualism did not exist in the first place does not mean that, as we shall see in the next section, it did not come into being in the second or third. But this analysis suggests that we are no longer locked into the categories that perhaps we thought we were, and that free from these inherited constraints, we can now try to work out an epistemology that will be peculiar and appropriate to professional disciplines, including education.

The Theory–Practice Dualism

Lobkowicz (1967, 1977) traces what happened to Aristotle's scheme subsequently. It is a long and complex story in the history of ideas, which can only be referred to here, and which even he regards as selective. It takes in not only some of the major figures of Arab and European philosophy — Alfarabi, Ibn Sina, Aquinas, Francis Bacon, Descartes, Kant, Hegel and eventually Marx — but many minor ones as well, such as the twelfth-century Hugh of St Victor, in relation to whom the author notes: 'From this brief survey, we may draw two important conclusions: first, in the twelfth century the notion of an immediate relevance of theoretical insights to "practice" certainly was not absent and, second, from about the same time the expression "practical" ceased to refer exclusively to the ethicopolitical realm' (ibid., p. 84). Perhaps it is to Hugh rather than Aristotle that modern educationists should be appealing.

Lobkowicz shows how Aristotle's original and in some ways now alien trichotomy gradually metamorphosed into the familiar dualism of today. (In addition to Lobkowicz's chapter, there are several other relevant chapters in the book edited by Ball, 1977.) Two things in particular seem to have brought this about. First of all, the third form of *dianoia* — *poiesis* and the associated concept of *techne* — began to drop out of account, perhaps because it was too strongly associated with art and craft and therefore not really seen as a form of thinking or knowledge. Even today, creative disciplines such as art and design, music and drama fit rather uneasily within the general canons of academic disciplines; curiously Hirst's essay on the problem does not refer back to Aristotle (Hirst, 1974, pp. 152–64).

The second thing that happens is that over a period of time, theory and practice begin to be seen as two aspects of the same thing, two dimensions of the same discipline or activity. The reasons for this are complex, but there can be no doubt that the growth of modern science, and the growing awareness of the possibilities of applying it, gave a major boost to the new dualistic conception. This reaches its logical conclusion in the philosophy of positivism, in which science provides the basis or underpinning for all forms for natural and social activity, including even the arts. So by the nineteenth century, and with important exceptions such as the Kantian treatment of practical reason, the hegemony of theory seems well established, and practice has become merely a derivation of it.

There have been three modern attempts to redress the balance, each of which has had some impact on educational thinking, and each of which needs to be briefly addressed here. The first stems from Marx's resuscitation of the concept of *praxis*, the second from the emphasis on practice in the American pragmatists such as Peirce and Dewey, and the third from the detailed analysis of the world-as-experienced or lived in the phenomenological tradition, in particular in the work of Heidegger and Merleau-Ponty.

It is over-simplifying things to call the first of these attempts Marxist, because it has become intertwined with other strands of thinking, in particular that of the Frankfurt School and critical social theory: Horkheimer (1972) and Habermas (1974) are key points of reference, and contemporary advocates include Giroux (see Welker, 1992, pp.101–28). Some writers (see Carr, 1995, pp. 120–8) see it as a continuation of the Enlightenment project. However, it owes much to Marx in the sense that it treats consciousness as the product of social situation, rather than the reverse, although in a less deterministic way than its originator did.

Therefore (the argument goes) since it is teachers who actually do teaching, it is they (rather than academic theorists) who are in the best position to talk about it. They will know most about it, and provide the most real accounts of it. Academic theory thus gives way to practitioner or personal 'theorizing', in which the situated experiences of teachers are articulated to the point where they can in turn inform their teaching again. Theory arises out of, and returns to, practice in a continuing dialectical relationship. Such practitioner research or action research can enlighten, emancipate and empower the teacher, not just as an individual, but as someone who shares in a collective and historically located consciousness.

The second attempt to revalue practice stems from the very different ethos of the American pragmatist tradition. Here, practice is seen as the ultimate validation of theory: Does it work? (Equally, if it works, don't fix it.) One might argue that this was no accident in a culture that could produce a quite un-European theoretical-cum-practical figure like Benjamin Franklin, and which from its early days had to be concerned with the workability of a new society in a 'new' continent. Be that as it may, I argued in Chapter 1 that writers such as Schon (1983, 1987) should be seen in the light of that tradition, as someone who is driven by the fact that technical rationality patently does not work a lot of the time (see also Argyris, 1982).

Hence the new interest in and respect for the practitioner rather than the scientist or technologist (as distinct from theorist). Practitioners clearly manage to do things, to get things done, so it is important to watch them and listen to them to find out how. Reflection is the process of subjecting that practice to meta-cognition in order to refine it (Eraut, 1995). Again, this wisdom of practice is not simply an individual thing, but often shared in and by 'communities of practice' (Brown and Duguid, 1996).

The third approach to revaluing practice is different again. Its roots lie in the phenomenologists' attempt to dis-cover the nature of the world-as-lived, without prestructuring or prejudging this through presuppositions. Existence precedes essence: so it is important to capture our encounter with the world in as direct a way as possible. Of course, this proves to be a complex and elusive task, since it is difficult if not impossible not to bring things to this encounter. So our portrayal of the world inevitably and equally becomes a portrayal of consciousness, of our being-in-the-world.

Although phenomenology as a substantive philosophy has had much less influence on education than either Marxism or pragmatism, as a method it has influenced educational research, initially through the Swedish work of Marton (1977) and subsequently through a range of other European and Australian writers (Entwistle and Marton, 1994; Marton, Hounsell and Entwistle, 1984; Prosser, Trigwell and Taylor, 1994; Ramsden, 1992). 'Phenomenography' does not have the powerful reflexive thrust of phenomenology, but it does aim at achieving a detailed account of how teaching and learning are experienced by those involved. It does this to redress the long-standing habit of educational psychologists of treating teachers and students as objects. In valuing the subjectivity of those involved, it asserts that teaching and learning are intentional activities, concerned with the construction of meanings.

Each of these three traditions attempts to revalue practice and practitioners, but each does so in a different way. This can be seen most clearly by asking what each is against. The Marxist's emphasis on situated *praxis* is set against the false consciousness of abstract theory. The pragmatist's emphasis on the practitioner is set against the bogus claims of technical rationality. The phenomenographer's emphasis on subjectivity is set against the crudities of objectivism.

And although all three share the same end-purpose, they are implicitly and sometimes explicitly critical of one another. Marxists complain that the pragmatist approach is decontextualized, individualistic and historically and politically naïve. Pragmatists might reply that Marxism is itself an ideology discredited by its practical politics. Phenomenography (and its cousin ethnomethodology) are criticized as ignoring the wider social structures and norms that permeate individual experience, as refusing to recognize how the social world is constituted.

The wider problem is that however we attempt to recast or revalue the notion of practice, it remains implicitly an antithesis. The modern emphasis on practice and practitioners in educational research seems always to be at the expense of something else, in relation to something else, in reaction to something else; see for example the determinedly grounded approach of Brown and McIntyre (1993) or the attack on theory by Thomas (1997). Significantly, it is easier to say what each of the three movements is against — abstract theory, technical rationality, methodological objectivism — than what each is for. That is hardly an adequate basis on which to build an epistemology of professions.

Decision-Making and Expertise

Does the concept of expertise offer a better basis for thinking about professional disciplines than the notions of theory and practice? Might this unitary concept avoid some of the problems associated with the dualism of the latter?

The last three decades have seen an enormous growth of interest in and research into expertise. There seem to have been several reasons for this. One is perhaps a general shift of emphasis in the field of learning psychology from what people cannot do to what they can do. For a long time, research on learning has been concerned with learning problems of one kind or another, and this focus has been relatively productive. But there is much to be gained also by studying success and achievement in learning and performance, and what better example of this than the complex and exceptional achievements of experts in various fields.

There have also been negative stimuli. The increased questioning of the 'applied science' paradigm mentioned in Chapter 1 has led people to explore how far expertise goes beyond the principle-based, rule-governed or algorithmic. Even if there are rules, it seems, experts sometimes bend them; even if there are procedures, experts sometimes bypass or jump them. But the interest in expertise has also stemmed from a critique of the 'rational activity' paradigm: the idea that professional activities are based on a rational process of identifying aims, making plans, selecting resources, implementing decisions and evaluating the results. Experts, it seems, do not always have a clear set of objectives, nor do they always rationally consider alternative strategies. They do not always formulate plans and even if they do, they sometimes change them as they go along, or abandon them altogether.

A third and quite different stimulus for the work on expertise has been the development of computing, and the attempts to mimic or replicate human expertise in computer systems. This has led to attempts to create programmes that would do everything from solve puzzles and play chess, through diagnose medical conditions or optimize design options, to 'general problem-solving'. Although some writers in the field are deeply sceptical about the ultimate ambitions of this work (notably Dreyfus, 1992), there has been a rapid development of 'expert systems' in various fields.

The work on expertise has focused on one central question — How do experts do what they do? — and a number of related, subsidiary questions: How do novices become experts? How domain-specific or transferable is expertise? How far can expertise be articulated? How far can computers replicate or improve on human expertise? In order to explore these issues, researchers have developed new methodologies, such as 'think-aloud protocols' in which experts articulate in detail what they are doing as they are doing it or soon afterwards. And even the difficulties of writing computer programs to mimic human expertise have thrown light on the process.

The field remains, however, one that is very difficult to review or summarize. This is partly because of its sheer scope: studies range from expertise in 'ordinary' jobs such as restaurant waiting, through more complex activities such as weather-forecasting, to broad professional fields such as medicine, engineering and management, and cover both limited-possibility problems (such as puzzles or games) and open-ended ones, where there is no boundary to the 'frame' of possible considerations. There is also a basic contrast and conflict between those who adopt a 'soft' reflective-heuristic approach and those who construct 'hard' computer-based expert systems. It would be foolhardy therefore to try to summarize the state of the art in the pages that follow. What can be done, however, is to try to indicate how this work is changing the way we talk about professional expertise, and the kind of language it is introducing: one that is very different from the traditional categories of theory and practice explored in the two previous sections. Even if we are still a long way from arriving at an agreed account of how experts do what they do, having a new vocabulary at our disposal is a step forward. The discussion will draw eclectically on a number of key sources in the field, such as Baskett and Marsick (1992), Benner (1984), Boreham (1989, 1994), Chi, Glaser and Farr (1988), Dreyfus (1992), Dreyfus and Dreyfus (1986), Eraut (1994, 1995), Klein et al. (1993), Schon (1983, 1987), Simon (1956, 1969, 1979, 1996), Suchman (1987) and Williams, Faulkner and Fleck (1998). The discussion will also refer to the useful recent overview by Ericsson and Lehmann (1996).

If there is one concept that lies at the heart of the research on expertise, it is that of *decision-making*, a term that neatly captures the essentially dynamic and active nature of the phenomenon. (It also makes the useful, implicit distinction between decision-orientated and conclusion-orientated.) Writers on expertise have explored the process of decision-making, the kinds of knowledge that inform it, and the kinds of action that flow from it.

A distinction is often drawn between formal and naturalistic decision-making (Klein et al., 1993). The former is the domain of classical decision theory and refers to decisions where there is a finite number of procedures and possibilities. The distinction may be overstated; even in professional work, there can be pockets of formal decision-making where people are operating in a quite structured environment with determinate options. It is significant that even in everyday conversation, professionals sometimes refer to 'the rules of the game'.

However, people in the professions are more likely to be involved in naturalistic decision-making, which has been described in terms of four key features: 'dynamic and continually changing conditions, real-time reactions to these changes, ill-defined goals and ill-structured tasks, and knowledgeable people' (Klein et al., 1993, p. vii). According to Orasanu and Connolly, research on naturalistic decision-making has yielded a number of broad findings:

> In naturalistic dynamic settings, experts frequently generate and evaluate a single option rather than analyse multiple options concurrently.
> Experts are distinguished from novices mainly by their situation assessment abilities, not their general reasoning skills.
> Because most naturalistic decision problems are ill-structured, decision-makers choose an option that is good enough, though not necessarily the best.
> Reasoning is 'schema-driven,' that is, guided by the decision-maker's knowledge, to search and assess information, and to build causal models of events.
> Deciding and acting are interleaved. (Orasanu and Connolly, 1993, p. 20)

However, a number of writers have pointed out that not all naturalistic decision-making is of the same kind. Rasmussen (1993, pp. 158–71) distinguishes between skill-based, rule-based and knowledge-based decision-making. The first involves subconscious and quasi-automatic behaviours, the second involves conscious application of a rule or approach based on past or predicted scenarios, and the third requires the development of a bespoke conceptual, structural model for that particular situation. All three are interrelated and may come into play in a single case.

Hammond's cognitive continuum theory holds that the process of decision-making is largely driven by the nature of the task and the cues it offers. Thus some kinds of decision will induce rather intuitive decision processes and other more analytic ones, while in between there will be a wide range of quasi-rational decisions. The continuum depends on the number, distribution, weighting, display and timing of the available cues. Hammond's 'lens model' of social judgment offers a framework for the analysis not only of the nature of decision-cues but their utilization, and its formal structure contrasts with the reliance of other naturalistic researchers on more embedded or situated forms of analyses such as case studies and verbal protocols (Hammond, 1993, pp. 205–27).

After reviewing nine models of decision-making, Lipshitz concludes that 'real world decisions are made in a variety of ways' (Lipshitz, 1993, pp. 131–7). The implication of such work is that decision-making is not in fact a single, unitary process, but rather a composite or componential one involving a number of different kinds of elements. The use of these may reflect not only the nature of the task or situation, but also variables related to the decision-maker (preferred style, influence of training) and organizational or social norms. Lipshitz points out that the various current models of decision-making do in fact manifest a number of common features, such as an emphasis on situational assessment, the use of mental imagery, dependence on context and a dynamic relationship with action. Other writers have also stressed the importance of self-monitoring (Chi, Glaser and Farr, 1988, p. xx) and meta-cognition (Eraut, 1994, pp. 145–6).

But these are rather general features, and what may be more interesting and researchable are the ways in which decision-makers combine various sub-processes in their decisions. Some studies in medicine and management seem to point towards a 'mixed mode' of decision-making that is both knowledge-driven and sensory-driven (Boreham, 1989; Elstein, Shulman and Sprafka, 1978; Eraut, 1994, pp. 138–41). Thus one might explore the roles of conceptual analysis (What are we talking about here?), pattern recognition (Have I seen this before?), formal reasoning (What relates to what?), rules (What principles can I apply here?), routines (What procedures can I use?), empirical investigation (What more do I need to find out?) and metacognitive monitoring (How am I getting on?). Not all of these processes may be present in every case; a lot will depend on the initial familiarity with the situation, the time available and perhaps the stakes involved. Likewise, there is no obviously fixed order in the above list, and one can imagine the process involving not merely a number of sub-processes but sometimes an iterative pattern of shuttling back and forth between them, to explore, frame, explore, check, reframe. But such a pluralistic view might help to move us beyond the rather blunt dichotomies of intuitive versus analytic, knowledge versus experience, semantic versus situational, algorithm versus judgment.

A further aspect of decision-making is the extent to which it is an explicit or tacit process (Senker, 1998). Experts, it is sometimes said, are not always aware of making decisions at all, so the concept of decision-making may thus imply a process that is more explicit and conscious than it really is. Or they may find it difficult to explain the decisions they do make, resorting to the sensory metaphors of intuitive judgment such as 'clinical nose', 'gut sense' or 'feel for the problem.' Thus their behaviour can appear rather artistic, veiled, mysterious, spontaneous: where the novice doctor will work painstakingly through a systematic diagnostic procedure, her experienced colleague may quickly jump to a probable hypothesis, and then spend the rest of the time checking that out (Elstein, Shulman and Sprafka, 1978, pp. 278–9).

If an expert finds it difficult to articulate the nature of his or her decision, it could be for one of three reasons. First, it might be because the process has become so condensed and compacted with practice that it has now become very difficult to disaggregate or deconstruct it again, bit by bit, step by step. However, in this case, one would expect the expert eventually to be able to reconstruct the decision, given time and patient questioning by an interviewer. The second possibility is that the decision is difficult to articulate because it was not framed in a verbal form in the first place, but rather in a sensory-situational-enactive one. It is thus difficult to give a verbal account of it, just as it is difficult to give verbal accounts of wine, music, paintings, movements or sometimes even an encounter with another person. The third possibility is that what was originally learned in a verbal or symbolic form has eventually become stored in a non-verbal iconic or enactive one; it is worth remembering here that Fitts's theory of skill acquisition posits the transition from an initial cognitive phase, through an associative phase, to a final autonomous phase (Fitts and Posner, 1973). In Anderson's terms, we are talking about the conversion of declarative into procedural knowledge (J.R. Anderson, 1995, pp. 280–3). Thus when people say that professional expertise is 'tacit', they may mean one of three different things.

However, Ericsson and Lehmann state that:

> Contrary to the belief that expert performance is highly automatized, most types of expert performance are mediated by reportable thoughts involving planning, reasoning, and anticipation. Even perceptual-motor activities have been successfully monitored with concurrent and retrospective verbal reports that reveal considerable planning and generation of expectations. . . . That experts' incidental memory for task-relevant information is superior to that of novices also implies that most forms of expert performance remain mediated by attention-demanding cognitive processes. (Ericsson and Lehmann, 1996, p. 291)

The emphasis on the tacit dimension of expertise, which often refers back to Polanyi (1958) sometimes forms part of a wider social and moral critique of the rationalistic or technocratic connotations of the concept of expertise (see, for example, Olson, 1992, pp, 45–52; Welker, 1992, p. 131). In one way, this sends us back to Aristotle's distinction between *praxis* and *poeisis*, *phronesis* and *techne*. However, the situation may not be quite as dichotomous as that. If decision-making is a composite or componential process, then it is likely that some aspects of it will be easier to explicate than others. One would expect people to be able to give some account of the conceptual analysis, formal reasoning or meta-cognitive monitoring that they went through. On the other hand, it might be much more difficult to unpack the process of pattern recognition or routinized procedures, for the kinds of reasons suggested above. The extent to which the overall decision-making process appears tacit or explicit would thus depend on the relative importance of the various components of it.

A second key aspect of decision-making is the *knowledge* that informs it. Chi, Glaser and Farr (1988, p. xvi) argue that expertise is strongly knowledge-based. This is not the banal statement that it might sound, because it counters the earlier assumption that expertise could be taught in terms of general problem-solving or reasoning. By contrast, these authors assert that expertise in a domain depends on knowing a lot about that domain. Moreover, that knowledge typically takes a long time to acquire: people speak of a 'ten-year rule' of necessary preparation, although Ericsson and Lehmann argue that experience *per se* correlates weakly with expertise and what really matters is the amount of time spent in deliberate practice (1996, pp. 278–9). In addition, since the knowledge is domain-specific, expertise is domain-specific. It does not transfer to other fields.

Such ideas are likely to disappoint those who would like to speed up professional training or make it more economical. They also place a question-mark beside the notion of generic skills. They imply that there are no short-cuts, no easy ways. But if this is so, the interesting question is why. One implication of this research is that abstract, conceptual knowledge has its limits: that while one should obviously equip the professional with as powerful analytic tools as possible, there is no substitute for actually doing it. For experience. For practice.

There could be two reasons for this. One is that, as suggested above, a good deal of this knowledge may be acquired and stored not in verbal or symbolic form, but in iconic-enactive templates, patterns, scenarios or scripts, and that these can only be accumulated through experience (for example all the sore throats one has ever looked down, all the students who have ever walked in late). Somehow — and the process is elusive — we build up a very large stock of these scenarios, and this allows us both to recognize things when they come along again, and to pick up the exceptions when occasionally we encounter them. As pointed out above, such pattern matching is only one aspect of expertise, but it may be an important one.

However, Ericsson and Lehmann also cite evidence that professionals not only know more, but order their knowledge better than novices; they have managed to develop more powerful ways of selecting, organizing and accessing that information. Presented with a problem, they will go straight to the deeper aspects of it, rather than waste time on surface characteristics; their analysis is more powerful and penetrating (see also Chi, Glaser and Farr, 1988, pp. xviii–xix; Hoffman, 1998, pp. 85–90; Orasanu and Connolly, 1993, p. 18). Sometimes this manifests itself as perceptual skill; experts 'see more' than novices, and are able to pick out key cues or features of a scene or situation. This suggests that cognitive representation — mental models, maps, schemata, frameworks, concepts — has an important role to play in the interpretation of experience and selection of important features or cues, a view that moves us away from the purely empirical emphasis on pattern acquisition and recognition, and has particular relevance for the model presented in this book.

A second possible reason why the development of expertise takes time is that it involves both declarative/propositional knowledge and procedural knowledge. As noted before, the distinction is associated with J.R. Anderson (1995) but reflects Ryle's (1949) earlier distinction between knowing-that and knowing-how. We can acquire propositional knowledge through formal study, and to some extent this process can be condensed, streamlined or speeded up; but procedural knowledge — knowing how things happen, how to get things done — is usually picked up through experience or simulations of it.

As with decision-making, the notion of expert knowledge thus seems to break down into a number of finer categories or types. It is not a single, unitary thing. Eraut (1994, pp. 40–58) provides a detailed discussion not only of the different kinds of professional knowledge, but of the different ways in which such knowledge may be used, in terms of replication, application, interpretation and association. Some kinds of knowledge are needed to make use of other kinds, and context is an important factor in their use. Expert knowledge is therefore partly situational knowledge (see Lipshitz, 1993, pp. 132–3).

Fleck (1998, pp. 152–61) proposes a useful breakdown of expert knowledge into six kinds: (1) formal knowledge, which is embodied in codified theories; (2) instrumentalities, which are embodied in the use of tools and instruments; (3) informal knowledge, which is embodied in verbal interaction; (4) contingent knowledge, which is embodied in specific contexts; (5) tacit knowledge, which is embodied in people; and (6) meta-knowledge, which is embodied in organizations and to some extent in the wider society. All these kinds of knowledge exist within three kinds of context: domains of specific expertise; situations comprising assemblages of components, people and domains; and milieus, which are the immediate environments in which the expertise is exercised.

The reference to exercise leads on to the third key notion related to decision-making, that of *action.* The whole purpose of expertise is to act, but describing the nature of that action is not easy. Two general points can, however, be made. The idea of 'situated action' as explored by writers like Suchman (1987) sees action not simply as the product of planned intention, but as an ongoing response to contextual circumstances. This may seem an obvious enough point to any teacher who has faced a room full of 12-year olds, but it does help us to put planning into perspective. Suchman sees plans as merely one input to action. The emphasis on plans in teaching and in particular in teacher training — lesson plans, curriculum plans, development plans, career plans — can all too easily give the impression that the world is plannable. But experience usually teaches us otherwise, and it is important to acknowledge that responsiveness and improvisation may have at least as big a part to play in teaching as 'planfulness'.

The second interesting gloss on the notion of action is the concept of 'productions' (J.R. Anderson, 1995, pp. 248–9; Simon, 1979, 1996). Productions are specific, linked if–then statements, which relate to a particular situation or episode, for example: if he turns up late again, then I will tell him off. They can take a more general form, for example: if students turn up late, I tell them off; or include some conditions within the statement, for example: if students turn up late, and if they do not have a good excuse, then I tell them off; if students turn up late, and if they do not have a good excuse, and if they are in the habit of turning up late, then I tell them off. One can see how quite complex sequences of conditions and actions can be built up in this way.

Again, this might seem a rather banal idea, and it has certainly attracted criticism as an attempt to codify what is actually far more fluid. But its interest lies in the implication that, far from being a generically or hierarchically ordered thing, expertise in fact consists of networks of large numbers of rather loosely connected behaviours, which constitute the expert's 'repertoire'. The development of expertise thus involves the building up of a larger and more complex repertoire, rather than the application of general principles to particular situations.

However, the idea that expertise consists of a large repertoire of specific productions runs into the problem of where the rules for these productions come from. Even the simple example given above invokes more general ideas of time and authority, and these in themselves form part of a general view of teaching that can be discussed (Does punctuality matter? What kind of authority does a teacher have?

What kinds of excuse are reasonable? and so on). The same problem arises with the idea of pattern recognition. How do we know what to look for? On what basis do we decide that some features of a pattern or script are important and others are not? How do we even recognize that a pattern is a pattern? The specificities of patterns and productions involve some kind of more general framework, and all that can be said here is that this problem sends us back to the view, expressed earlier, that expertise may be a composite business that involves a number of different kinds of processes.

Rather like our revisitation of Aristotle, this brief and incomplete discussion of some of the current work on expertise has yielded both negative and positive results. On the one hand, it has not simplified the epistemology of the professions; in fact it has made it worse. Far from being the neat, unitary or integrative concept that we had hoped, expertise seems to divide into a large number of components or elements. Where 'theory' and 'practice' dichotomize, 'expertise' multiplies. The process of decision-making seems to consist of a number of sub-processes that are themselves related in complex ways; there is not one, but several kinds of expert knowledge, and various ways of using these; and expert action may comprise literally tens of thousands of discrete 'productions'.

However, all this multiplicity and plurality is in fact congruent with the kind of model being presented in this book. Far from being a single or simple thing, teaching (like other professions) can be seen in terms of not one but a number of dimensions, each of which involves a number of headings, which can in turn be related to one another in numerous ways. The picture is a complex one. What this section suggests is that the plurality of the model itself may be matched by a plurality of ways of using it, a point that leads on to the final stages of this chapter.

Six Scenarios

Let us imagine six scenarios.

In the first, the Novice — we'll call him that — is told that he must meet with a group of about 20 young people in a designated room on Monday, Wednesday and Friday mornings from 9.15 to 10.05. These meetings are to go on for 12 weeks. He is not told why he should meet these young people, and neither are they. Apart from some tables and chairs, the room is empty, with nothing to suggest what it might be used for. And the rest of the building seems to be deserted; there are no signs anywhere. He is told that he can ask for anything he needs, though he may not get it. And that is all.

The second scenario is the same as the first except that this time the Novice is told that he must teach the group history, which happens to be his subject. He is given a list of student names, a syllabus, textbooks, two rather old videos and details of an examination that the group will have to take at the end of the course, but no other information or advice. Never having taught before, nor been trained to, he asks if he might borrow one or two books about teaching, but is told that none has ever been written.

In the third scenario, the Novice is not only given the above materials, but detailed plans for every class. These set down exactly what he should do, in what order, and for how many minutes. Precise instructions are given for tasks to be completed in the class and outside, and he must adhere to these exactly. The marking of assessed work must follow a prescribed scheme, and he must choose from a list of approved comments. In addition, he is provided with a thick manual (arranged alphabetically), which tells him what to say and do in every conceivable classroom situation, for example if someone asks an irrelevant question, or if there is too much noise at the back, or if the window-cleaners appear at the window.

The fourth scenario begins differently with the Novice attending a one-year full-time teacher-training course after his first degree. This takes place entirely in a local university, and is extremely rigorous in academic terms. It covers all the main concepts and models of teaching (including of course this model) and the research literature bearing on them. It involves a detailed analysis of educational ideas, curriculum issues, and of the bases and processes of assessment. However, there is no case-study work, simulation or story-telling, and the Novice never actually sees any teaching taking place; in fact he never sets foot in a classroom, and often wonders what it will be like. Then one afternoon he is informed that he will begin teaching the next day.

In the fifth scenario, the Novice undergoes what might be regarded as a normal course of teacher training, involving both university-based 'theory' and school-based 'practice'. However, when he begins to teach he finds that he has not one group but ten. No sooner has he finished one class than it is time to go on to the next, and any spare time he has is taken up with preparation, (extensive) record-keeping and marking. Moreover, when he talks to other teachers, he finds that they are in exactly the same predicament, and barely have time to answer his most basic questions, let alone talk about what goes on in class. In fact, he forms the distinct impression that teaching is regarded as a private matter, and that attempts to raise it in the staff-room are rather frowned upon.

In the final scenario, the Novice not only undergoes a normal course of teacher training, but has a 'normal' teaching job. However, when he begins work, he finds that nothing stays quite the same for long. No sooner has he started a course than someone leaves the group or someone else joins. There are continual, small modifications to the syllabus and the pattern of assessment. Room changes are quite frequent and even the timetabling of his classes is altered one week. Half-way through the term, the decision is taken that all sessions should last 45 rather than 40 minutes. Periodically he receives memos urging him to focus on certain aspects of his work, now to make good use of information technology, now to emphasize the importance of teaching the class as a whole, now to make sure that what he is doing develops core skills. And there are constant physical changes too. The seating keeps being rearranged overnight and the bookcases are repositioned without warn-ing. The podium on which he is used to standing disappears, making it a bit more difficult for him to write on the board. Each overhead projector that he borrows seems to have slightly different controls. Then one day he arrives to find the whole class sitting on the floor because all the furniture has been removed.

The Model in Use

The six scenarios represent situations that in various ways would be less than perfect for the development of expertise in teaching. In the first, the very notion of teaching, and all its associated concepts, has not even been established. The Novice and his group might decide to spend their time gambling or watching soap operas or telling stories (but are these totally unrelated to teaching?). In the second, the idea of teaching has been established but the assumption is that it can be learned entirely on the job. The third scenario leaves no room for the development of judgment, and the fourth allows no time for reflection. The fifth scenario provides organized knowledge but no practical experience, and the last continually breaks down the little routines that we all develop to cope with our work.

Other scenarios are possible. But the general point here is the same as was made at the end of the section on decision-making and expertise, which is that teaching like other professional activities is a composite of different kinds of knowledge and know-how. It is not reducible simply to one or two elements, and this pluralistic message seems to fit well with the pluralism of the model set out in this book.

What kind of epistemology of professions is suggested by the model? What does it imply about theory and practice, knowledge and know-how? What place does it assign to rules, judgment, skills or reflection in teaching or other professions? The model implies that there are six main elements of professional expertise.

First, professionals need a *general framework* for thinking about what they do. This is implicit in the *form* of the model. Other models with other forms will imply other views of teaching, and indeed it would be important to expose teachers (or other professionals) to a variety of such models and associated concepts. But the essential point is that without some such general framework, mental model or schema, it is difficult if not impossible for teachers (and other professionals) to think about their work as a whole. The lack of some means of getting their minds round what they do potentially incapacitates them not only in practical but in moral terms. They are not equipped to formulate the more general questions or engage in the more general ethical and social issues.

Secondly, professional expertise involves *specific knowledge* about all the different aspects of the work. This is implied by the *headings* in the model, each of which has its own knowledge-base. Without such knowledge, the practitioner cannot understand the nature of his or her work, or make informed decisions about it. Not all the headings are immediately relevant to all teachers, but over time one would expect most teachers to be reasonably conversant with the main research and thinking related to each. Thus teachers should be aware of the main theories of motivation, the writing on educational tasks, the work on individual differences and group processes, not to mention the general thinking on curricular rationales and the content of their own field. They should be familiar with the relevant work on selection, course design, assessment and evaluation as and when they need it.

Thirdly, expertise in teaching, as in other professions, involves *routinized skills* that have to be acquired, practised and refined to the point where they can be 'run off' competently and efficiently. Most of these relate to the Procedures dimensions, at the level of both the course and the class. Skills in teaching are usually most effective when they are least noticed. There may be relatively few skills in teaching that are wholly routine — most involve a degree of fine-tuning — but the importance of competence in skills is that it releases time and attention for more complex aspects of the work and the processes of interpretation and judgment.

Fourthly, expertise involves *contingent analysis*, which is implied by the *relationships* between the three dimensions. Teaching involves the proceduralization of variable functions. This means that each teaching decision is situationally specific, involving a reading of and judgment on the conditions that pertain at that moment, which will always be different (if only in the flow of time) from those at any other moment. The teacher is continually involved in decision-making at the micro and macro levels, as the research on expertise suggests.

An epistemology of teaching can thus be derived directly from the form, headings and relationships of the model. However, these four elements — general frameworks, specific knowledge, routinized skill and contingent analysis — are not simply applied to or brought to bear on the *action* of teaching, but interpreted and modified through it and *reflection* on that action. The model comes alive in its use, and such use affects people's perception of it. Each person thus has his or her own 'version' of the model, in which certain headings loom larger than others, and certain relationships stand out against others. But it is important that these private versions are shared with other practitioners, since it is through this kind of exchange that the various meanings and relationships can be explored and deepened. The model provides a public framework and language for the communication of private perceptions and priorities; public not just in terms of one's immediate colleagues, but in terms of the whole research and practitioner community, and its historically accumulated wisdom.

These six elements — general frameworks, specific knowledge, routinized skill, contingent analysis, action and reflection — are not particularly novel or unusual. However, this kind of approach may be useful in steadying up our conception of teaching in two ways. First, it makes it easy to ask questions about gaps. If there are no general frameworks or ideas, if the knowledge related to certain headings is missed out, if particular skills are not practised, if there is a lack of case analysis in the training of the practitioner, if there are inadequate opportunities for action or reflection, we can quickly see these and ask why. There may be a good answer — the scheme does not prescribe any particular balance between the various elements — but at least one will have to be forthcoming.

Secondly, the scheme does imply a need for 'balance' of a more general kind. 'Balance' is not always a virtue in and of itself, but educational thinking is so prone to pendulum swings and fashions that balance has a particular relevance to it. The elements set out point to the need not only to strike the right balance between frameworks, knowledge, skills and judgment, but between the general and the specific, the routine and the contingent.

How does all this relate to the analysis in the previous sections of this chapter? It will be evident, first, that the various elements of professional expertise have not been divided into 'theory' and 'practice'. Some aspects of teaching will always be more general than others, some analyses will be more abstract than others. But that is no reason to erect a basic distinction between theory and practice, which was not, as we have seen, Aristotle's intention in the first place. One might argue that the form of the model represents a kind of 'theory' about professions, but what about the knowledge specific to the various headings? Is that 'theory'? If one uses case studies or story-telling to develop contingent analysis, is that theory or practice? Case studies are grounded in the particular, but to make sense of them we need to draw in more general issues and ideas. And where do 'skills' fit in terms of a theory–practice divide? Such a dualistic approach seems neither valid nor useful.

In terms of the research on expertise, the model assumes a similarly mixed or pluralistic view. Expertise comprises not one, but a number of things. The model as a whole offers a particular 'cognitive representation' of teaching, a way of thinking about it. The various headings constitute the knowledge bases, to be acquired not simply through formal study, but through experience and 'deliberate practice'. The model offers a multitude of 'frames' for the analysis of patterns and scenarios. Routinized skills have their place, and the contingencies reflect the dependence on context. There is an interplay between decision and action, and reflection is a means to meta-cognition and self-monitoring. Thus although the literature on expertise does not (as yet anyway) provide a coherent epistemology of professional disciplines, the model seems to be generally consistent with the pluralistic thrust of that work.

Novices and Experts

All this should apply to both the novice and the expert, but it still leaves un-answered the intriguing question of how it is that novices turn into experts, of how raw recruits eventually become highly effective professionals (Benner, 1984). Here, one runs into the great paradox of expertise: that experts know more, but take less time. Logically, as experts accumulate more and more information about their field, it should take them longer and longer to process it, and to come to decisions. But in fact the reverse is the case: experts seem to be able to condense, short-cut or by-pass some of the slower, laborious decision-making processes of the novice.

One can only speculate here about how this is possible. The knowledge that the expert accumulates about his or her field is so easily and rapidly accessible that it seems likely that it is stored not in logical hierarchies and levels, but in clusters and networks that allow multiple kinds of connections; the idea of neural networks comes to mind here (Alexsander and Morton, 1990). However, two things may make the processing of such information quicker. The first is some kind of 'chunking' of the information, which allows it to be treated in larger units (Chi, Glaser and Farr, 1988, p. xvi; Miller, 1956). Miller's now old but still influential idea suggests that the built-in limits to human information-processing can be overcome by process-ing that information in larger 'chunks', each of which may contain or subsume a number of items; thus experienced chess players can take in a whole board at a glance compared to the segment registered by the novice (and my own three or four pieces). Likewise, the experienced teacher may be able to take in a whole class-room situation the moment he or she walks in the door, while the novice is concentrating on the fracas in the second row. The second possibility is that the storing of such information occurs in situational rather than semantic form. Here, the metaphors are revealing. We say of the expert that he or she has 'seen it all'. If accumulated expertise is stored partly in the form of 'scenarios', each of which contains a lot of immediately accessible information, these might be quicker to call up and process than linear, verbal text.

Such a notion raises an interesting question about this model. If I am saying that much of teachers' expertise is in fact stored in situational or iconic-enactive form, how does a rational-verbal construct such as this model relate to such scenarios? Rather than posit the kind of dual cognitive architecture suggested by Boreham (1994), we need to find some ways in which cognitive representations such as this intervene in and relate to situational knowledge. In the section on decision-making, it was noted that expertise depends partly on the possession of powerful conceptual and analytical frameworks that allow one to go beyond the surface characteristics of situations and engage quickly in a deeper level of analysis (Ericsson and Lehmann, 1996, p. 284). The model as a whole may function in this way, its form helping teachers to home in on the fundamentals of what they do. But through its detailed headings, it may also provide structures and triggers for the identification and interpretation of specific situational cues in the manner suggested by Hammond (1993). Ideally, therefore, the model should provide enough structure to facilitate analysis, but not so much as to inhibit it.

It is impossible here to get into a detailed discussion of how this may happen, and it is in any case the proper province of cognitive psychologists. But two points can be made. First, it should now be clear that the model should be regarded not as a construct that is to be imposed on experience, but as one that may help us to interpret it. What matters in the end is not the model on the page but the construct in the teacher's mind, and the way teachers use it to analyse their own work. In practice, this is how it has been mainly used in its training form and it seems to generate a lot of perceptive, concrete case-analysis and penetrating discussion in groups. Paradoxically, perhaps, people often describe it as 'practical'. Secondly, the emphasis on the situated specifics of experience has brought us back to where this chapter began: with the search for a way to describe the knowledge of things that can be otherwise than they are. We seem to have come full circle.

Chapter 6

Research, Training and Evaluation

I began this book by setting out a number of different paradigms of teaching. The point was made that a paradigm involves not just a particular way of conceptualizing a field or problem, but comprises a whole package of associated attitudes, assumptions, habits and practices. So what comes in the package associated with the model set out in Chapters 3 and 4? What kind of paradigm is being suggested here?

There are implications for research into teaching, the training of teachers and the evaluation of teaching, and these will be sketched out in a moment. First, however, something must be said about the idea of teaching as a professional discipline. Education has long had a rather uncertain place in the academic scheme of things. There are doubts about where it belongs, indeed whether it belongs at all. Probably some of this uncertainty is a result of historical and social factors: it has not always been part of higher education, and teaching does not have the unambiguous professional status that medicine, law and even engineering have. But there are deeper, more academic worries as well. It has not been clear what kind of a discipline education is, and some have wondered whether it is actually a proper discipline at all.

If one accepts the analysis presented in this book, then the answers to both questions are quite clear. Education is a discipline, a professional discipline. Teaching shares with other professional disciplines the three basic characteristics of instrumentality, contingency and procedurality. Of course, there is more to education and the study of education than teaching, but the activity of teaching lies at its core, and as long as this cannot be conceptualized, there is a fatal weakness at the heart of the subject. I have offered an ontology of teaching, an account of what it is. Much of the detail of that account — the various headings in the model — is open to dispute, but the model as a whole makes, I would argue, a coherent case.

What does this imply for the relationship between education and other disciplines? In the past, the closest links tend to have been with those disciplines that were often regarded as providing the foundations for the study of education: philosophy, history, psychology and sociology. The model presented here implies a different pattern. The idea that teaching (and by extension, education) can be seen as an autonomous professional discipline eliminates the need for foundations; we have our own building now. Indeed, the idea that education needs to be founded on other disciplines simply delays the process of working out its own nature. Clearly, such disciplines will always inform the process of teaching, but we do not need the hybrids to which this gives rise. If someone is researching into a particular aspect of learning such as cognitive style or skill acquisition, that is properly the domain of psychology. If someone is researching into the learning of a subject by students in an educational setting, that is education; and there seems no need for anything in between.

Conversely, if education is seen as a professional discipline, one would expect to see the growth of links between it and other professional disciplines. Of course, there is much that distinguishes one profession from any other, and one cannot simply assume that getting (say) doctors and teachers together will yield useful mutual insights. But at a deeper level, the kinds of epistemological issues discussed in the previous chapter, such as the nature of professional decision-making, the balance of routine and contingency, the relationship between organized knowledge and accumulated experience, or the transition from novice to expert, are not only of common interest to all professions, but have a bearing on the way they train and retrain their members. One would expect, therefore, to see the growth of inter-professional work, first perhaps at the research level, and then over time spreading out to influence professional practice. And it may be useful to compare systematic-ally the patterns of training and accreditation across the different professions.

Research

The mention of research brings us to the first of our three headings. What does a professional paradigm of teaching imply for research in the field? At the time of writing, educational research in the UK has recently come under direct, public attack for being of poor quality and dubious relevance. And, according to one writer there is apparently a pervasive sense of disillusion in the US also (Kennedy, 1997).

The assumption lying behind this book is that our understanding of teaching moves forward through a combination of conceptual analysis and empirical invest-igation. The main thrust of the book has been conceptual: it represents an attempt to *rethink* teaching. But that should not be taken as in any way downgrading the importance of empirical research. The justification of the various headings set out in the model, and the potential relationships between them, are proper matters of empirical study, and indeed I have been quite cautious about the status of these headings and relationships precisely because many of them need further empirical investigation. The hope is that the model will provide a framework that allows the empirical questions to be formulated more precisely and productively than they have sometimes been in the past. For example, the model implies that straight comparisons of the effectiveness of different teaching methods or technologies are likely to yield little unless they are seen in relation to the functions and variables as well.

Unfortunately, research into teaching has often been guided by a rather crude empiricism: the belief — and it is no more than that — that if one carried out enough empirical studies, they would somehow all gradually come together, and one would eventually be able to aggregate the results to form a general picture of teaching. The more recent shift of emphasis from experimental to naturalistic research does nothing to alter this fundamentally empirical bias.

The problem with teaching is not that there has not been enough research, for there has been an enormous amount, but that it has too often been carried on in a kind of conceptual vacuum, what the Americans sometimes call 'dust-bowl empiricism', although some recent writing of a more 'philosophical' kind in that country may signal a change of ethos (see, for example, Fenstermacher, 1994; Greene, 1994). The continuing empirical drive is evident in the announcement at the time of writing of a new research programme to be organized by the Economic and Social Research Council (ESRC) and Higher Education Funding Council for England (HEFCE) into teaching and learning in higher education. This states that the programme will be geared at least in part to 'evidence-based teaching'. It is likely that this idea has come from the field of medicine, where it has now been around for some years. Hammersley (1997) and Hargreaves (1997) have presented sharply contrasting views on the subject, and some years ago the US Department of Education attempted to summarize the available evidence on school teaching and learning in a little booklet entitled *What Works*, setting out 59 findings 'from some of the best research about what works when it comes to educating a child'. They included only findings 'about which research evidence and expert opinion were consistent, persuasive, and fairly stable over time' (US Department of Education, 1987, pp. v, 2). The booklet was widely distributed but came in for substantial academic criticism, mainly on the grounds of over-generalization — in terms of this model, a failure to recognize contingency.

I have recently been involved in an NHS-funded study of the attitudes of medical general practitioners to evidence-based medicine, and so have some knowledge of the field. Basing medicine or teaching on research findings is a sensible idea if it means that decision-making is based on solid evidence rather than mere habit or hearsay. However, the whole thrust of the argument in this book suggests why there are limits to this. Professional practice is typically contingent and contextualized, and even for doctors, narrower clinical decisions typically have to take account of wider medical considerations, including the availability of provision and the wishes of the patient, one of whom in our study rejected some new pills because she did not like the colour of them — a trivial, perhaps, but still significant example. In the end, it usually comes down to a matter of judgment. Evidence-based teaching is simply a new way of restating the applied science paradigm, and should be seen in those terms. It therefore seems unwise to place too much emphasis on it.

The other general point about educational research is that to some extent it still seems to be a prisoner of its own past, and in particular still reacting against the 'failure of theory' associated with the 1960s and 1970s. This reaction is evident in the strong current emphasis on craft or reflective paradigms, naturalistic or phenomenographic methods, and grounded or action research. I have argued that the 'foundations approach' did not involve educational theory at all, but theories in education, and that therefore to react against it is to react against the wrong thing. The implication is not that we should reject or abandon 'theory', but try to find general ways of thinking about teaching that do justice to the complex and contingent nature of the activity. This model can be seen as one attempt to do that.

Training

The origins of the modern system for training schoolteachers now go back over a century (Evans, 1978, pp. 119–20). Provision for Further Education is still patchy, although most lecturers now take a City and Guilds basic course, and an increasing number possess a full, professional qualification in teaching in further education. A national framework for training university lecturers is only now being put in place, by the newly created Institute for Learning and Teaching. By contrast, both short and longer courses on teaching in adult education have existed for several decades. In discussing the implications of this model for teacher training, therefore, it seems obvious that I should focus on the school sector, as being both the largest and the best developed.

The latest regulations governing school teacher training are set out in Annex A of the Department for Education and Employment Circular 4/98 (*Teaching: High Status, High Standards*) titled *Standards for the Award of Qualified Teacher Status*. These amend slightly those set out in Circular 10/97, which constituted the first-ever 'national curriculum' for Initial Teacher Training in the UK. It is also worth noting that these recent documents have appeared in the context of a much more elaborate system of inspections of Initial Teacher Training courses than existed previously.

It is interesting to try to map Annex A onto the model in this book. Of course, such a form of content analysis is relatively crude; one has to allow for differences of terminology and interpretation, and in any case Circular 4/98 is intended to provide only a general (though obligatory) framework for institutions to work from:

> the curricula do not specify a course model or scheme of work and it is for providers to decide how training is best delivered. Providers should use the curricula as the basis for designing courses which are coherent, intellectually stimulating and professionally challenging. (ibid., p. 5)

I shall focus just on the standards for secondary school teachers. There are 52 different headings in the Macro and Micro Models (most of the variables are repeated, though in macro and micro terms). Allowing for differences in terminology and organization, the secondary school standards listed in Annex A cover about 38 of these. Some of the 'gaps' are easily explicable in terms of the situation and responsibilities of the newly trained schoolteacher: for example there is nothing that appears to correspond to the macro functions of *selection* or *induction*, or to the macro procedures of *analysis, proposal* and *marketing*. Conversely, there are some items in Annex A for which there is no obvious corresponding heading in the macro or micro models. Most of these come under the general heading of 'Other Professional Requirements' and lie beyond the scope of a model of teaching *per se*; others, such as health and safety could perhaps be accommodated under the broad function of *environ*. In some cases, a degree of translation is involved; for example, one can class 'parents' as *clients*. Occasionally, there is no obvious parallel: it is worth noting the statement that teachers should teach through 'listening carefully to pupils, analysing their responses and responding constructively in order to take the pupils' learning forward' — a case perhaps for nominating *responding* as a function.

The first point to be made, therefore, is that there is a fair degree of congruence between the two schemes in terms of what they cover. Indeed, it would be worrying if this were not so, since each in its different way aims to give a comprehensive view of teaching. However, there are differences, and it is these that are more interesting. Annex A places a particular emphasis on certain aspects of teaching. First, it foregrounds the what of teaching: *content, process, level* and the curricular frameworks that embody these. The impression is of a curriculum-driven view of teaching, with a heavy emphasis on subjects and key skills. This is complemented by a strong emphasis on *accreditation* and the procedures of *assessment*.

In terms of the actual teaching process, the aspects that seem to loom largest are *motivation* (and the associated concerns with expectations and targets), the need for clear *orientation* and structure and the importance of maintaining a good learning *environment* (classroom management, discipline and relationships). There is also a good deal of emphasis on teacher *input* (presentation and demonstration) and on *explaining* (partly in terms of learners' errors and misconceptions), though rather less on *exploring*.

Conversely, there seems to be very little emphasis on *rationale* (the 'why' of teaching), although this is conceivably covered by the references to 'understanding' the curriculum. There is no explicit reference to the need to *audit* students' existing learning (though there are references to 'progression') and little evidence of concern with student *interaction* or *groups*. *Individual* differences and *social setting* are referred to mainly as aspects that should not impede learning ('setting high expectations for all pupils notwithstanding individual differences, including gender, and cultural and linguistic backgrounds'). The impact of the *physical setting* on teaching is not mentioned at all, although one should not perhaps read too much into that.

Such differences of emphasis can be seen as reflecting current policies and issues: the overall shift away from a child-centred to a subject-centred approach; the focus on whole group teaching; the move away from 'progressive' methods; the relegation of 'contextual' concerns; the development of a national framework of testing and qualifications. It is the job of a national ministry to make policy, and therefore natural that such a scheme should reflect these policies. In that respect, the point of this analysis here is simply to clarify the scheme so that it can be discussed more easily.

However, the deeper question is whether this kind of scheme represents an adequate model of teaching. In one sense, it is not a model at all, but simply an inventory, and the Circular emphasizes this point:

each standard has been set out discretely. Professionalism, however, implies more than a meeting of discrete standards. It is necessary to consider the standards as a whole to appreciate the creativity, commitment, energy and enthusiasm which teaching demands, and the intellectual and managerial skills required of the effective professional. (Annex A, p. 2)

However, even a basic list or inventory carries its own messages. The broad division of the standards into four sections — *Knowledge and Understanding*; *Planning, Teaching and Class Management; Monitoring, Assessment, Recording, Reporting and Accountability*; and *Other Professional Requirements* — projects a certain view of teaching. From the perspective of this model, there are several problems with such a view. First, it privileges one set of variables — the what — as against the why, who or where of teaching. Secondly, it confuses function and procedure, regularly mixing statements about the underlying functions of teaching with ones about particular methods. This erodes the important professional distinction between what one does and how one does it. Thirdly, despite periodic use of the word 'appropriate' (which I shall come back to), it underplays the inherent contingency of teaching. Finally and most importantly, it does not set the various aspects of teaching in a consistent relationship with one another. And as a result of all these, it yields a framework that is comprehensive but not coherent.

My model has implications for two other aspects of training, each of which is a matter of current concern. The first is the balance between on-the-job, school-based training and off-the-job university or college-based; the second is the relationship between inititial and continuing professional education. The relationship between university-based and school-based training has often acted as a kind of surrogate for the theory–practice debate, and the greater proportion of time now spent in schools reflects the increased emphasis on 'practice'. This book has argued against that simple dichotomy, so the important question becomes not 'Where should teachers do their training?' but 'What kind of things do they learn in each place?' A balanced training programme would thus be one that developed all the necessary aspects of teaching set out in the model, rather than one that assigns a particular proportion of time to each setting.

However, this leads on to the second question, about what is necessary at the initial stage, and what is better left to continuing professional development. Again, one cannot give a simple answer to this question, but the model allows one to formulate the issues and track the development patterns more precisely. For example, one can ask to what extent a teacher is involved in the various Macro Procedures at each stage of his or her career. A common pattern is for new teachers to be primarily involved with the most direct procedures (delivery, assessment) and then as they gain experience to take on added responsibilities to do with design, enrolment and organization. Senior members of staff may be concerned mainly with the 'higher-level' activities of analysis, proposals, marketing, evaluation and development, and may indeed move away from direct teaching. Whatever the rights and wrongs of this — and it is an issue in terms of career development and reward structures — the model allows one to pin down the arguments. Likewise, it offers a general map for teachers to look at their own development needs. Where one person might decide to deepen his or her knowledge of the 'what' of teaching, another might want to focus on the 'where' and the management of the organizational setting, thus leading to different career paths.

In all this, it is important to recognize that continuing professional development happens not only formally through attendance at courses, workshops and the like, but informally through everyday contacts and activities and self-directed learning. Indeed, my own research has discovered a preference among some professionals for the latter (Gear, McIntosh and Squires, 1994, p. 14). Again, the model can be used to map the latter, and see what areas or aspects of work people are learning about of their own volition, and how those relate to organized provision.

What has been said about training in this section applies *pari passu* to other sectors of education, such as higher education. At the time of writing, the plans for this are on the drawing-board, so not much can be said. Clearly, the situation will differ in some respects from that in the schools. The current proposals are for two levels of training, leading to two levels of membership of the Institute for Learning and Teaching. This reflects what has now effectively become a dual labour market in higher education, with a core of full-time lecturing staff complemented by large numbers of short-contract graduate teaching assistants; a situation quite unlike that in the schools. Another important difference is that by the time lecturers begin any teaching, they have undergone a thorough education in and socialization into their discipline. It is hardly surprising, therefore, that so many of them begin by seeing teaching through the lens of their subject, and need to complement this focus on the 'what' with a greater awareness of the 'who' and the 'where' (see Kugel, 1993).

However, in general, what has been said here about training for schoolteaching should also apply to higher education, with appropriate   differences of emphasis. But one additional point needs to be made. It is sometimes argued that training for academics to teach should be kept to the bare minimum, and be as practical as possible, because they are more likely to tolerate, if not actually like it, that way. The view taken here is the opposite. Unless teaching can be shown to have a coherent academic basis, which goes beyond mere tips and techniques, it will never be taken seriously in higher education. It may be built into the structures, but it will never become part of the culture. The view of teaching implicit in some current developments in the higher education sector trivializes it by adopting the simplest form of craft model. While in the short term some academics may welcome this as the least possible distraction from their research, it is unlikely to satisfy most of them in the longer term, or even to do justice to their own experience of what they do.

Evaluation

Approaches to evaluation tend to reflect views of teaching. If one sees teaching as a rational activity, then the evaluation of teaching is likely to focus on the achievement (or not) of objectives, the quality of planning and the deployment of resources, as in the well-known Tylerian model (Tyler, 1949). If teaching is seen as a craft, evaluation tends to concentrate on design, methods and techniques. If teaching is regarded as an art, evaluation is conducted in terms of artistry, interpretation and connoisseurship. McCormick and James (1983, pp. 171–203) have provided a good overview of these various general approaches, and in many ways they mirror the various paradigms described in Chapter 1.

The view of teaching presented in this book implies that evaluation should focus above all on the functions of teaching, and whether or not they are being fulfilled. It is worth reminding ourselves that the functions may be fulfilled by the teacher, by the learner, by his or her peers or by others, or by some combination of these: what is important is that they are fulfilled. The reason why we should concentrate on the functions is that it is they that we can link, conceptually and empirically, most directly with learning.

Evaluating the 20 (or however many) functions is not necessarily easy. Enquiries and observations will need to be framed quite carefully to get at them. Learners may need to understand something of them before they can adequately respond to questions or statements about them. And questions can certainly be asked about other aspects of teaching. But the focus on functions will draw in the other two dimensions anyway, since if the functions are not being fulfilled it is usually either because they have not been properly fine-tuned in relation to the variables, or because they have not been competently translated into procedures. By homing in on the functions, as a first step, we can pick up the headings on the other two dimensions as well, though it is likely that further evaluation will then be needed to explore issues to do with these.

Clearly, one cannot spell out what this will mean in practice, because evaluation, like teaching, is a rather contingent activity, and the answers to the general set of questions drawn up by Nevo (1986) will vary from case to case. However, the kind of approach presented in this book implies two things. First, that those involved — teachers and students — *understand* the basis and process of evaluation. Although common-sense responses and feedback can yield some useful data, evaluations of activities are much more likely to be insightful if the participants know what it is all about. It is the lack of such knowledge that makes it difficult for me (up to a point) to evaluate what my doctor, solicitor or surveyor is doing for me, and the same applies to teaching. Learners, as well as teachers, need to be equipped to evaluate.

Secondly, the complexity of the process as represented by the three dimensions of the model and the relationships between them means that evaluation is not simple, because teaching is not simple. Thus even where one is carrying out a 'quick and dirty' survey (which is sometimes necessary), one has to remind oneself that it is precisely that, and not place too much weight on it. A thorough evaluation is likely to take time, and as pointed out above, may be best planned in a series of stages that allow for the initial identification of issues or problems, and ways of following them up subsequently.

How do current evaluation practices look in the light of the model? The external evaluation of teaching in schools ('inspection') has been established for a very long time, though has recently changed dramatically in organization and approach. Periodic external inspection is also normal in Further Education. Higher Education is in the odd position of having its teaching externally evaluated ('assessed') before having its teachers trained. In addition to these formal or statutory evaluations, there may be other kinds carried out by specific agencies, such as professional bodies, and internal evaluation through student feedback is now the norm in post-school education, though not in the schools.

Generalization is thus hazardous, and the remarks that follow will apply mainly to the more formal, external inspections or assessments, and even then must be treated with caution. The schemes and guidelines set out in evaluators' handbooks may not tell the whole story (see, for example, Higher Education Funding Council for England, 1993, 1994, 1996). What goes on in practice may differ from or go beyond these in various ways. After all, the evaluators bring to the job not simply the formal frameworks they are given, but their own experience and accumulated wisdom. However, in general terms, it appears that evaluation both in the school and post-school sectors currently concentrates primarily on procedures, rather less on variables, and pays very little attention to the functions (Squires, 1997a, 1997b).

The focus on procedures is evident at the macro level in terms of the emphasis on the planning, design, organization and evaluation of courses, and the documentation of these ('paper trails'). The focus on procedures at the micro level is evident in the concern with classroom methods and management, usually based on direct observation of teaching, which forms a key part of all the 'official' evaluation processes. Thus at the level of both the course and the class, evaluation may be said to be concerned chiefly with the procedural aspects of teaching; indeed the implication is that this is what teaching *is*.

However, there is some evidence of awareness of and concern with variables. This appears in two ways: first in terms of the emphasis in evaluation guidelines on the relationships between various aspects of teaching; and secondly through the recurring use of the word 'appropriate'. As noted earlier, this word has a special place in the official vocabulary of teaching. It signals a recognition that teaching is not the same across the board, that it has to be adapted to circumstances and context, and take account of various things: but it does not usually say what. Thus while it implies that teaching is a contingent activity, it does not spell out the range of variables in the way that I have attempted to do. 'Appropriateness' is therefore likely to be a rather hit or miss affair, depending on the particular perspective of the evaluator.

There is little explicit evidence in the public evaluation frameworks of concern with functions, basically because teaching is not conceived in these terms at all. As in the training framework, functions and procedures — what one does and how — tend to get mixed up together, so that one will come across reference to a function (motivation, feedback, reinforcement) in the middle of a list of methods (whole group teaching, discussion, projects). However, it is interesting that the language of the reports on evaluations in higher education (by subject) tends to be more concerned with functions than the guidelines given to the evaluators, and to comment on aspects of teaching that are not simply reducible to methods or techniques. So it may be that what evaluators actually do goes beyond what they are said or told to do. This is hardly surprising, since it is difficult to observe a class with any degree of perceptiveness without being aware of the functions: of what is happening in terms of motivation, orientation, task-setting, feedback, and so on.

If one accepts the framework set out in this book, then the emphasis in evaluation needs to be turned around. It needs to focus primarily on the functions of teaching, drawing in the variables and procedures as necessary. However, since this is difficult to do in the kind of snapshot evaluation conducted over a few hours or days, we need to shift the balance between external and internal evaluation as well. The aspects of teaching that are important in the model can only really be explored and tracked through an internal, continuing process. However, one cannot leave it at that; internal evaluation can too easily become domesticated and tame over time. So periodic external 'inspections' and 'assessments' conducted by officials or peers will still also be needed, but their role should change from that of a direct evaluation of teaching to the indirect role of ensuring that the internal evaluations remain rigorous and honest. That, in any case, would be the arrangement one would expect in a profession.

Beyond Dualism

I shall end with one final, more abstract point about the kind of approach set out in this book. A good deal of the discussion in it has been concerned with what might be called the grand dualisms of education: arts and science, pure and applied, theory and practice. But once one begins to reflect on it, educational thinking is permeated by smaller dualisms: didactic versus facilitative, subject-centred versus student-centred, discipline-based versus problem-based, whole group versus small group, mediated versus face-to-face, examined versus assessed, and so on.

In one way, this is quite natural. The debate on any issue tends to get polarized, so the arguments of the day typically take this antithetical form. But that is no reason to assume that educational, and more specifically teaching, issues are inherently dualistic, matters of either/or, and therefore best formulated in these terms. Such deeper dualism, I have argued, results in the longer-term pendulum swings and oscillations that tend to mark policy, thinking and practice in the field.

The model set out here implies a shift from dualism to something more complex and relativistic; a change of visual metaphor. Teaching, as represented in the model, is a multi-dimensional and multi-faceted thing, involving a large number of aspects and relationships. Expertise in teaching is similarly pluralistic. The hope is that such a model will offer us a steadier, general framework within which to work out the specifics of current arguments and decisions.

The limitation of the model is of course that it leaves so much still open, to be worked out, to be decided. The choice of headings, their interpretation, the weight placed on them, the relationships between them, the actions flowing from them: all these are matters in the end for the practitioner — the teacher — to judge and decide. But it is a limitation characteristic of and shared by all the professions.

References

ABERCROMBIE, M.L.J. (1960) *The Anatomy of Judgement*, London: Hutchinson.

ACKRILL, J.L. (1981) *Aristotle the Philosopher*, Oxford: Oxford University Press.

ALEKSANDER, I. and MORTON, H. (1990) *An Introduction to Neural Computing*, London: Chapman and Hall.

ANDERSON, J.R. (1995) *Cognitive Psychology and its Implications*, 4th edn, San Francisco: W.H. Freeman.

ANDERSON, L.W. (ed.) (1995) *The International Encyclopaedia of Teaching and Teacher Education*, 2nd edn, Oxford: Pergamon.

ANDERSON, L.W. (1998) 'Models and the improvement of teaching and learning', *Teaching and Teacher Education*, **14**, 3, pp. 353–7.

ANDO, T. (1965) *Aristotle's Theory of Practical Cognition*, 2nd edn, The Hague: Martinus Nijhoff.

ARENDT, H. (1959) *The Human Condition*, New York: Doubleday.

ARGYRIS, C. (1982) *Reasoning, Learning and Action*, San Francisco: Jossey-Bass.

ARGYRIS, C. (1994) 'Good communication that blocks learning', *Harvard Business Review*, July–August, pp. 77–85.

ARGYRIS, C. and SCHON, D.A. (1996) *Organizational Learning II: Theory, Method and Practice*, Reading, Mass.: Addison-Wesley.

AUSUBEL, D.P. (1963) *The Psychology of Meaningful Verbal Learning*, New York: Grune and Stratton.

AXELROD, J. (1973) *The University Teacher as Artist*, San Francisco: Jossey-Bass.

BALL, T. (ed.) (1977) *Political Theory and Praxis: New Perspectives*, Minneapolis: University of Minnesota Press.

BANDURA, A. (1971) *Social Learning Theory*, New York: General Learning Press.

BANDURA, A. (1986) *Social Foundations of Thought and Action*, Englewood Cliffs, NJ: Prentice-Hall.

BANNISTER, D. and FRANSELLA, F. (1986) *Inquiring Man*, 3rd edn, London: Routledge.

BARNES, J. (1976) *Aristotle*, London: Methuen.

BARNETT, R. (1994) *The Limits of Competence: Knowledge, Higher Education and Society*, Buckingham: Open University Press.

BASKETT, H. and MARSICK, V. (eds) (1992) *Professionals' Ways of Knowing* (New Directions for Adult and Continuing Education No. 55), San Francisco: Jossey-Bass.

BECHER, T. (1989) *Academic Tribes and Territories*, Milton Keynes: Open University Press/Society for Research into Higher Education.

BECHER, T. (ed.) (1994) *Governments and Professional Education*, Buckingham: Open University Press/Society for Research into Higher Education.

BENNER, P. (1984) *From Novice to Expert: Excellence and Power in Clinical Nursing Practice*, Menlo Park, Calif.: Addison-Wesley.

BERGER, P. and LUCKMANN, T. (1971) *The Social Construction of Reality*, Harmondsworth: Penguin.

BERNSTEIN, B. (1971) 'On the classification and framing of educational knowledge', in YOUNG, M.F.D. (ed.) *Knowledge and Control*, London: Collier-Macmillan, pp. 47–69.

BIEHLER, R. and SNOWMAN, J. (1993) *Psychology Applied to Teaching*, 7th edn, Boston: Houghton Mifflin.

BIGGS, J. (1993) 'What do inventories of student learning really measure? A theoretical review and clarification', *British Journal of Educational Psychology*, **63**, 1, pp. 3–19.

BINES, H. and WATSON, D. (eds) (1992) *Developing Professional Education*, Milton Keynes: Open University Press/Society for Research into Higher Education.

BLUMENFELD, P.C., MERGENDOLLER, J.R. and SWARTHOUT, D.W. (1987) 'Task as a heuristic for understanding student learning and motivation', *Journal of Curriculum Studies*, **19**, 2, pp. 135–48.

BOBBITT, F. (1924) *How to Make a Curriculum*, Boston: Houghton Mifflin.

BOREHAM, N. (1989) 'Modelling medical decision-making under uncertainty', *British Journal of Educational Psychology*, **59**, pp. 187–99.

BOREHAM, N. (1994) 'The dangerous practice of thinking', *Medical Education*, **28**, pp. 172–9.

BOUD, D., COHEN, R. and WALKER, D. (eds) (1993) *Using Experience for Learning*, Buckingham: Open University Press/Society for Research into Higher Education.

BROADIE, S. (1991) *Ethics with Aristotle*, New York: Oxford University Press.

BROCKETT, R.G. and HIEMSTRA, R.L. (1991) *Self-direction in Adult Learning: Perspectives on Theory, Research and Practice*, London: Routledge.

BROPHY, J. and GOOD, T. (1986) 'Teacher behavior and student achievement', in WITTROCK, M. (ed.) *Handbook of Research on Teaching*, 3rd edn, New York: Macmillan, pp. 328–75.

BROWN, G. (1978) *Lecturing and Explaining*, London: Routledge.

BROWN, G. and ATKINS, M. (1988) *Effective Teaching in Higher Education*, London: Routledge.

BROWN, J.S. and DUGUID, P. (1996) 'Organizational learning and communities of practice', in COHEN, M.D. and SPROULL, L. (eds) *Organizational Learning*, London: Sage, pp. 58–82.

BROWN, S. and McINTYRE, D. (1993) *Making Sense of Teaching*, Buckingham: Open University Press.

BRUNER, J.S. (1968) *Toward a Theory of Instruction*, New York: Norton.

BUCKLEY, R. and CAPLE, J. (1992) *The Theory and Practice of Training*, 2nd edn, London: Kogan Page.

BURKE, J.J. (ed.) (1989) *Competence-Based Education and Training*, Lewes: Falmer Press.

BURKE, J.J. (ed.) (1995) *Outcomes Learning and the Curriculum*, Lewes: Falmer Press.

BURNS, R.B. (1995) 'Paradigms for research in teaching', in ANDERSON, L.W. (ed.) *The International Encyclopaedia of Teaching and Teacher Education*, 2nd edn, Oxford: Pergamon, pp. 91–6.

BURNYEAT, M.F. (1980) 'Aristotle on learning to be good,' in RORTY, A.O. (ed.) *Essays on Aristotle's Ethics*, Berkeley: University of California Press, pp. 69–92.

CALDERHEAD, J. (1984) *Teachers' Classroom Decision-Making*, London: Holt, Rinehart and Winston.

CALDERHEAD, J. (1987) 'Introduction', in CALDERHEAD, J. (ed.) *Exploring Teachers' Thinking*, London: Cassell, pp. 1–19.

CALDERHEAD, J. (1995) 'Teachers as clinicians', in ANDERSON, L.W. (ed.) *The International Encyclopaedia of Teaching and Teacher Education*, 2nd edn, Oxford: Pergamon, pp. 9–11.

CALDERHEAD, J. and GATES, P. (eds) (1993) *Conceptualizing Reflection in Teacher Education*, Lewes: Falmer Press.

CANDY, P. (1991) *Self-direction for Lifelong Learning: A Comprehensive Guide to Theory and Practice*, San Francisco: Jossey-Bass.

CARLEY, M. (1980) *Rational Techniques in Policy Analysis*, London: Heinemann.

CARR, W. (1995) *For Education: Towards Critical Educational Inquiry*, Buckingham: Open University Press.

CARR, W. and KEMMIS, S. (1986) *Becoming Critical: Education, Knowledge and Action Research*, London: Falmer Press.

CHARTERS, W.W. (1929) *Curriculum Construction*, New York: Macmillan.

CHECKLAND, P. (1981) *Systems Thinking, Systems Practice*, Chichester: John Wiley.

CHI, M., GLASER, R. and FARR, M. (eds) (1988) *The Nature of Expertise*, Hove: Lawrence Erlbaum.

CLANDININ, D.J. and CONNOLLY, F.M. (1996) 'Teachers' professional knowledge landscapes', *Educational Researcher*, **25**, 3, pp. 24–30.

CLARK, C.M. and YINGER, R.J. (1987) 'Teacher planning', in CALDERHEAD, J. (ed.) *Exploring Teachers' Thinking*, London: Cassell, pp. 84–103.

COOK, T.G. (ed.) (1973) *Education and the Professions*, London: Methuen.

CRUICKSHANK, D.R. and METCALF, K.K. (1995) 'Explaining', in ANDERSON, L.W. (ed.) *The International Encyclopaedia of Teaching and Teacher Education*, 2nd edn, Oxford: Pergamon, pp. 232–8.

DE VILLE, H.G. (1986) *Review of Vocational Qualifications in England and Wales: A Report by the Working-Group*, London: Department of Education and Science/ Manpower Services Commission.

DELAMONT, S. (1995) 'Teachers as artists', in ANDERSON, L.W. (ed.) *The International Encyclopaedia of Teaching and Teacher Education*, 2nd edn, Oxford: Pergamon, pp. 6–8.

DEPARTMENT FOR EDUCATION AND EMPLOYMENT (1998) *Teaching: High Status, High Standards (Circular 4/98)*, London: DfEE.

DESFORGES, C. and MCNAMARA, D. (1979) 'Theory and practice: Methodological procedures for the objectification of craft knowledge', *British Journal of Teacher Education*, **5**, 2, pp. 139–52.

DORE, R. (1976) *The Diploma Disease*, London: George Allen and Unwin.

DOYLE, W. (1986) 'Content representation in teachers' definitions of academic work', *Journal of Curriculum Studies*, **18**, 4, pp. 365–79.

DOYLE, W. (1988) *Curriculum in Teacher Education*, Vice-Presidential address to the annual meeting of the American Educational Research Association, New Orleans, April. Revised version, mimeo.

DOYLE, W. and CARTER, K. (1984) 'Academic tasks in classrooms', *Curriculum Enquiry*, **14**, 2, pp. 129–49.

DREYFUS, H.L. (1992) *What Computers Still Can't Do*, 2nd edn, Cambridge, Mass.: MIT Press.

DREYFUS, H.L. and DREYFUS, S.E. (1986) *Mind over Machine*, Oxford: Blackwell.

DUBIN, R. and TAVEGGIA, T. (1968) *The Teaching–Learning Paradox: A Comparative Analysis of College Teaching Methods*, Eugene: University of Oregon Center for Advanced Study of Educational Administration.

DUNKIN, M.J. (ed.) (1987a) *The International Encyclopaedia of Teaching and Teacher Education*, Oxford: Pergamon.

DUNKIN, M.J. (1987b) 'Teaching: art or science?', in DUNKIN, M.J. (ed.) *The International Encyclopaedia of Teaching and Teacher Education*, Oxford: Pergamon, p. 19.

DUNKIN, M.J. and BIDDLE, B.J. (1974) *The Study of Teaching*, New York: Holt, Rinehart and Winston.

EBLE, K.E. (1976) *The Craft of Teaching*, San Francisco: Jossey-Bass.

EDEL, A. (1982) *Aristotle and His Philosophy*, London: Croom Helm.

EISNER, E.W. (1985) *The Educational Imagination: On the Design and Evaluation of School Programs*, 2nd edn, New York: Macmillan.

ELLIOTT, J. (1991) 'Competence-based training and the education of the professions: Is a happy marriage possible?', in ELLIOTT, J. (ed.) *Action Research for Educational Change*, Buckingham: Open University Press, pp. 118–34.

ELLIOTT, J. (ed.) (1993) *Reconstructing Teacher Education*, Lewes: Falmer Press.

ELLIS, P. (1995) 'Standards and the outcomes approach', in BURKE, J. (ed.) *Outcomes, Learning and the Curriculum*, London: Falmer Press, pp. 83–95.

ELSTEIN, A.S., SHULMAN, L.S. and SPRAFKA, S.A. (1978) *Medical Problem Solving: An Analysis of Clinical Reasoning*, Cambridge, Mass.: Harvard University Press.

EMERY, F. (ed.) (1969) *Systems Thinking: Vol. 1*, Penguin: Harmondsworth.

ENTWISTLE, N. (1992) 'Student learning and instructional principles in higher education', in MACFARLANE, A. (ed.) *Teaching and Learning in an Expanding Higher Education System*, Edinburgh: Committee of Scottish University Principals, pp. 52–62.

ENTWISTLE, N. and MARTON, F. (1994) 'Knowledge objects: Understandings constituted through intensive academic study', *British Journal of Educational Psychology*, **64**, pp. 161–78.

ERAUT, M. (1994) *Developing Professional Knowledge and Competence*, London: Falmer Press.

ERAUT, M. (1995) 'Schon-shock: A case for reframing reflection-in-action?', *Teachers and Teaching*, **1**, 1, pp. 9–22.

ERICSSON, K.A. and LEHMANN, A.C. (1996) 'Expert and exceptional performance: evidence of maximal adaptation to task constraints', in SPENCE, J.T., DARLEY, J.M. and FOSS, D.J. (eds) *Annual Review of Psychology*, **47**, pp. 273–305.

ETZIONI, A. (1969) *The Semi-Professions and Their Organization*, New York: Free Press.

EVANS, K. (1978) *The Development and Structure of the English Educational System*, London: Hodder and Stoughton.

EVANS, N. (1992) *Experiential Learning: Assessment and Accreditation*, London: Routledge.

FENSTERMACHER, G. (1994) 'The knower and the known', *Review of Research in Education*, **20**, pp. 3–56.

FIEDLER, F.E. (1967) *A Theory of Leadership Effectiveness*, New York: McGraw-Hill.

FITTS, P.M. and POSNER, M.I. (1973) *Human Performance*, London: Prentice Hall.

FLECK, J. (1998) 'Expertise: Knowledge, power and tradeability', in WILLIAMS, R., FAULKNER, W. and FLECK, J. (eds) *Exploring Expertise: Issues and Perspectives*, London: Macmillan, pp. 143–71.

FLETCHER, S. (1991) *Designing Competence-Based Training*, London: Kogan Page.

FONTANA, D. (1995) *Psychology for Teachers*, 3rd edn, London: Macmillan/British Psychological Society.

FREIRE, P. (1970) *Pedagogy of the Oppressed*, New York: Herder and Herder.

GAGE, N. (1996) 'Confronting counsels of depair for the behavioral sciences', *Educational Researcher*, **25**, 3, pp. 5–15, 22.

GAGNÉ, R.M. (1965) *The Conditions of Learning*, New York: Holt, Rinehart and Winston.

GAGNÉ, R.M. (1975) *Essentials of Learning for Instruction*, expanded edn, Hinsdale, Ill.: Dryden Press.

GAGNÉ, R.M. (1985) *The Conditions of Learning and Theory of Instruction*, 4th edn, Fort Worth: Holt, Rinehart and Winston.

GAGNÉ, R.M. (ed.) (1987) *Instructional Technology: Foundations*, Hove: Lawrence Erlbaum.

GAGNÉ, R.M., BRIGGS, L. and WAGER, W. (eds) (1988) *Principles of Instructional Design*, 3rd edn, New York: Holt, Rinehart and Winston.

GEAR, J., McINTOSH, A. and SQUIRES, G. (1994) *Informal Learning in the Professions*, Hull: University of Hull School of Education.

GIBBS, G. (1981) *Teaching Students to Learn*, Milton Keynes: Open University Press.

GOODLAD, S. (ed.) (1984) *Education for the Professions*, Guildford: Society for Research into Higher Education.

GOODNOW, W.E. (1982) 'The contingency theory of education', *International Journal of Lifelong Education*, **4**, pp. 341–52.

Gow, L. and Kember, D. (1993) 'Conceptions of teaching and their relationship to student learning', *British Journal of Educational Psychology*, **63**, pp. 20–33.

Greene, M. (1994) 'Epistemology and educational research: The influences of recent approaches to knowledge', *Review of Research in Education*, **20**, pp. 423–64.

Grimmett, P. and MacKinnon, A. (1992) 'Craft knowledge and the education of teachers', *Review of Research in Education*, **18**, pp. 385–456.

Gudmundsdottir, S. (ed.) (1997) 'Narrative perspectives on research on teaching and teacher education', *Teaching and Teacher Education*, **13**, 1, entire issue.

Habermas, J. (1974) *Theory and Practice*, J. Viertel (trans.), London: Heinemann.

Hammersley, M. (1997) 'Educational research and teaching: A response to David Hargreaves' TTA lecture', *British Educational Research Journal*, **23**, 2, pp. 141–61.

Hammond, K.R. (1993) 'Naturalistic decision-making from a Brunsvikian viewpoint: Its past, present, future', in Klein, G.A. et al. (eds) *Decision-Making in Action: Models and Methods*, Norwood, NJ: Ablex, pp. 205–27.

Hargreaves, D. (1993) 'A common-sense model of the professional development of teachers', in Elliott, J. (ed.) *Reconstructing Teacher Education*, Lewes: Falmer Press, pp. 86–92.

Hargreaves, D.H. (1997) 'In defence of research for evidence-based teaching: A rejoinder to Martyn Hammersley', *British Educational Research Journal*, **23**, 4, pp. 405–19.

Harries-Jenkins, G. (1991) *Human Resource Development* (Newland Papers No 19), Hull: University of Hull Department of Adult Education.

Haselgrove, S. (ed.) (1994) *The Student Experience*, Buckingham: Open University Press/Society for Research into Higher Education.

Heidegger, M. (1962) *Being and Time*, J. MacQuarrie and E. Robinson (trans.), Oxford: Basil Blackwell.

Higher Education Funding Council for England (1993) *Assessment of the Quality of Education (Circular 3/93)*, Bristol: HEFCE.

Higher Education Funding Council for England (1994) *The Quality Assurance Method from April 1995 (Circular 39/94)*, Bristol: HEFCE.

Higher Education Funding Council for England (1996) *Assessors' Handbook*, Bristol: HEFCE.

Highet, G. (1963) *The Art of Teaching*, London: Methuen.

Hilgard, E.R. and Bower, G.H. (1975) *Theories of Learning*, 4th edn, Englewood Cliffs, NJ: Prentice-Hall.

Hirst, P.H. (1973) 'What is teaching', in Petters, R.S. (ed.) *The Philosophy of Education*, Oxford: Oxford University Press, pp. 163–77.

Hirst, P.H. (1974) *Knowledge and the Curriculum*, London: Routledge and Kegan Paul.

Hirst, P.H. (ed.) (1983) *Educational Theory and its Foundation Disciplines*, London: Routledge and Kegan Paul.

Hoffman, R.R. (1998) 'How can expertise be defined? Implications of research from cognitive psychology', in Williams, R., Faulkner, W. and Fleck, J.

(eds) *Exploring Expertise: Issues and Perspectives*, London: Macmillan., pp. 81–100.

HOPE, R. (1952) *Aristotle's Metaphysics*, New York: Columbia University Press.

HORKHEIMER, M. (1972) 'Traditional and critical theory', in HORKHEIMER, M. *Critical Theory: Selected Essays* (trans. J.O. O'CONNELL), New York: Herder and Herder, pp. 188–243.

HOUSTON, W.R. (1987) 'Competency-based teacher education', in DUNKIN, M.J. (ed.) *The International Encyclopaedia of Teaching and Teacher Education*, Oxford: Pergamon, pp. 86–94.

HOUSTON, W.R. (ed.) (1990) *Handbook of Research on Teacher Education*, New York: Macmillan.

HOYLE, E. (1995) 'Teachers as professionals', in ANDERSON, L.W. (ed.) *The International Encyclopaedia of Teaching and Teacher Education*, 2nd edn, Oxford: Pergamon, pp. 11–15.

HYLAND, T. (1997) 'Reconsidering competence', *Journal of Philosophy of Education*, **31**, 3, pp. 491–503.

ILLICH, I. et al. (1977) *Disabling Professions*, London: Marion Boyars.

JACKSON, J. (ed.) (1970) *Professions and Professionalisation*, Cambridge: Cambridge University Press.

JACKSON, P.W. (1986) *The Practice of Teaching*, New York: Teachers College Press.

JARVIS, P. (1983) *Professional Education*, London: Croom Helm.

JESSUP, G. (1991) *Outcomes*, Lewes: Falmer Press.

JOYCE, B.R. and WEIL, M. (1996) *Models of Teaching*, 5th edn, Boston: Allyn and Bacon.

KELLY, G.A. (1955) *The Psychology of Personal Constructs, Vols I and II*, New York: Harper Row.

KENNEDY, M. (1987) 'Inexact sciences: Professional education and the development of expertise', *Review of Research in Education*, **14**, pp. 133–67.

KENNEDY, M. (1997) 'The connection between research and practice', *Educational Researcher*, **26**, 7, pp. 4–12.

KENNY, A. (1978) *The Aristotelian Ethics*, Oxford: Clarendon.

KESSELS, J. and KORTHAGAN, F. (1996) 'The relationship between theory and practice: Back to the classics', *Educational Researcher*, **25**, 3, pp. 17–22.

KIRKPATRICK, D. (1987) 'Evaluation of training', in CRAIG, R. (ed.) *Training and Development Handbook*, 3rd edn, New York: McGraw-Hill, pp. 301–19.

KLEIN, G., ORASANU, J., CALDERWOOD, R. and ZSAMBOK, C.E. (eds) (1993) *Decision-Making in Action: Models and Methods*, Norwood, NJ: Ablex.

KNOWLES, M. (1978) *The Adult Learner: A Neglected Species*, 2nd edn, Houston: Gulf.

KOLB, D. (1984) *Experiential Learning*, Englewood Cliffs, NJ: Prentice-Hall.

KUGEL, P. (1993) 'How professors become teachers', *Studies in Higher Education*, **18**, 3, pp. 315–28.

KUHN, T.S. (1962) *The Structure of Scientific Revolutions*, Chicago: University of Chicago Press.

KYRIACOU, C. (1997) *Effective Teaching in Schools: Theory and Practice*, 2nd edn, Cheltenham: Stanley Thornes.

LAKATOS, I. and MUSGRAVE, A. (eds) (1972) *Criticism and the Growth of Knowledge*, Cambridge: Cambridge University Press.

LEINHARDT, G. (1990) 'Capturing craft knowledge in teaching', *Educational Researcher*, **19**, 2, pp. 18–25.

LEINHARDT, G. (1993) 'Weaving instructional explanations in history', *British Journal of Educational Psychology*, **63**, pp. 46–74.

LENS, W. (1995) 'Motivation and learning', in ANDERSON, L.W. (ed.) *The International Encyclopaedia of Teaching and Teacher Education*, 2nd edn, Oxford: Pergamon, pp. 395–402.

LINDBLOM, C.E. (1959) 'The science of "muddling through"', *Public Administration Review*, **19**, 2, pp. 79–88.

LINDBLOM, C.E. (1979) 'Still muddling, not yet through', *Public Administration Review*, **39**, 6, pp. 517–26.

LIPSHITZ, R. (1993) 'Converging themes in the study of decision-making in realistic settings', in KLEIN, G. et al. (eds) *Decision Making in Action: Models and Methods*, Norwood, NJ: Ablex, pp. 103–37.

LOBKOWICZ, N. (1967) *Theory and Practice: History of a Concept from Aristotle to Marx*, Notre Dame: University of Notre Dame Press.

LOBKOWICZ, N. (1977) 'On the history of theory and praxis', in BALL, T. (ed.) *Political Theory and Praxis: New Perspectives*, Minneapolis: University of Minnesota Press, pp. 13–27.

MAGER, R.F. (1962) *Preparing Instructional Objectives*, Palo Alto: Fearon.

MARLAND, M. (1975) *The Craft of the Classroom*, London: Heinemann.

MARLAND, P.W. (1995) 'Implicit theories of teaching', in ANDERSON, L.W. (ed.) *The International Encyclopaedia of Teaching and Teacher Education*, 2nd edn, Oxford: Pergamon, pp. 131–6.

MARRIS, P. (1964) *The Experience of Higher Education*, London: Routledge and Kegan Paul.

MARTON, F. (1977) 'What does it take to learn?', in ENTWISTLE, N. and HOUNSELL, D. (eds) *How Students Learn*, Lancaster: University of Lancaster, Institute for Research and Development in Post-Compulsory Education, pp. 125–38.

MARTON, F., HOUNSELL, D. and ENTWISTLE, N. (eds) (1984) *The Experience of Learning*, Edinburgh: Scottish Academic Press.

MASTERMAN, M. (1972) 'The nature of a paradigm', in LAKATOS, I. and MUSGRAVE, A. (eds) *Criticism and the Growth of Knowledge*, Cambridge: Cambridge University Press, pp. 59–89.

McCORMICK, R. and JAMES, M. (1983) *Curriculum Evaluation in Schools*, 2nd edn, London: Routledge.

McGILL, I. and BEATY, L. (1992) *Action Learning: A Practitioner's Guide*, London: Kogan Page.

McKEACHIE, W. (1986) *Teaching Tips*, 8th edn, Lexington, Mass.: D.C. Heath.

McNAMARA, D. (1994) *Classroom Pedagogy and Primary Practice*, London: Routledge.

MEIGHAN, R. and SIRAJ-BLATCHFORD, I. (1997) *A Sociology of Educating*, 3rd edn, London: Cassell.

MERRIAM, S.B. and CAFFARELLA, R.S. (1991) *Learning in Adulthood*, San Francisco: Jossey-Bass.

MEZIROW, J. (1977) 'Perspective transformation', *Studies in Adult Education*, **9**, 2, pp. 153–64.

MILLER, G.A. (1956) 'The magical number seven plus or minus two: Some limits on our capacity for processing information', *Psychological Review*, **63**, pp. 81–97.

NEEDHAM, J. (1956) *Science and Civilisation in China, Vol. II*, Cambridge: Cambridge University Press.

NEVO, D. (1986) 'Conceptualisation of educational evaluation: An analytical review of the literature', in HOUSE, E. (ed.) *New Directions in Educational Evaluation*, Lewes: Falmer Press, pp. 15–29.

NISBET, J. and SHUCKSMITH, J. (1986) *Learning Strategies*, London: Routledge.

NUSSBAUM, M.C. (1986) *The Fragility of Goodness*, Cambridge: Cambridge University Press.

OAKSHOTT, M. (1962) *Rationalism in Politics: And Other Essays*, London: Methuen.

OECD (ORGANISATION FOR ECONOMIC CO-OPERATION AND DEVELOPMENT) (1977) *Selection and Certification in Education and Employment*, Paris: OECD.

OLSON, J. (1992) *Understanding Teaching: Beyond Expertise*, Buckingham: Open University Press.

ORASANU, J. and CONNOLLY, T. (1993) 'The reinvention of decision making', in KLEIN, G. et al. (eds) *Decision Making in Action: Models and Methods*, Norwood, NJ: Ablex, pp. 3–20.

OXENHAM, J. (1984) *Education versus Qualifications*, London: George Allen and Unwin.

PASCARELLA, E. and TERENZINI, P. (1991) *How College Affects Students*, San Francisco: Jossey-Bass.

PATRICK, J. (1992) *Training: Research and Practice*, London: Academic Press.

PHENIX, P.H. (1964) *Realms of Meaning*, New York: McGraw-Hill.

POLANYI, M. (1958) *The Study of Man*, Chicago: University of Chicago Press.

PRATT, D.D. (1989) 'Three stages of teacher competence: A developmental perspective', in HAYES, E. (ed.) *Effective Teaching Styles* (New Directions for Continuing Education, No. 43), San Francisco: Jossey-Bass, pp. 77–87.

PROSSER, M., TRIGWELL, K. and TAYLOR, P. (1994) 'A phenomenographic study of academics' conceptions of science teaching and learning', *Learning and Instruction*, **4**, pp. 217–31.

RAMSDEN, P. (1992) *Learning to Teach in Higher Education*, London: Routledge.

RANDALL, J.H. (1960) *Aristotle*, New York: Columbia University Press.

RASMUSSEN, J. (1993) 'Deciding and doing: Decision-making in natural contexts', in KLEIN, G. et al. (eds) *Decision Making in Action*, Norwood, NJ: Ablex, pp. 158–71.

READER, W.J. (1966) *Professional Man*, London: Weidenfeld and Nicolson.

REEVE, C.D.C. (1992) *Practices of Reason*, Oxford: Clarendon Press.

REIGELUTH, C.M. and CURTIS, R.V. (1987) 'Learning situations and instructional models', in GAGNÉ, R.M. (ed.) *Instructional Technology: Foundations*, Hillsdale, NJ: Lawrence Erlbaum, pp. 175–206.

REVANS, R. (1982) *The Origins and Growth of Action Learning*, Bromley: Chatwell-Pratt.

RICHARDS, C. (1984) *Curriculum Studies: An Introductory Annotated Bibliography*, Lewes: Falmer Press.

RICHEY, R. (1992) *Designing Instruction for the Adult Learner*, London: Kogan Page.

ROGERS, C. (1983) *Freedom to Learn for the 1980s*, Columbus: Merrill.

ROMIZOWSKI, A.J. (1988) *Producing Instructional Systems*, London: Kogan Page.

ROSENSHINE, B. and MEISTER, C. (1995) 'Direct instruction', in ANDERSON, L.W. (ed.) *The International Encyclopaedia of Teaching and Teacher Education*, 2nd edn, Oxford: Pergamon, pp. 143–9.

ROSENSHINE, B. and STEVENS, R. (1986) 'Teaching functions', in WITTROCK, M. (ed.) *Handbook of Research on Teaching*, 3rd edn, New York: Macmillan, pp. 376–91.

ROSS, W.D. (ed.) (1921) *The Works of Aristotle: Vol. X*, Oxford: Clarendon Press.

ROSS, W.D. (ed.) (1925) *The Works of Aristotle: Vol. IX*, Oxford: Clarendon Press.

ROSS, W.D. (ed.) (1928) *The Works of Aristotle: Vol. VIII*, 2nd ed., Oxford: Clarendon Press.

ROSS, W.D. (1949) *Aristotle*, 5th edn, London: Methuen.

RYLE, G. (1949) *The Concept of Mind*, Penguin: Harmondsworth.

SCHEIN, E.H. (1972) *Professional Education: Some New Directions*, New York: McGraw-Hill.

SCHILLING, M. (1986) 'Knowledge and liberal education: A critique of Paul Hirst', *Journal of Curriculum Studies*, **18**, 1, pp. 1–16.

SCHON, D.A. (1983) *The Reflective Practitioner*, San Francisco: Jossey-Bass.

SCHON, D.A. (1987) *Educating the Reflective Practitioner: Towards a New Design for Teaching and Learning in the Professions*, San Francisco: Jossey-Bass.

SCHUELL, T.J. (1992) 'Designing instructional computing systems for meaningful learning', in JONES, M. and WINNE, P.H. (eds) *Adaptive Learning Environments*, Berlin: Springer-Verlag, pp. 19–54.

SCHUTZ, A. (1970) *Collected Papers III: Studies in Phenomenological Philosophy*, The Hague: Martinus Nijhoff.

SCHWAB, J.J. (1969a) 'The practical: A language for curriculum', in LEVIT, M. (ed.) *Curriculum*, Urbana: University of Illinois Press, pp. 306–30.

SCHWAB, J.J. (1969b) 'Structure and dynamics of knowledge', in LEVIT, M. (ed.) *Curriculum*, Urbana: University of Illinois Press, pp. 181–214.

SENKER, J. (1998) 'The contribution of tacit knowledge to innovation', in WILLIAMS, R., FAULKNER, W. and FLECK, J. (eds) *Exploring Expertise: Issues and Perspectives*, London: Macmillan, pp. 223–44.

SHORT, E.C. (1984) *Competence*, Lanham, MD: University Press of America.

SHULMAN, L. (1987) 'Knowledge and teaching: Foundations of the new reform', *Harvard Educational Review*, **57**, 1, pp. 1–22.

SIMON, H. (1956) 'Rational choice and the structure of the environment', *Psychological Review*, **63**, pp. 129–38.

SIMON, H. (1969) *The Sciences of the Artificial*, Cambridge, Mass.: MIT Press.

SIMON, H. (1979) *Models of Thought*, London: Yale University Press.

SIMON, H. (1996) 'Bounded rationality and organizational learning', in COHEN, M.D. and SPROULL, L.S. (eds) *Organizational Learning*, London: Sage, pp. 175–87.

SKINNER, B.F. (1954) 'The science of learning and the art of teaching', *Harvard Educational Review*, **24**, pp. 88–97.

SNYDER, B. (1971) *The Hidden Curriculum*, New York: Knopf.

SORABJI, R. (1980) 'Aristotle on the role of intellect in virtue', in RORTY, A.O. (ed.) *Essays on Aristotle's Ethics*, Berkeley: University of California Press, pp. 201–19.

SQUIRES, G. (1982) *The Analysis of Teaching* (Newland Papers No. 8), Hull: University of Hull Department of Adult Education.

SQUIRES, G. (1987) *The Curriculum Beyond School*, London: Hodder and Stoughton.

SQUIRES, G. (1988) *Teaching and Training: A Contingent Approach* (Newland Papers No. 15), Hull: University of Hull Department of Adult Education.

SQUIRES, G. (1989) *Pathways for Learning: Education and Training from 16 to 19*, Paris: Organisation for Economic Co-operation and Development.

SQUIRES, G. (1990) *First Degree: The Undergraduate Curriculum*, Milton Keynes: Open University Press/Society for Research into Higher Education.

SQUIRES, G. (1993) 'Education for adults', in THORPE, M., EDWARDS, R. and HANSON, A. (eds) *Culture and Processes of Adult Learning*, London: Routledge, pp. 87–108.

SQUIRES, G. (1994) *A New Model of Teaching and Training*, Hull: Geoffrey Squires, loose-leaf in binder.

SQUIRES, G. (1996a) 'Analysing the teaching-learning process: A new model', in *Using Open Learning in Health and Social Care*, London: Open Learning Foundation, pp. 24–32.

SQUIRES, G. (1996b) 'Modularisation, mobility and the inner curriculum', *Reflections on Higher Education*, **8**, pp. 26–39.

SQUIRES, G. (1997a) 'Evaluating teaching and improving learning', *Lifelong Education in Europe*, **2**, 2, pp. 86–91.

SQUIRES, G. (1997b) *The Evaluation of Teaching in the United Kingdom*, Paper presented at the Annual Conference of the Consortium of Higher Education Researchers, Alicante, mimeo.

SQUIRES, G. (1997c) 'A three-dimensional model of course design', in RUST, C. and GIBBS, G. (eds) *Improving Student Learning through Course Design*, Oxford: Brookes University, Oxford Centre for Staff and Learning Development, pp. 254–264.

STAMMERS, R. and PATRICK, J. (1975) *The Psychology of Training*, London: Methuen.

STENHOUSE, L. (1975) *An Introduction to Curriculum Research and Development*, London: Heinemann.

STONES, E. (1994) *Quality Teaching: A Sample of Cases*, London: Routledge.

SUCHMAN, L. (1987) *Plans and Situated Actions*, Cambridge: Cambridge University Press.

TABA, H. (1962) *Curriculum Development: Theory and Practice*, New York: Harcourt Brace and World.

TANNENBAUM, S. and YUKL, G. (1992) 'Training and development in work organizations', *Annual Review of Psychology*, **43**, pp. 399–441.

TAYLOR, P.H. and RICHARDS, C.M. (1985) *An Introduction to Curriculum Studies*, 2nd edn, Slough: NFER-Nelson.

TENNANT, M. (1997) *Psychology and Adult Learning*, 2nd ed., London: Routledge.

THOMAS, G. (1997) 'What's the use of theory?', *Harvard Educational Review*, **67**, 1, pp. 75–104.

THOMPSON, J.A.K. (1976) *The Ethics of Aristotle*, London: Penguin.

TOM, A.R. (1984) *Teaching as a Moral Craft*, London: Longman.

TOM, A.R. and VALLI, L. (1990) 'Professional knowledge for teachers', in HOUSTON, W. (ed.) *Handbook of Research on Teacher Education*, New York: Macmillan, pp. 373–92.

TOUGH, A. (1971) *The Adult's Learning Projects*, Toronto: Ontario Institute for Studies in Education.

TURNER, J.D. and RUSHTON, J. (eds) (1976) *Education for the Professions*, Manchester: Manchester University Press.

TUXWORTH, E. (1982) *Competence in Teaching*, London: Longmans/Further Education Unit.

TYLER, R. (1949) *Basic Principles of Curriculum and Instruction*, Chicago: University of Chicago Press.

URMSON, J.O. (1988) *Aristotle's Ethics*, Oxford: Basil Blackwell.

US DEPARTMENT OF EDUCATION (1987) *What Works: Research about Teaching and Learning*, 2nd edn, Washington, DC: Department of Education.

VON BERTALANFFY, L. (1968) *Organismic Psychology and Systems Theory*, Barre: Clark University Press.

WARD, J. (1926) *Psychology Applied to Teaching*, Cambridge: Cambridge University Press.

WEIL, S.W. and MCGILL, I. (eds) (1989) *Making Sense of Experiential Learning*, Buckingham: Open University Press/Society for Research into Higher Education.

WEINSTEIN, C.E. and MAYER, R.E. (1986) 'The teaching of learning strategies', in WITTROCK, M. (ed.) *Handbook of Research on Teaching*, 3rd edn, New York: Macmillan, pp. 315–27.

WELKER, R. (1992) *The Teacher as Expert: A Theoretical and Historical Examination*, Albany: State University of New York Press.

WIENER, N. (1948) *Cybernetics*, New York: John Wiley.

WILKIN, M. (1996) *Initial Teacher Training: The Dialogue of Ideology and Culture*, London: Falmer Press.

WILLIAMS, R., FAULKNER, W. and FLECK, J. (eds) (1998) *Exploring Expertise: Issues and Perspectives*, London: Macmillan.

WILSON, J.D. (1981) *Student Learning in Higher Education*, London: Croom Helm.

WINNE, P.H. (1995) 'Information-processing theories of teaching', in ANDERSON, L.W. (ed.) *International Encyclopaedia of Teaching and Teacher Education*, 2nd edn, Oxford: Pergamon, pp. 107–12.

WINTER, R. and MAISCH, M. (1996) *Professional Competence and Higher Education: The ASSET Programme*, London: Falmer Press.

WITKIN, H. and GOODENOUGH, D.R. (1977) *Field Dependence Revisited*, Princeton, NJ: Educational Testing Service.

WITTROCK, M. (ed.) (1986) *Handbook of Research on Teaching*, 3rd edn, New York: Macmillan.

Index